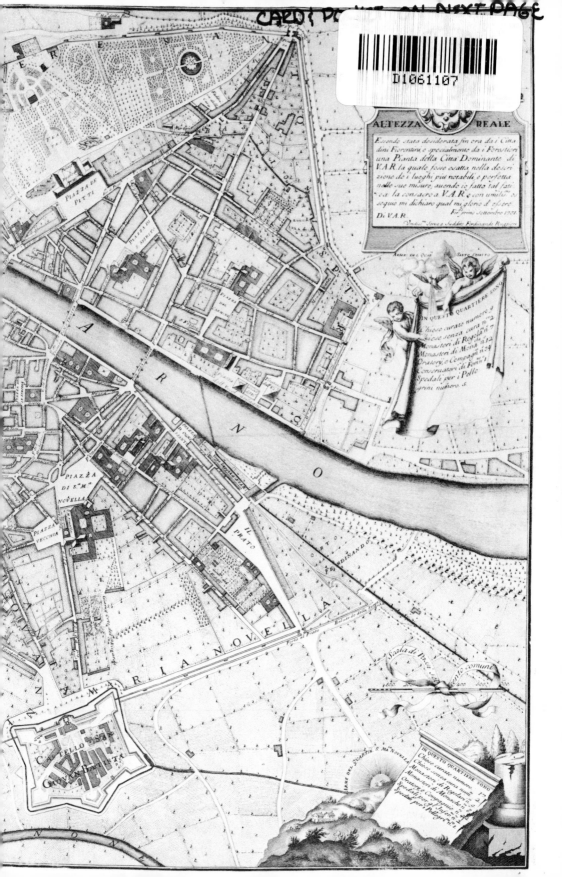

PIAZZA DE' PITTI

PIAZZA S. SPIRITO

A R N O

PIAZZA DI S.ta M.a NOVELLA

PIAZZA VECCHIA

IL PRATO

S.ta M.a NOVELLA

CASTELLO GIOVAN BATTISTA

The Laboring Classes in Renaissance Florence

Laborers in the late fourteenth century. Reproduced with the permission of the British Library.

Laborers in the mid-fifteenth century. Reproduced with the permission of the British Library.

The Laboring Classes in Renaissance Florence

Samuel Kline Cohn, Jr.

Department of History
Brandeis University
Waltham, Massachusetts

and

Center for European Studies
Harvard University
Cambridge, Massachusetts

ACADEMIC PRESS
A Subsidiary of Harcourt Brace Jovanovich, Publishers
New York   London   Toronto   Sydney   San Francisco

This is a volume in

STUDIES IN SOCIAL DISCONTINUITY

A complete list of titles in this series appears at the end of this volume.

ACADEMIC PRESS, INC.
111 Fifth Avenue, New York, New York 10003

United Kingdom Edition published by
ACADEMIC PRESS, INC. (LONDON) LTD.
24/28 Oval Road, London NW1 7DX

Library of Congress Cataloging in Publication Data

Cohn, Samuel Kline.
    The laboring classes in Renaissance Florence.

    (Studies in social discontinuity)
    A revision of the author's thesis, Harvard University,
1978.
    Bibliography: p.
    Includes index.
    1. Labor and laboring classes--Italy--Florence--
History. 2. Florence--History--1421–1737. I.
Title. II. Series.
HD8490.F6C63 1980   305.5'6   80–1096
ISBN 0–12–179180–7

PRINTED IN THE UNITED STATES OF AMERICA

80 81 82 83   9 8 7 6 5 4 3 2 1

To

30 ESSEX STREET, CAMBRIDGE, MASSACHUSETTS

and

VIA DELL'AGNOLO 58. PRESSO: LELLA PELLEGRINI

Contents

List of Figures and Tables

Acknowledgments

This book is a much-revised version of a doctoral dissertation that I submitted to Harvard University in August 1978. I wish first to thank my advisor, David Herlihy, whose encouragement at certain critical moments in my graduate career kept alive a desire to pursue social questions within a preindustrial milieu. His shrewd judgment, moreover, often saved me from unwarranted speculation and theoretical entanglements.

The research and much of the conceptual work for this book took place in Florence, where I received funds from the Renaissance Society of America, National Science Foundation, Krupp Foundation, and Fulbright–Hays Program. To the archival staff and to those who regularly consulted materials at the Archivio di Stato, Firenze during my year-and-a-half of research, I owe a debt of gratitude for providing a pleasant, cooperative, and stimulating intellectual environment. In particular, I would like to single out Anthony Molho, whose assistance and enthusiasm for archival matters and social, political, and economic questions—both past and present—has been, in my opinion, the single most important influence on a new generation of American historians of medieval and Renaissance Florence. His encouragement and patient scrutiny of my work since 1975 has been indispensable for the development of ideas elaborated in this book. In addition, John Najemy (who first suggested that I study the Notarile), Richard Trexler, Christine Klapisch, Enzo Settesoldi, F.W. Kent and Dale Kent (who offered valuable suggestions for the final draft of this book), Frederich Krantz, Marvin Becker, Jeff Newton, Ronald Weissman, Yoram Milo, Carlo Corsini, Humphrey Butters, and Gino Corti often came to my assistance in deciphering paleographical difficulties or in explaining peculiarities in the organization of various archives. They were always willing to share with me their vast knowledge of Florentine history and made the

Sala di Consultazione more than a place simply for ordering, reading, and depositing documents.

Beyond the archives, I discussed statistical and sampling problems with Carlo Corsini at the Istituto Sperimentale-matematico of the Università degli Studi di Firenze, and with Gregory Schnell and Douglas Hibbs at Harvard University. Julia Sheehan, Tom Kelly, Larry Poos, and Paul Drolet endured the tedious labor of punching and proofreading IBM cards. Lynn McKay typed and proofread several versions of this manuscript. Molly Nolan, James Henretta, Dieter Wuerth, Carlo Corsini, Oscar Di Simplicio, Anthony Molho, and Robert Burr Litchfield read with care and critical insight my first efforts in writing this book. These scholars, together with John Bohstedt and Charles Tilly (who read later versions of the manuscript), offered valuable suggestions from their perspectives in the modern world. They forced me to conceive of my empirical findings within the larger framework of European labor history. My colleague at Wesleyan University, David Konstan, took time off his summer vacation, read my manuscript thoroughly, offered editorial and stylistic criticisms, and suggested changes in organization and content. Finally, I wrote various drafts of the manuscript while I was a research associate at the Center for European Studies at Harvard University. I owe special thanks to the camaraderie of my coworkers, in particular, Abby Collins, Peter Lange, Joel Krieger, Molly Nolan, Paschalis Kitromilides, and Keitha Fine.

This book is dedicated to two addresses, two residential and political collectives—30 Essex Street, Cambridge, Massachusetts, and Via dell' Agnolo, 58 Presso: Lella Pellegrini—where I spent much of my energies (1975–1978) while not writing this book.

And among other things which
disgraced the city (Florence)
even more was a term, which the
popolo minuto took from the
French, courtiers and soldiers.
In French they are accustomed to
saying "comrade"; and just in
speaking to their comrades, they
go willingly to the taverns.
And the gente minuta make use of wine and
the tavern. It was fashionable
to go there together to drink.
And the French would say "Compar,
allois a boier (Comrade, let's
get a drink)." And the popolo
rozzo would garble the French
saying, "Ciompo, Ciompo," and
suddenly they were all Ciompi,
that is, comrades.

—MARCHIONNE DI COPPO STEFANI

Introduction

THE title of this book, *The Laboring Classes in Renaissance Florence*, may seem anomalous. The idea of the Renaissance in Florence evokes high culture—art history, then literature, then humanism—matters, to be sure, which were far removed from the laboring classes. This work investigates the other side of Renaissance history, that side which pertained to the mass of men and women and which the current historiography concludes in effect had no history—no history in the sense that the collective and individual actions of these men and women in any way helped to shape their own lives or society as a whole.[1] To reconstruct that other side of the Renaissance in Florence, this book examines sources that never before have been studied systematically—the notarial and criminal archives of Florence. Yet this work is more than just an empirical dusting of certain shelves in the Archivio di Stato, Firenze. It considers the laboring classes in the larger context of class relations and concludes that to understand the broad political and social changes from the fourteenth through the fifteenth centuries in Florence, the historian must consider changes both within the laboring classes (the *popolo minuto*) as well as the interaction between the laboring classes and the ruling elite—or, to be more direct, class struggle.

From its inception, two considerations "extra-fonti"[2] preceded the chores of deciphering paleographical difficulties, coding and computer manipulation of the archival resources and structured by inquiry into the documentation. First, I came to the Renaissance with some interest

---

1. Samuel Cohn, Jr., "Rivolte popolari e classi sociali nella Toscana del Rinascimento," *Studi Storici*, vol. 20, (1979), 747–758.
2. See Jerzy Topolski, *Metodologia della ricerca storica*, translated by R. C. Lewanski (Bologna, Naukowe, 1973).

in comparative labor history and the rise of capitalism. I felt uneasy
with the results of modernization theory and certain demographic
studies of early modern Europe, which had relegated the preindustrial
past (certainly from the perspective of the laboring classes) to a "pre-
Malthusian" continuum without significant variations over time or across
societies. In other words, the history of peasants, artisans, and workers,
according to this tradition of social and historical research, was an
unconscious history structured on the one hand by the vicissitudes of
climate and harvests, and on the other by the unremitting fact of biological reproduction. To break from the presumptions behind this
"unconscious history," I have transposed for an examination of the
Renaissance certain modes of analysis developed principally for the
study of late nineteenth- and early twentieth-century labor history.
Through the use of models and comparative perspectives devised by
George Rudé, Charles Tilly, E. P. Thompson, John Foster, Eugene
Genovese, Eric Hobsbawm, and others, the historian of the Renaissance
can do more than dismiss the *popolo minuto* of the fourteenth and
fifteenth centuries, their history and their impact on shaping society
as a whole, simply because these preindustrial laboring classes did not
meet some (unstated) standards imagined for a fully blown nineteenth-
or twentieth-century Western proletariat. In the works of these modern
social historians, we do not find a simple either/or proposition and the
implication that all preproletarian, pre-nineteenth-century populations
lacked consciousness about the social and political problems that confronted them as classes and about the means through which to resolve
these difficulties. Instead, we find sensitive reconstructions of the political strategies, repertoires of protest, and consciousness of artisans and
laborers in preindustrial milieux. Although the tax revolt, the food
riot, and rural rebels resisting encroachments by landlords and the
state on their rights in common did not require the organizational and
ideological sophistication of the strikes and mass political demonstra-
tions later waged by nineteenth-century proletarians, these incidents
cannot be explained simply by variables that are exogenous to these
laboring classes. Instead, these incidents reflect the resources of these
preindustrial plebeian populations and were made possible often through
their own organization and consciousness of lost rights and rights in
common. In summary, class struggle is not something over which the
nineteenth century has a monopoly, and it is not anachronistic to consider the development of class struggle in periods preceding the Industrial Revolution. With this labor historiography, I thus have at my
disposal a finer instrument (than common sense) for discerning and

exposing the variation and richness in the history of Florentine artisans and workers in the fourteenth and fifteenth centuries.

Second, I wanted to make use of the documents—such as baptismal registers and marriage acts—that over the past 20 years have become the staple and domain of demographic historians of early modern Europe. I wanted to use these documents, however, in an altogether different way. I sought to remove their analysis from the Durkheimian mold, where "social facts" (rates of fertility or nuptiality, for instance) automatically produce "collective representations" (or what the Annalists call "mentalités"), and vice versa. Rather than reducing social relationships to series of discrete data, historians could study the marriage relationship, for instance, as a social relationship, and from the patterns and networks cast by the aggregation of these relationships, might thus examine social and political solidarities and interactions. Thus, social relationships themselves (and not the aggregation of individual facts extracted from their social contexts) are the objects of my inquiry. The analysis of marriage associations in this study provides the basis for examining the dynamics of class and power.

The eight chapters of this book divide into two parts. The first concerns the presuppositions of the political actions and consciousness of the Renaissance laboring classes. I investigate networks of associations, the emergence of ethnic ghettos, the impact of immigration, the distribution of population, wealth, and occupational groupings. Chapter 1 concerns the documentation pertaining to the Florentine laboring classes. I seize upon the marriage contracts found scattered through the notarial protocols as the one notarial act that reasonably represents the world of the *popolo minuto*. The chapter concludes with an aggregate analysis of two marriage samples, one drawn from the revolutionary epoch of the middle and late Trecento, the other from a period of apparent social quiescence, the late fifteenth century. At this point in the analysis, significant differences between the two periods do not emerge. I then begin to extract various classes from the amalgam of classes embodied in these aggregate figures. Chapter 2 examines the patriciate, Chapter 3 the laboring classes. Here, the evidence unveils striking changes in the worlds of patricians and laborers over the long period of our analysis. In Chapters 4 and 5, I consider other variables in an attempt to control for these changes. What begins as a method of statistical analysis ends with new findings on migration, the ethnic compositions of neighborhoods, and the class structure of Florentine urban geography.

To compile these new materials on the laboring classes in preindustrial

Florence, it was necessary to proceed along the margins, to consider documents which read individually reveal little indeed. Through statistical means we have nonetheless reconstructed from these monotonous records new information that sketches out for the first time the vague outlines of the heretofore hidden world of the *popolo minuto*—their neighborhoods and communities of social interaction. Hopefully, the reader who is not particularly enamored of demographic findings—facts on migration and statistics of local endogamies—will persevere through the first five chapters. The political significance of the social structures described in the first part became clear by Chapter 6.

In the second part (Chapters 6–8), I chart (primarily from the immense and rich archives of the criminal tribunals) the changes in the composition of insurrectionary crowds and transformations in the forms of popular protest from wide-scale insurrections to individual outbursts of violence. From the perspectives of studies of crowds in eighteenth- and nineteenth-century France and Britain, I found tucked back in the late Middle Ages patterns and repertoires of insurrectionary activity that would have appeared surprisingly "modern" in Paris in 1789. In fourteenth-century Florence, there were fraternities of workers, industrial strikes, and insurrections that followed falling instead of rising bread prices. By the latter half of the fifteenth century, this picture of the *popolo minuto* had changed radically. The laboring classes turned inward, retreating into communities of parochial protection, and their forms of protest reflected these changes in social structure and the ecology of the Renaissance city. Isolated, individualistic outbursts of violence against their social betters and the strong arm of the state had taken the place of organized mass insurrection and practical plans for capturing the state apparatus.

I then seize upon this history of the demobilization and decline of the working classes in Chapter 7 as an opportunity for writing a more complete and more organic history of the Florentine *popolo minuto* than has been previously achieved in those studies which isolate the turbulent period of the Ciompi as the unit of investigation. First, I can demonstrate that the laboring classes over the long term from the period of the Ciompi insurrections (1343–1383) to that of Medicean hegemony (1434–1492) did change, and that the changes were not simply the results of forces outside the *popolo minuto*—strategies of the patriciate or dire economic conditions. Instead, the *popolo minuto* itself—its casual as well as political relationships—changed. Second, the demobilization of the laboring classes in the Quattrocento presents an opportunity to depart from a tendency that is prominent in working-class historiography. Instead of studying only the peaks of labor history, here is an opportunity to examine a trough. And in addition to understanding another, albeit a less glamorous, phase of labor history, it is possible from the perspective of this fifteenth-century trough to ask new questions about the grand events of that more dramatic period of Trecento Ciompi revolt. It is possible to discover new relationships in documents which in some cases have now been scrutinized by scholars for over a century (Chapter 6). In comparison to the parochial associations of insurgents during the mid-Quattrocento, the citywide array of participants found in various insurrections, both large and small, during the 1342–1383 period appear striking. The differences in these networks between the two periods, moreover, suggest that there were fundamental changes in social structure, organization, and the consciousness of the Florentine *popolo minuto* which indeed underlay and made possible certain political events (e.g., insurrections and protests) during both centuries.

To comprehend what happened to the revolutionary Ciompi during the period of Medicean control, my work—which begins with a quantitative analysis of the structure and composition of artisan and laboring communities in the final chapter—concludes by addressing rather traditional questions regarding the rise of the Medicean state. If nothing else, I have learned that just as the old political history, which chronicles the events of the ruling class, cannot be understood fully except in relation to developments of the laboring classes, the Florentine *popolo minuto* is incomprehensible in and of itself, that is, in isolation from the development of other classes.

The trajectory of research that this study of the laboring classes of Florence follows has been the inverse of that behind Eugene Genovese's already classic work on U.S. slavery, *Roll, Jordan, Roll.* While Genovese found after 20 years of research that "the world the slaveholders made" was not fully comprehensible without a study of "the world the slaves made," I am now discovering the other side of this dialectical relation: To understand class struggle in Renaissance Florence, the historian of the *popolo minuto* must search beyond those glorious events of the Revolt of the Ciompi or even the insurrections and associations that antedated their temporary victory. From the ghettos of artisans and laborers, we must consider the patriciate, the consequences of their palace building, the changes in their political sociology, and that problem raised over a hundred years ago, but which Renaissance historians persist in describing solely from one side—"the state as a work of art." In summary, this book uses demographic materials to do what is ultimately political history.

Chapter 1

The Sources

*F*ROM analyses of materials on taxation, the composition of insurrectionary crowds, and criminal records, historians of late medieval and Renaissance Florence have bracketed the sociological
character and the political behavior of the *popolo minuto* or the popular
classes with single sets of descriptions.[1] These descriptions have in effect
denied the *popolo minuto* a history. The most authoritative works [2] now
describe them with the same backhanded sympathy with which the
French historian, Hippolyte Taine [3] described the *sans-culottes* on the
eve of the French Revolution. Historians of Renaissance Florence have
characterized the working classes as "the poor . . . without roots . . .
and no genuine link to any urban collectivity." [4] Seen from this per-

---

1. Cf. Lauro Martines (editor), *Violence and Disorder in Italian Cities, 1200–1500* (Berkeley, 1972).

2. The exceptions to this historiographical tendency have been the works of Victor Ruten-burg, *Popolo e movimenti popolari*, translated by G. Borghini (Moscow, 1958; Bologna, 1971); and of Charles de la Ronciére, "Pauvres et Pauvreté à Florence au XIVᵉ siècle," in *Études sur l'histoire de la Pauvreté, Moyen Age—XVIᵉ siecle*, edited by Michel Mollat, Vol. II (Paris, 1974), 661–745; and *Florence: Centre économique régional au XIVᵉ siècle: Le marche des denrées de première necessité à Florence et dans sa campagne et les conditions de vie des salaries, 1320–1380*, Vol. III (Aix-en-Provence, 1977), pp. 1289–1307.

3. "Theoretically, through humanity and through good sense, there is, doubtless, a desire to relieve the peasant and pity is felt for him. But, in practice, through necessity and routine, he is treated according to Cardinal Richelieu's precept, as a beast of burden to which oats are measured out for fear that he may become too strong and kick, 'a mule which accustomed to his load, is spoiled by more long repose than by work'" (Hippolyte A. Taine, *The Ancien Régime*, translated by John Durand, New York, 1876; p. 388). For a critical evaluation of Taine's place in the historiography of the French Revolution, see George Rudé, *Paris and London in the Eighteenth Century: Studies in Popular Protest* (London, 1974), pp. 135–137; and Gustone Manacorda's introduction to Jean Juares, *Storia socialista della Rivoluzione Francese*, Vol. I (Milan, 1953), ix–liii.

4. Gene A. Brucker, "The Florentine *Popolo Minuto* and Its Political Role, 1340–1450," in *Violence and Civil Disorder*, edited by Martines, p. 170.

spective, their role in shaping the political life and structure of society could only have been a passive one; they came to the fore in politics only under the most dire material conditions and after some faction or other jockeying for control within the oligarchy had successfully manipulated them into action.[5] The Renaissance historian, Sergio Bertelli, concluded an article on oligarchies and government in the Renaissance city:

> We must then refuse in our methodological approach all *a priori* constructions. For above all else, the political struggle in the Renaissance city unfolded exclusively within the very restricted world of the patriciate. Outside of this world there was nothing, the nihilism of the jacqueries. When the subordinate class penetrated into the political theater (I am not speaking of the historical theater), it is really only a part of the oligarchy that has appealed to the people in order to serve its own ends for its own particular struggle within the world of the *cives*. At the termination of the confrontation, the masses fall back into oblivion. The waters of the sea fold over them as though they were a sunken ship.[6]

In this book I plan to reconsider the sociological basis from which these political judgments on the character of the *popolo minuto* have been drawn. Over the period of the later Middle Ages and the Renaissance (roughly 1300–1600) were the formations and communities of the laboring groups of Florence so static? Were the structures of their political and social life (structures that presupposed changes in political and social consciousness) indeed unchanging? Were they, in other words, merely a ship in the waters of the sea, that overwhelming context that engulfed their history—the occasional riot or insurrection?

The Marxist Historiography and the Mode of Production

The materials pertaining to the laboring classes of Florence are slim indeed. For the most part, the *popolo minuto* have been studied either in relation to the economic structure of fourteenth-century Florence or in relation to that political event, the Revolt of the Ciompi (the Florentine wool workers) in 1378. After Karl Marx's notes on the

---

5. In addition to the work of Brucker, see Marvin Becker, "Florentine Politics and the Diffusion of Heresy in the Trecento: A Socioeconomic Inquiry," *Speculum*, 34 (1959), p. 66; and Raymond de Roover, "Labour Conditions in Florence around 1400: Theory, Policy and Reality," in *Florentine Studies,* edited by N. Rubinstein (London, 1968) p. 312.

6. Sergio Bertelli, "Oligarchies et gouvernement dans la ville de la Renaissance," *Social Science: Information sur les sciences sociales,* XV-4/5 (1976), p. 623. Lauro Martines echoes similar sentiments: "Plebeian uprisings in fourteenth century Perugia, Florence, and Siena threatened to be more revolutionary (than the thirteenth century *popolo*) and promised a more radical cargo of reforms, but they were a will-o'-the-wisp, all glow and no substance," *Power and Imagination: City-States in Renaissance Italy* (New York, 1979; p. 59).

historian Gino Capponi,[7] research on the laboring classes and the mode of production of late medieval and Renaissance Florence was developed through the latter part of the nineteenth century in the works of Robert Pöhlmann, Alfred Doren, and Niccolò Rodolico.[8] Since World War II, the Soviet historian, Victor Rutenburg, has returned to and developed this earlier approach to Florentine history, which can be loosely identified as being within a Marxist tradition.[9]

From this historical research we can conclude that sometime during the last decades of the thirteenth century and the early part of the fourteenth the corporate guild structure in wool production disintegrated. Skilled artisans who, heretofore, had been independent and who had possessed the right to make certain decisions about production, the buying of their raw materials, and the selling of the finished products were stripped of these political–economic rights and were pressed into a mass of wage earners. Concomitantly, a number of political and technological changes intermeshed to create a revolution in the material conditions of work. With the expansion of the Florentine wool industry in the late Dugento, more efficient and costly tools—the loom and the spinning wheel—were diffused through the cloth industry.[10] More steps of production were created; old skills were fragmented into menial tasks; and more positions were removed from the home and placed under the close supervision of management.

At the same time, the wool guild of Florence (the Arte della Lana) in collaboration with the Commune disbanded all other guilds organized around the various skills involved in wool production and prohibited even casual or religious association among workers.[11] *Discepoli* ('apprentices'), *fattori* ('clerks'), and *sottomaestri* ('managers') no longer signified a division of labor by age. Workers could no longer expect, through marriage or tenure, to inherit the ownership and management of a small shop. Instead, they became the foremen who supervised the new relations of wool production.[12] As a result, at the time of the Ciompi revolt, two classes faced one another at the point of production.

---

7. See Rutenburg, *Popolo e movimenti popolari*, p. 15.

8. Robert Pöhlmann, *Die Wirtschaftspolitik der Florentiner Renaissance und das Prinzip der Verkehrsfreiheit* (Leipzig, 1878); Alfred Doren, *Studien in der Florentiner Wirtschaftgeschicte: I. Die Florentiner Wollentuchindustrie vom 14. bis zum 16. Jahrhundert* (Stuttgart, 1908); *Le arti fiorentine*, 2 vols., translated by G. B. Klein (Florence, 1940); Niccolò Rodolico, *La democrazia fiorentina nel suo tramonto, 1378–1382* (Bologna, 1905); *Il popolo minuto: Note di storia fiorentine, 1343–1378* (Bologna, 1899).

9. Rutenburg, *Popolo e movimenti popolari*.

10. *Ibid.*, 17.

11. *Ibid.*, 47.

12. *Ibid.*, 41–42.

On the one hand, there were the *soci* or 'partners' who were matriculated in the Arte della Lana. By the middle of the fourteenth century, they were a class (in the objective sense of their relation to the means of production) completely divorced from the actual daily toil involved in wool production. They were interested in production principally as a means of capital accumulation, and the reaping of surplus value.[13] On the other side, despite certain graduations in status and skill there stood a mass of artisans and wage earners, who were legally barred from guild matriculation.[14]

For the period after the Ciompi through the sixteenth century, historians have not devoted the same attention to the structure of industry, the nature of work, and the development of the urban economy that the earlier transition was given. Rutenburg and Pöhlmann suggest that the tendencies toward capitalist accumulation spread horizontally during the fifteenth century, revolutionizing the relations of production in other Florentine craft industries.[15] Doren, on the other hand, argues that by the 1480s the trajectory of capitalist development in Florence was stultified.[16] More recently, however, Hidetoshi Hoshino has refuted the conclusions of Doren.[17] He argues that employment and production in the wool industry, instead of declining during the Quattrocento, increased at the very time that the silk industry, and its relation of capital to wage labor were expanding rapidly. Thus, according to the most recent literature on the economic history of urban Florence, the Florentine economy during the fifteenth and early sixteenth centuries certainly did not regress into an earlier mode of production; rather, it appears that the capital sector and wage-labor relations of production developed through the Renaissance.[18]

---

13. *Ibid.*, 19, 32, 65, and 76.

14. This general schema of the development of Florentine industry and economy can be found in the non-Marxist literature as well; see E. Carus-Wilson, *The Cambridge Economic History*, Vol. II, edited by M. M. Postan and E. E. Rich (Cambridge, 1952), 396ff.; Raymond de Roover, "Labour Conditions in Florence Around 1400: Theory and Reality," *Florentine Studies: Politics and Society in Renaissance Florence*, edited by Nicolai Rubinstein (London, 1968), 279ff; and la Roncière, *Florence, centre économique régional*, pp. 1289–1307. Nonetheless, it must be recognized that the above is no more than an outline. Florentine industry and capital must be perceived in a context in which the principal sources of wealth were still derived from commerce and finance. For a criticism of this schema and evidence of economic and social cleavages within the ranks of wool workers and artisans, see also Brucker, "The Ciompi Revolution," in *Florentine Studies*, pp. 314–356.

15. Rutenburg, *Popolo e movimenti popolari*, p. 76, Pöhlmann, *Die Wirtschaftspolitik*, p. 43.

16. Doren, *Le arti fiorentine*, Vol. I, 118–119.

17. Hidetoshi Hoshino, "Per la storia dell'Arte della Lana in Firenze nel Trecento e nel Quattrocento: Un riesame," *Istituto Giapponese di Cultura*, X (1972–1973) pp. 33–80.

18. The status of weavers in the silk industry during the Quattrocento was, however, certainly different from wool and linen weavers of the previous century. The masters were careful

To understand the revolt of the Ciompi, the Marxist tradition of Florentine history has concentrated on the development of capitalist relations of production during the Trecento. Especially in the work of Victor Rutenburg, the Revolt of the Ciompi has been explained (*a*) in terms of the immiserization of the laboring poor, which resulted from the transformation of the social relations of production, and (*b*) in terms of class development. But class is here defined almost exclusively in terms of its objective manifestations, that is, the definition of groups simply in terms of their relationship to the means of production. This economistic notion of class and class conflict leaves out or minimizes severely the subjective character of class and the formation of structures (such as the shape and character of community life) beyond the point of production. It, moreover, neglects other forces that affect class consciousness and class struggle. While the deterministic relationship between changes in the social relations of production and the formation of class consciousness might provide a framework for understanding the political and social developments that led up to the Revolt of the Ciompi, it is certainly insufficient for an understanding of the Ciompi in the ensuing period of the Medicean Republic: the breakdown of working class solidarity and the decline of militancy.

In this book I will entertain the possibility of crucial changes in the community structures, organization, and consciousness of the Florentine *popolo minuto* within a time span in which there seem not to have been any fundamental transformations in the mode of production. Between the fourteenth and sixteenth centuries the wool industry might have declined in importance, but capitalist relations of production and the employment of wage labor certainly expanded in the silk industry. Throughout the period 1340–1530, a form of wage-labor relationship characterized from a third to a half of the work force of urban Florence.[19] The questions now become: How do we begin to grasp the subjective nature of class in the late middle ages; how do we study the communities and social organization of those groups so faintly enshrined in the documentation of late medieval and Renaissance Florence?

---

to handle silk weavers as though they were independent craftsmen; yet, at the same time, they did not permit them to enter the guild (*Por Santa Maria*) and thereby to have any real voice in the decisions of production. "The *setaioli* or silk manufacturers, who owned the raw material, were in complete control. . . ." (Raymond de Roover, "Labour Conditions in Florence around 1400," pp. 306–307).

19. For the Trecento see Giovanni Villani, *Cronica*, edited by F. Dragomani (Florence, 1844–1845), XI, cap. 94, p. 325; for the latter half of the Quattrocento, we find approximately half the occupations specified in the *Notarile* as those of *sottoposti* in the wool and silk industries.

The Sources

The narrative sources left by this population are almost nonexistent. We know, however, that in the Trecento 80% of all Florentine children were taught to read, and that in fact artisans and even laborers kept account books, which like the *ricordanze* of the patriciate contained jottings concerning their family histories, economic and political opinions, and difficulties.[20] But unlike those of their social betters very few of these documents survive. Impressions and information can be garnered from chronicles, poetry, and political statements found in the discussions of the Commune's governmental affairs, the *Consulte e Pratiche*. Almost exclusively, these sources were written by the patriciate and were unsympathetic to the fate and fortunes of the laboring classes. In general as one moves through this literature from the late Trecento to the end of the Quattrocento, the comments of the patriciate become more detached and more hostile at the same time that they become less frequent. The occasional sympathy of a merchant chronicler, a Dino Compagni, or chroniclers who were partisans of the small artisan and worker disappears.[21] In the literary circles of the humanists Leonardo Bruni and Poggio Bracciolini, hostility to the participation of the lower orders in Communal life became more ardent.[22] "No longer were anonymous chroniclers in evidence which exhibited Franciscan overtones of sympathy for the plight of the lower classes."[23]

The vast bulk of these precious scraps of literary sources which pertain to and describe popular life have been published and studied over the last century. From them we can see a psychological polarization of Florentine society from the late Trecento through the Quattrocento. But these sources provide little information from which the historian can reconstruct the sociological nature of the communities of artisans and laborers and their development from the Trecento through the Quattrocento. Only recently have historians turned to other materials— tax records and considerations of fiscal policy—to study Florentine society as a whole and how changes in demography, economy, and

---

20. G. Villani, *Cronica*, XI, cap. 94, p. 324.

21. See, for instance, John Najemy, "Guild Republicanism in Trecento Florence: The Successes and Ultimate Failure of Corporate Politics," *American Historical Review*, 84 (1979) p. 60; and *Cronaca Prima d'Anonimo*, in *Il tumulto dei Ciompi cronache e memorie*, edited by G. Scaramella in Italicarum Scriptores, new ed., XVII, Pt. 2 (Bologna, 1934).

22. See Rutenburg, *Popolo e movimenti popolari*, p. 231.

23. Marvin Becker, "Florentine Politics and the Diffusion of Heresy in the Trecento: A Socio-economic Inquiry," *Speculum*, 34 (1959), 68; Cf. Eugenio Garin, *L'Umanesimo Italiano* (Bari, 1952), 6off.

fiscality might have changed the lives and social structure of the lower orders.[24] Although continued research for direct references to the *popolo minuto* in sources such as the *Consulte e Pratiche* and the legal commentaries of the late fifteenth century would certainly be beneficial to our understanding of the popular classes, for the major artery of research we must proceed along the margins. The researcher must consider aggregate series, which do not exist conveniently organized in any particular source; serial data must be created and their interpretation must rely on quantitative methods.

Historians have for a long time considered the *Notarile antecosimale* ('notarial archives') of the Archivio di Stato of Florence (whose records originate in the middle of the thirteenth century and continue through the first half of the sixteenth century) a central source for the study of Florentine social history. The problems, however, of carrying out a systematic investigation through these documents—which with more than 22,000 volumes comprise the largest single archive in the Archivio di Stato—have been overwhelming. Immediately, the researcher is faced with the problem of isolating a manageable portion of this vast collection for concentrated study. Notarial practice in Renaissance Florence makes certain obvious methods of sampling or studying this documentation infeasible. The researcher might break off a single parish, *gonfalone,* or even quarter of the city for investigation for example, and then follow the notarial business of the geographical unit. In Florence and its suburban parishes, however, the notaries seldom concentrated on a particular neighborhood; more often their business assumed a wide geographical arc through the neighborhoods of the city, sometimes roving in and out of the neighboring villages and towns of the *contado.* From the fourteenth to the fifteenth centuries the tendency of business to draw away from a neighborhood base accentuated; increasingly notaries became specialists, and the type of business—testimonies, business contracts, or dowries—determined their itineraries more and more.

For a study of the *popolo minuto,* moreover, it is difficult to follow the business of any group of notaries or even a single notary over the duration of their careers. There were very few notaries who concentrated on contracts that consistently involved the popular classes. In searching through over 400 notarial books, I found only five notaries with long careers who concentrated on the popular classes and their

---

24. See Becker, *Florence in Transition,* 2 vols. (Baltimore, 1967–1968); David Herlihy and Christiane Klapisch, *Les Toscans et leurs familles: Une étude du catasto florentin de 1427* (Paris, 1978); and Herlihy, "The Distribution of Wealth in a Renaissance Community: Florence, 1427," in *Towns in Societies,* edited by Abrams and Wrigley (Cambridge, 1978), pp. 131–157.

communities,[25] but in each case I found over time a distinct amelioration in the clientele of these notaries. After a decade of redacting petty contracts for artisans, laborers, and peasants who resided in the rural suburbs of the city, these notaries, toward the end of their careers, shifted decisively to the affairs of the merchant class. The researcher who attempts to trace in detail, through all the contracts of a small number of notaries, the outline of a popular urban community, risks confusing the fortunes of a particular group of *popolo minuto* with the individual fortunes of the notaries and their careers.

We have, therefore, sampled our data not by the notary or group of notaries nor by the neighborhood; rather we shall draw a sample through the protocols redacted by notaries who resided in the city of Florence. We shall not attempt to reconstruct in detail the contractual life of a community; instead we shall focus on a single relation: the marriage act, the engagement, and the dowry.[26] We have selected these acts because first, more than any other act in the *Notarile*, they reasonably represent the population as a whole, from the patriciate parishes of the central city to the ghettos of wool workers and small artisans who contracted dowries of as little as a few florins and resided in the large parishes on the city's periphery.[27] Second, more than any other contractual act, the social meaning of the marital relation was probably the most stable over the fourteenth and fifteenth centuries and the easiest to discern. In contrast, a debtor–creditor relationship could signify various different relations between individuals and groups. The indebtedness of a wool carder to a patrician *lanaiolo* in one instance might

---

25. Michelangelo di Silvestro Contadini, 1329–1381 [N(otarile) A(nte)c(osimo)] C 599–C 605; Filippo di Cristofano di Leonardo di Lippo (NAC F 297–305, 1401–1453); Antonio Nardi (NAC, N 19, 1461–1497); Bartolommeo Gerino (NAC, G 122–123, 1495–1547); Francesco di Dino (NAC, F 498, 1441–1491); Francesco Leoni (NAC, L 141–143, 1488–1521); Paolo di Lorenzo (NAC, P 128–130, 1426–1473).

26. Concerning the importance of the marriage relation (at least for the elites) in constructing the social and political fabric of Renaissance Florence, see Dale Kent, *The Rise of the Medici: Faction in Florence 1426–1434* (Oxford, 1978), pp. 48–67; F. W. Kent, *Household and Lineage in Renaissance Florence: The Family Life of the Capponi, Ginori, and Rucellai* (Princeton, 1977) pp. 91–97; Brucker, *The Society of Renaissance Florence: A Documentary Study* (New York, 1971), 28–42; and *Renaissance Florence* (New York, 1969), 92–94, "In a society thus organized around the family, the marriage contract was a document of supreme significance. First, it was an important financial transaction. The size of the dowry was an indication of the economic status of the contracting parties. . . Marriages were also indices of social status, and of the rise and decline of particular families. . . The accounts of births, deaths, and marriages bulk large in the private records of any society, but the space devoted to marriage negotiations in Florentine letters and diaries is conclusive evidence of the importance of this activity in patrician circles. . . Together with wealth, antiquity, and the possession of high communal office, marriage connections were the most important criteria for determining social status."

27. See pages 39–41 and 148–151.

reflect the intimacy of a patron–client relationship; in another instance, it might represent the hard economic relation of an emerging wage-labor organization of society. From several volumes of the deliberations of the Arte della Lana, it appears that there was a shift in the debtor–creditor relationships which were adjudicated in the courts of this guild. In the late Trecento there were more of these relationships between *sottoposti* and artisans in the industry than one finds in the latter part of the fifteenth century at the same time that the number of cross-class relationships (between *lanaiolo* and *sottoposti*) increased.[28]

If we assume that the creditor–debtor relationship represented ties of mutual assistance (as they very well might in a precapitalist or an early capitalist milieu), then the change from the fourteenth- to fifteenth-century data might reflect a growing trust and social interdependence between classes. More plausibly, the increase in prosecutions in the guild courts of debtors who were laborers by patrician creditors reflects the hardening of social bonds into economic bonds of dependency and the breakdown of reciprocity of customary means among neighbors for financial help. Similarly, solidarities such as confraternity membership (which characterized very few poor artisans or *sottoposti* before the middle of the fifteenth century, at least according to the surviving documentation)[29] might, on the one hand, reflect the voluntaristic association of workers and artisans; in another period it might instead have been imposed from above and therefore represent the social policy of the Commune or a major guild.[30] The marriage relationship over this period is less ambiguous. Although it may not always have reflected the intimacy of the spouses individually, it must have always represented a particularly close relationship between either the individuals or the individual families. Of all the notarial acts, moreover, we can argue that marriages represent the most concrete social relationships beyond the point of production for members of the *popolo minuto*; individually and collectively these relationships linked and interlaced occupational groups, classes, and neighborhoods.

---

28. These impressions are based on a small sample of sentences for indebtedness tried in the tribunals of the *Arte della Lana* for two years, 1345–1346 and 1458, *Arte della Lana*, no. 75 and no. 203.

29. Massimo Papi, "Per un censimento delle fonti relative alle confraternite laiche fiorentine: Primi resultati," in *Da Dante a Cosimo I: Ricerche di storia religiosa e culturale toscana nei secoli XIV–XVI*, edited by Dominico Maselli (Pistoia, 1976), pp. 92–121, does not mention a single confraternity of wage earners, *discepoli* of the minor guilds, or *sottoposti* of the wool or silk industries. Several, however, are known to have exited as early as the third decade of the fifteenth century, such as S. Caternina dei tessitori tedeschi and S. Croce (Societas tessitorum drapporum et filatariorum siricis), whose transactions appear in the Notarile (G 122, 1495–1515).

30. Richard Trexler, *Public Life in Renaissance Florence* (New York, 1980).

The Marriage Relation

The historian might argue that the marriage relation reflected only one dimension of the social world of the patriciate or of the *popolo minuto* and from only a single point in time, a single contract. Christiane Klapisch, for instance, has delineated three contours of social relation and interaction from the *ricordanze* of the Niccolini family.[31] Residential patterns among *parenti* or kin cut out the narrowest and most closely knit relationships; then there were the geographical ties between *amici* or those who witnessed and celebrated the baptismal ceremonies of the Niccolini children. The most expansive geography for this family was drawn by its relations of consanguinity; the marriage relationship.

For the *popolo minuto,* however, a three-dimensional study of their networks of social interaction would be much more difficult, if not impossible, to reconstruct. *Ricordanze* which might note detailed social exchanges and solidarities of *amici* among the poor do not exist. But even for the patriciate our study of the marital contract can contribute to a broader understanding of its sociology. Unlike recent studies which have concentrated on the complex web and interaction of familial, social, and financial relations of a handful of families, our study will take a global outlook of the patriciate and its development from the middle of the Trecento through the early part of the sixteenth century.[32] Finally, the marriage relationship was not a single relationship contracted at a single point in time. Its conception and planning, certainly in patrician families, reached back in time well before the initial contractual promise or the dowry. Technically, it was most often two separate acts—the *actum matrimonium* and the dowry—and occasionally, three separate contracts (the *sponsalitium* in addition to the two other contracts).[33] Moreover, the dowry itself might be strung through a series of acts extending back to the initial investment which the father placed in the *Monte delle doti,* when the daughter was an infant, and possibly reaching through the lifetime of the couple: from the original confession of the dowry, through various installments in payment, and

---

31. Christiane Klapisch, "Parenti, amici e vicini': il territorio urbano d'una famiglia mercantile nel XV secolo," *Quaderni Storici,* 33 (1976), pp. 953–982.

32. Klapisch, "Parenti, amici e vicini," considers only one family at the beginning of the Quattrocento; Richard Goldthwaite's *Private Wealth in Renaissance Florence* (Princeton, 1968) is a study of four patrician families from the late Trecento through the early part of the Cinquecento; and the recent anthropological study of F. W. Kent, *Household and Lineage* derives a very different picture of patrician life and social structure from the one drawn by Goldthwaite. Kent's study concerns three families over the course of the Quattrocento.

33. A team of researchers directed by Anthony Molho and Julius Kirschner are now studying the relationships between these various acts; for their initial findings, see "The Dowry Fund and the Marriage Market in Early Quattrocento Florence, "*Journal of Modern History,* 50 (1978), pp. 403–438.

possibly through long years of litigation between the families following the death of one of the spouses. The marriage contracts which bound together two individuals usually and theoretically for life were ties which had religious, social, and familial as well as financial overtones. In late medieval and Renaissance Florence, the dowry often served as the means for purchasing a house for the new couple or the tools for a laborer, a shop for a master artisan or the capital for the new merchant to establish a business partnership.[34] In addition, it was the essential welfare system that provided support for the widow and her offspring. As the study of the Catasto of 1427 by Herlihy and Klapisch shows, the number of truncated families composed of widows living with or without their offspring comprised an important portion of Florentine society.[35]

In summary, the marriage relation and the dowry were central to the complex web of social networks of association not only of individuals but of families, occupational groups, neighborhoods and classes. This phenomenon, moreover, applied not only to the elites of Renaissance Florence, but cut through the social and economic fabric of Florentine society. Critical changes in the aggregate statistics of this social relation would in Renaissance Florence have affected the whole of social interaction for the *popolo minuto* as well as for the patriciate.

To investigate the sociology of the *popolo minuto* in Florence over that period labeled the Renaissance, 1300–1600, I will consider two periods: (*a*) 1343–1383 and (*b*) 1450–1530. Since the work of Niccolò Rodolico, the period 1343–1383 has been considered the period of the Ciompi. It begins with the expulsion of the Duke of Athens from Florence—an event which coincides with the survival of the earliest records from the Florentine criminal archives of the *Podestà*, the *Capitano* and the *Esecutore degli Ordinamenti di Giustizia*. A cursory glance through the criminal archives of the period which culminates in the Revolt of the Ciompi and the establishment of a broadly based government of artisans and laborers, shows that the entire period was punctuated by periodic large-scale insurrection and class war. In contrast, the period of the middle and late Quattrocento and the early part of the Cinquecento seems to have been one of considerable social peace. Even the brief religious and political upheavals surrounding Savonarola and the expulsion of the Medici in 1494 did not mobilize the masses of Florence into the political formations of the previous century.[36]

The first part of this book considers whether changes in social struc-

---

34. See, for instance, Gregorio Dati, *Il libro segreto*, edited by Carlo Gargiolli (Bologna, 1865), and note n. 25.

35. Herlihy and Klapisch, *Les Toscans*, p. 472.

36. See Donald Weinstein, *Savonarola and Florence: Prophecy and Patriotism in the Renaissance* (Princeton, 1970).

ture and changes in networks of association accompanied the political changes from the period of the Ciompi through the rule of the Medici under Republican forms. After evaluating the aggregate statistics on the networks of casual association cast by the analysis of marriage ties, we will question whether these statistics might not obscure fundamental changes in class formation and consciousness of both the *popolo minuto* and the Florentine elites. For this analysis, we will first differentiate and isolate the patriciate and then the laboring classes. Finally, we will evaluate changes in social structure—immigration, the composition of neighborhoods, the distribution of wealth—that may have affected the endogamy patterns of various groups, and the implications of changes in community and consciousness. One thing we will find is that a reading of social structure and community life from the top of society alone will not yield an accurate portrayal of Florentine society in general or of the *popolo minuto* in particular. Rather than parallel developments among classes, a model of antagonistic relations and class conflict reveals much more about the nature of community structures during the Quattrocento.

In this section, I shall describe how the statistical sample of marriages was assembled. Readers who are not concerned with the technical aspects of my research should proceed to the following section (p. 25).

The Selection of Marriages

The selection of marriages for this study could be neither random nor systematic. According to the voluminous survey of demographic sources in Italy there are no extant marriage registers for an integral population in Italy until the Council of Trent, 1563.[37] From the thirteenth century, however, Communal law in Florence required the civil notarization of all marriages. These still exist, in part, scattered through one of the largest *fondi* in the Archivo di Stato. They were not kept in separate *protocolli;* rather, the researcher must search for them through the existing volumes of everyday contractual life in Florence and its surrounding countryside. By the fifteenth century, nevertheless,

---

37. Comitato Italiano per lo studio dei problemi della popolazione, *Fonti archivistiche per lo studio della popolazione fino al 1848* (Rome, 1933–1941); and Roger Mols, *Introduction à la démographie historique des villes d'Europe du XIVᵉ au XVIIIᵉ siècle,* 3 vols, (Gembloux-Louvain, 1954–1956). Actually, the *Fonti archivistiche* does cite a book of marriages from the Sienese parish of S. Salvatore a San Giusto whose records supposedly begin in 1500. However, this citation is mistaken; see *L'Archivio arcivescovile di Siena,* edited by G. Catoni and S. Fineschi (Rome, 1970), p. 76.

one finds considerable specialization in notarial business. Some notaries simply did not handle marriages or dowries, whereas, for a precious few, it was their principal business. For instance, to collect the 3150 separate marriage relations for the later sample, it was necessary to search through over 200 notarile books, redacted by over 100 notaries; however, the business of only 10 notaries constituted over a third of the marriages found.

The compilation of samples of marriage contracts did not proceed along exactly the same lines for both periods. For the fourteenth-century sample it was possible to draw on the protocols of all the notaries who (according to the nineteenth-century inventories) resided in the city of Florence and whose business is extant in the Archivio di Stato. After selecting a single *filza* from each of the 72 notaries, 1343–1383, additional *filze* were chosen from a particular notary if five or more marriages between Florentines were found in the volume first selected from his business. (For a list of these Trecento notaries, see Appendix A.) Through these methods I estimate that 90% or more of those marriage contracts which involved at least one spouse from the city have been collected from the surviving protocols redacted by those notaries residing in the city of Florence, 1343–1383. On the other hand, for the later period, 1450–1530, well over 1000 separate *filze* redacted by notaries residing in the city of Florence survive in the inventories. Thus, in the selection of notarial books for this later period, only a little more than half of all the notaries now extant in the Archivio di Stato were considered. In order to accumulate more contracts, additional *filze* of a particular notary were selected if more than 10 Florentine marriages were found in the first volume of his business (see Appendix B).

For both periods these marital relationships were selected from one or more of three possible contracts concerning marriage in the notarial books: the marriage contract itself *(actum matrimonium)*, the dowry, and the engagement *(actum sponsalitium)*.[38] When more than one of these contracts was found for a particular marital relation, often the various acts were redacted on the same day or were separated only by several days; they are seldom found separated by more than a month. For the Trecento sample, 1221 separate contracts were found, which comprise 878 marital relations (see Table 1.1). Among the three types of marriage contracts, there were 92 acts of engagement, 523 marriage

---

38. For a description of the ceremonies that distinguished these various acts, see Christiane Klapisch, "Zacharie, ou le père évincé: Les rites nuptiaux toscans entre Giotto et le concile de Trente," *Annales: E.S.C.*, 34 (1979), pp. 1216–1243.

Table 1.1
Distribution of Types of Marriage Contracts, 1340–1383

Type	Before 1340	1340–1349	1350–1359	1360–1369	1370–1379	1380–1383	After 1383	Total
Sponsalitia	4	24	12	14	26	12	0	92
Matrimonia	14	44	107	130	141	62	25	523
Dotes	15	82	129	154	132	72	22	606
Total number of contracts	33	150	248	298	299	146 (= 365 decade)	47	1221
Total number of marital relationships	22	117	164	208	213	113 (= 282.5 decade)	41	878

contracts, and 606 dowry agreements. For the sample of the second half of the Quattrocento and early Cinquecento, 3150 separate marital relations were collected from 3860 contracts. There were 310 engagement acts, 2244 marriages, and 1306 dowry agreements (see Table 1.2).

The engagement (or *sponsalitium*) was almost always the earliest of the notarized contracts concerning a particular marital agreement. In this act (usually celebrated in the home or the parish of the bride), a promise of the dowry payment was given. In both periods this act was numerically the least important of the three contracts. Only 10% of all the notarized marriages in both the Trecento and the later period were engagements. This act appears, moreover, to have been a custom practiced (at least notarized) almost exclusively by the rich. For the Trecento the majority of the spouses found in these acts bore prominent Florentine names. In the later period, we find very few of the dowries promised in these contracts to be less than 200 florins; for the most part, they exceeded 500 florins.

The dowry, on the other hand, was an institution which by the Trecento had penetrated all social classes. Dowry payments in both periods ranged from as little as a few florins or 25 lire to 3000 florins by the beginning of the sixteenth century. We find *mezzadri* ('share-croppers') in the rural suburbs, weavers, and wool beaters contracting dowry agreements in basically the same formulaic language as those dowry contracts that tied together the important patriciate families: the Rucellai, the Medici, and the Strozzi. In the Trecento sample, in fact, the most common document concerning marriage in the *Notarile* was the dowry contract; of the spouses found in the *Notarile* 60% redacted marriage acts and 69% are found in dowry contracts. During the latter half of the fifteenth and early sixteenth centuries, however, the relative numbers of these two notarial acts shift in importance; 71% of the spouses can be found in marriage acts, and 41% negotiated dowry agreements.

This change may in part be explained by the appearance of the Monte delle doti (which originated in 1425). In the second part of the fifteenth century we find notaries of the Monte who, while entering the date and amount of the dowry payment in the ledgers of the Monte delle doti, kept notarial books filled exclusively with these dowry contracts of the elites of Florence. In order not to over represent the rich in our sample, these notarial protocols were not considered. Yet, well before the creation of the Monte delle doti, we find a tendency for the marriage act to become relatively more important than the dowry agreement in the mass of notarized documents concerning marriage. In the last full decade of our analysis of the Trecento sample (1370–1380), the num-

Table 1.2
The Distribution of Marriage Contracts by Decade

Type of Contract	1451–1460	1461–1470	1471–1480	1481–1490	1491–1500	1501–1510	1511–1520	1521–1530	Total
Sponsalitia	68	112	51	24	25	15	10	5	310
Matrimonia	260	543	362	336	304	197	106	116	2244
Dotes	138	220	127	209	239	202	111	60	1306
Total	466	875	540	569	588	414	227	181	3860

ber of marriage acts exceeded dowry contracts. We cannot, however, assert that this was a tendency that continued through the last decades of the Trecento and through the early Quattrocento. How do we interpret this evidence? Did the growing preponderance of marriage acts as opposed to dowry contracts in the later sample mean that there was a shift in the economic and social status of the population that notarized its marriage agreements? Did the increase in the relative numbers of isolated marriage contracts, in other words, signify that there was a growing number of individuals who married without exchanging a formally notarized dowry?

The evidence for the fourteenth century strongly suggests that this was not the case. Social historians have recently concluded that the family name generally indicates the attainment of notable social status as reliably as any other indicator which we find in notarial, tax, and other administrative documents.[39] This rule would, in fact, apply more rigorously to the middle and late Trecento than it would to the fifteenth century. In the fourteenth century it is safe to assume that in the vast majority of instances the appearance of a family name specifies that an individual was a member of a self-conscious *consorteria*.[40] In our marriage sample, as well as in the contemporaneous tax records (the *estimi*), the family names which we encounter are almost all names well known to the student of Florentine history. For the latter half of the fourteenth century only 7.8% of all the individuals in our sample possessed a family name.[41] And of those exchanging a dowry of 400 florins or more (which represented roughly the upper fifteenth percentile of all those exchanging dowries in the sample) only 28% bore a family name. Thus, if we consider the frequency in the appearance of family names for those found only with marriage contracts in our sample and without any indication of the value of the dowry, we might gain some insight into the social character of that population represented in our sample by only the marriage contract. Instead of a group of impoverished spouses, there was a higher percentage of individuals with family names (12%) within this group than for the population as a whole.

---

39. Herlihy and Klapsch, *Les Toscans,* pp. 251, 538–542.

40. On the meaning of *consorteria,* see F. W. Kent, *Household and Lineage,* pp. 1–17.

41. This figure might slightly underestimate the percentage of those Florentines who bore family names. When a family name is expressed in the ablative (the general form of the family name), it is easy to spot the family name. There are, however, other family names, which at least in form are more difficult to recognize: names such as di Como or del Bene or da Panzano. Unless the individual is well known, these names might be mistaken for patronymics, nicknames, and toponymics. As a rule, only family names in the ablative form were counted as family names, unless the individual bore a well known family name in another form.

When occupations are considered, a similar impression is given. Of those marriages for which we possess only the marriage agreement itself, 40 persons were identified by occupation in the Trecento sample. Eleven of them (28%) were members of the major guilds, and only five (13%) were *sottoposti* in the wool industry. All of these workers, moreover, were tailors, one of the most elevated positions outside but under the jurisdiction of the Arte della Lana. The majority of these spouses identified by profession belonged to the minor guilds. Thus, in the fourteenth-century sample, that group identified exclusively by the appearance of a marriage contract does not represent the most impoverished group of our sample, that is, a group that generally did not exchange dowries.

In some ways, the evidence for the fifteenth- and early sixteenth-century sample concerning this point is even more striking. Although we find exactly the same percentage of spouses (19%) who bore a family name among those represented in our sample only by a marriage contract as we find in the population at large, we find, of all the social groups in Florentine society, those bearing the most prominent family names (the Medici, Strozzi, Tornabuoni, Rucellai, etc.) represented most often by the marriage agreement alone. In addition, there are numerous spouses with upper guild professions for whom we find no indication of a dowry transaction.

In all likelihood, those represented in our samples by only a marriage agreement transacted dowries that were notarized in other notarial books, perhaps even by a different notary. Why a couple should have chosen to divide the marriage and dowry contracts between notaries (or over extended periods) would require a more detailed study of the social history of notarial practice during the late middle ages and the Renaissance. The slight change in the numerical importance of the marriage act over the dowry contract in the protocols of the latter half of the Trecento and the late Quattrocento and early Cinquecento perhaps reflects changes in the differentiation and separation of business among notaries (especially concerning the affairs of the wealthy) more than a change in the social composition of the two samples. At any rate from literary evidence, the work of Richard Trexler and, more recently, that of Anthony Molho and Julius Kirshner, it appears that the practice of exchanging a dowry ran through Florentine society during the Renaissance and accompanied almost every formal marriage.[42] Indeed,

---

42. Richard Trexler, "Le célibat à la fin du Moyen Age: les religeuses de Florence," *Annales, E.S.C.*, 27 (1972), p. 1339; and Anthony Molho and Jules Kirschner, "The Dowry Fund."

in the fifteenth-century sample (where the notaries identified by profession a significant number of spouses or the fathers of spouses), over half of those exchanging dowries were wage earners *(sottoposti)* of the wool and silk industries. And in the surrounding countryside, *mezzadri* contracted notarized dowries no matter how paltry the exchange.

The Aggregate Analysis of the Marriage Contracts

Let us now examine the internal consistency of the marriage data. First, we will consider the period from about 1340 to 1383. From the analysis of the frequency of contracts by decade (Table 1.1), we find that the period before the Black Death (1348) is seriously underrepresented, while 65% of the contracts found for the 45-year period pertain to the last 25 years of our analysis (1360–1385). Our conclusions on Florentine marriage behavior will therefore bear much more closely on the two decades preceding the Ciompi than on the years before and immediately after the Black Death of 1348. Nonetheless, does the time interval 1340–1383 constitute a period? How widely do the patterns of endogamy fluctuate over time within this interval? Unfortunately, the notarial documents of the latter part of the fourteenth century, unlike those of the later period, indicate only sporadically the professions of the spouses or those of the fathers of the spouses. In the fourteenth-century sample there are only 20 marriage relationships in which both spouses are identified by occupation. Thus, there are not enough statistics to evaluate fluctuations in occupational endogamy. On the other hand, the notaries of the middle and late Trecento identified persons in these contracts by their parish of residence with even greater regularity than did their colleagues a century later. In the fourteenth century 85% of the marriage relations possessed parish identifications for both spouses, whereas a century later the possibility of comparing the residences of spouses declines to 73% of all relationships.

The patterns of geographical endogamy and exogamy have been organized according to two overlapping principles. The central category for both schemes is the district of the parish church—which was the only geographical unit by which the notaries in both periods of our analysis customarily identified their clients. Beyond the parish there are certain problems for geographical demarcation within the city. First, the boundaries of the parish do not correspond or neatly fit into the civil jurisdictions of the 16 *gonfalone* (the basic units of taxation in the city). After the division of the city into sixths, there seems to have been a conscious attempt by the Commune to cut civil borders through the ecclesiastical jurisdictions. Not only the lines of the *gonfalone,* but also the boundaries of the *quartiere,* and even the city walls either crossed or completely ignored the jurisdictions of the parishes. In at least 10 city parishes part of the parish lay beyond the city walls and extended into the *contado.*[43] In most cases the extent lying "fuori le mura" did not exceed 5% of the parish population. In the case of S. Maria in Verzaia, however, the city walls split the parish in half. In the baptismal records of the fifteenth century, no less than 54 churches in the city appear as separate parish jurisdictions. Some appear extremely infrequently, less than once a year, which must have meant that their populations did not exceed 50 souls. On the other hand, the parish of S. Lorenzo was fully one-seventh of the city's population and remained that proportion through the eighteenth century.[44] Six parishes alone in the second half of the fifteenth century (S. Lorenzo, S. Frediano, S. Ambrogio, S. Niccolò, S. Pier Maggiore, and S. Lucia Ognissanti) comprised over 50% of the city population, and 10 churches (S. Maria in Verzaia, S. Pier Gattolino, S. Simone and S. Michele Visdomini) nearly 70%.[45]

Nonetheless, from materials provided by the Catasto of 1427 now organized by David Herlihy and Christiane Klapisch and from the *Estimo del Sega,* 1351–1352, it is possible to approximate which parishes lay in which *gonfaloni* (see Table 1.3).[46] From the parish identification and the administrative units of the city we can form four rings of marriage endogamy: within the parish, within the *gonfalone* (which usually was at least twice the territory and population of the parish), within the quarter (which comprised four *gonfaloni*), within the city,

---

43. These parishes were S. Lorenzo, S. Frediano, S. Pier Maggiore, S. Ambrogio, S. Niccolò, S. Maria in Verzaia, S. Pier Gattolino, S. Lucia Ognissanti, S. Michele Visdomini and S. Felice in Piazza.

44. See Table 1.6, and Piero Pieraccini, "Nota di demografia fiorentina: La parrocchia di S. Lorenzo dal 1625 al 1751," *Archivio Storico Italiano,* LXXXIII (1925), p. 60.

45. For the development of the parochial geography of Florence from the early Christian period through the middle ages, see Arnaldo Cocchi, *Le chiese di Firenze dal secolo IV al secolo XX* (Florence, 1903); Mario Lopes Pegna, *Le più antiche chiese fiorentine* (Florence, 1972); *La chiesa fiorentina* (Curia Arcivescovile) (Florence, 1970); and Luigi Santoni, *Raccolta di notizie storiche riguardanti le chiese dell'Arci-Diogesi di Firenze* (Florence, 1847).

46. We notice that several parishes lay in more than one *gonfalone,* and two parishes, S. Procolo and S. Michele Berteldi possessed territories in more than one quarter. For purposes of our study of geographical endogamy, the most lenient interpretation was always followed; that is, if a man married a woman from a parish which lay in more than one *gonfalone* and one of these *gonfaloni* also contained the parish of the husband's residence, we would conclude that the marriage was an intra-*gonfalone* relationship.

Table 1.3
A Code Sheet of the Popoli within the City of Florence [a]

I. Cluster of S. Frediano
.01 S. Frediano S.S. Drago
.02 S. Maria in Verzaia S.S. Drago
.03 S. Pier Gattolino S.S. Ferza
.04 S. Iacopo sopr'Arno S.S. Nicchio
.05 S. Felicità   S.S. Nicchio, (Scala)
.06 S. Felice ia Piazza S.S. Ferza
.07 S. Spirito S.S. Nicchio

II. Cluster of S. Niccolò
.10 S. Niccolò S.S. Scala
.11 S. Gregorio S.S. Scala
.12 S. Giorgio S.S. Scala
.13 S. Lucia dei Bardi (Magnoli) S.S. Scala
.14 S. Maria sopr'Arno S.S. Scala

III. Cluster of S. Lucia Ognissanti
.20 S. Lucia Ognissanti S.M.N. Unicorno
.21 S. Maria Novella S.M.N. L.Bianco
.22 S. Paolo S.M.N. L.Rosso
.23 S. Pancrazio S.M.N. L.Rosso
.24 S. Trinità S.M.N. Unicorno
.25 Ognissanti S.M.N.

IV. Cluster of S. Lorenzo
.30 S. Lorenzo S.I. L. d'oro
.31 S. Iacopo in Campo Corbolini S.I. Chiavi
.32 S. Marco S.I. Drago

V. Cluster of S. Ambrogio—S. Piero Maggiore
.40 S. Ambrogio—S. Piero Maggiore
.41 S. Pier Maggiore S.I. Chiavi
.42 S. Michele Visdomini S.I. Vaio
.43 S. Simone S.C. Bue
.44 S. Remigio (S. Romeo) S.C. L.Nero
.45 S. Iacopo tra le Fossi S.C. L.Nero
.46 S. Croce S.C. L. Nero, Bue

VI. The Central City Cluster
.50 S. Maria del Fiore S.I. L.d'oro, Drago (S. Reparata)
.51 S. Maria Maggiore S.I. Drago
.52 S. Rufillo S.I. Drago
.53 S. Michele Berteldi S.M.N. L.Bianco, S.I. Drago
.54 S. Leo S.I. Drago
.55 S. Donato dei Vecchietti S.M.N. L. Bianco
.56 S. S. Tommaso S.I. Drago
.57 S. Pier Buonconsiglio S.M.N. L.Bianco
.58 S. Maria in Campidoglio S.I. Chiavi
.59 S. Miniato fra le Torri S.M.N. L.Rosso

Table 1.3 *(Continued)*

.60 S. Andrea   S.M.N. L.Rosso
.61 Orsanmichele   S.C. Carro
.62 S. Biagio (S. Maria sopra Porta)   S.M.N. Vipera
.63 SS Apostoli   S.M.N. Vipera
.64 S. Stefano al Ponte   S.C. Carro
.65 S. Piero Scheraggio   S.C. Carro
.66 S. Cecilia   S.C. Carro
.67 S. Romolo   S.C. Carro
.68 S. Firenze   S.C. Bue
.69 S. Apollinare   S.C. Bue
.70 Badia (S. Stefano alla Badia) S.C. Ruote
.71 S. Procolo   S.C. Ruota, S.I. Chiavi, Vaio
.72 S. Margherita dei Ricci   S.I., Vaio
.73 S. Bartholommeo al Corso   S.I. Chiavi, Vaio
.74 S. Maria Nipotecosa   S.I., Drago, Vaio
.75 S. Michelle delle Trombe   S.I., Vaio (in Palchetta; S. Elisabetta)
.76 S. Maria degli Alberighi   S.I. Vaio
.77 S. Maria in Campo   S.I. Vaio
.78 S. Benedetto   S.I., Vaio
.79 S. Cristofano degli Adimari   S.I., Drago
.80 S. Maria degli Ughi   S.M.N. L.Rosso
.81 S. Piero Celoro   S.I., Vaio
.82 S. Salvatore   S.I., Drago
.83 S. Martino   S.C. Ruote

ᵃ S.S. = S. Spirito; S.M.N. = S. Maria Novella; S.I. = S. Giovanni;
S.C. = S. Croce; L. = Leon.

and then points beyond. We would thus find, generally, the following progression:

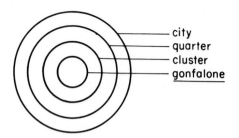

Because of the imprecise intermeshing of the parochial and civil jurisdictions and the possibility of changes in administrative boundaries between our two periods, we have carved up the ecclesiastical geography of the city into six ecological clusters. These divisions are based on observations of the distance between parishes, the population sizes of the parishes, and the appearance of certain physical divides, such as the Arno River, the Pitti Palace, and the street patterns within the old Roman walls. The large parish of S. Frediano and its adjacent parishes south of the Arno comprise cluster I.[47] (see Figure 1.1). The identification numbers of the churches correspond to the numbers in Table 1.3. The Pitti Palace (or, before its construction, the woods and farmland that lay beyond the first ring of walls built across the Arno)[48] divided this cluster from the other *sopr'Arno* area (cluster II), that of the parish of S. Niccolò and its adjacent parishes.[49]

The four clusters north of the Arno are of varying composition. The parish of S. Lucia Ognissanti, which stretches from S. Maria Novella south to the Arno and east to the Roman city walls dominates cluster III.[50] S. Lorenzo by itself constituted a significant chunk of Florentine territory and population (cluster IV).[51] The fifth cluster is not dominated by a single large parish, but instead comprises two of the city's largest parishes (S. Ambrogio and S. Piero Maggiore), four medium-size parishes (S. Simone, S. Michele Visdomini, S. Remigio, and S. Iacopo fra le fosse), and the very small community of S. Croce. Finally, the cluster of churches (cluster VI) within the central city forms a very different ecclesiastical composition. This area is not dominated by a single large parish but, instead, is composed of 34 closely bunched parishes that lie roughly within the Roman walls, extending north from the Arno to the Duomo and west from the Uffizi to the Porta Rosa.[52]

In distinguishing these geographical clusters some of the ecological divisions were clear: the Arno, the street patterns of the area within the Roman walls, and the distance separating the settled area around S. Niccolò from the area around S. Spirito. Other boundaries were more arbitrary. Certain decisions had to be made concerning several parishes

---

47. S. Frediano, S. Maria in Verzaia, S. Pier Gattolino, S. Iacopo sopr'Arno, S. Felicità, S. Felice in Piazza, S. Spirito.

48. Giuseppina C. Romby, *Descrizioni e rappresentazioni della città di Firenze nel XV secolo* (Florence, 1976), p. 33.

49. S. Niccolò, S. Gregorio, S. Giorgio, S. Lucia de'Bardi (dei Magnoli), S. Maria sopr'Arno.

50. S. Lucia Ognissanti, S. Maria Novella, S. Paolo, S. Pancrazio, S. Trinità.

51. S. Lorenzo, S. Iacopo in Campo Corbolini, S. Marco.

52. S. Maria del Fiore (S. Reparata), S. Maria Maggiore, S. Rufillo, S. Michele Berteldi, S. Leo, S. Donato de'Vecchietti, S. Tommaso, S. Pier Buonconsiglio, S. Maria in Campidoglio. S. Miniato fra le Torri, S. Andrea, S. Maria sopra Porta (S. Biagio), S.S. Apostoli, S. Stefano al Ponte, S. Piero Scheraggio, S. Cecilia, S. Romolo, S. Firenze, S. Apollinare, S. Stefano alla Badia, S. Procolo, S. Margherita de'Ricci, S. Bartolommeo al Corso, S. Maria Nipotecosa, S. Michele delle Trombe (in Palchetta, S. Elisabetta), S. Maria degli Alberighi, S. Maria in Campo, S. Benedetto, S. Cristofano degli Adimari, S. Maria degli Ughi, S. Pier Celoro, S. Salvatore, S. Martino.

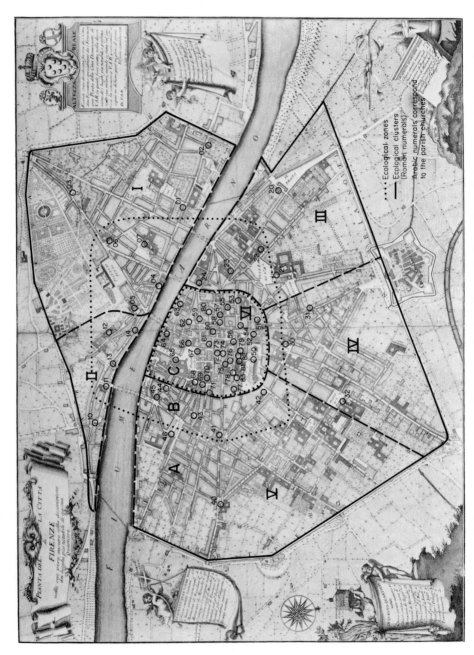

Figure 1.1. (For the names of churches and the ecological clusters, see Table 3.1.)

which lay between clusters (such as S. Iacopo fra le Fosse, S. Remigio, S. Michele Visdomini, and S. Trinità), where there were no decisive ecological boundaries. It was necessary, moreover, to draw the borders of certain clusters across the boundaries of *gonfaloni*. For instance, the *gonfalone* of Leon Bianco in the Quarter of S. Maria Novella extends from the city walls, crosses the territory of the parish of S. Maria Novella and then enters the northwestern corner of that area within the old Roman walls. The parish of S. Maria Novella, thus, was included within the cluster of S. Lucia Ognissanti, while the small parishes of S. Michele Berteldi and S. Donato de'Vecchietti were placed in the central city cluster. In summary, if we were to intersperse these two systems of geographical division, there would be the following progression: parish, *gonfalone*, cluster, quarter, and city.

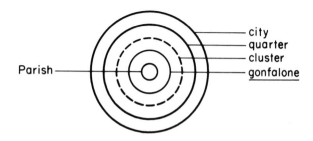

The difference in parish populations and territories, however, at times confounds the absolute rank ordering of these territorial demarcations. In the *gonfalone* of Viao, S. Giovanni, there were at least 10 parishes (according to the tax survey of del Sega, 1351–1352 and 1355); on the other hand, the parish of S. Lorenzo comprised almost the entirety of the considerably larger *gonfalone* of Leon d'oro. In the tables, therefore, we have kept the two systems of geographical endogamy separate (parish, *gonfalone*, quarter, cross-quarter, *contado* and parish, cluster, cross-cluster, *contado*), and we will consider social interaction and community across social classes from the perspective of both of the geographical grids—the ecclesiastical and civil districts, and the ecological territories. Although the ecclesiastical–civil districts (that is, parish, *gonfalone*, quarter) will be the predominant lens for viewing changes in association and community, the ecological districts will serve as a control to the problems of comparing various communities across the urban landscape of Florence. As we have seen, the historical development

of these ecclesiastical and civil districts by the fourteenth century created a conglomeration of intersecting boundaries demarcating districts
which were hardly uniform.

To consider changes in endogamy over the Trecento period, we have
divided the data into three historical periods: (*a*) the 8 years of our
sample preceding the Black Death, 1340–1348; (*b*) the period preceding the Revolt of the Ciompi, 1349–1378; and (*c*) the remaining years
of our sample, which run from the fall of the Otto di Santa Maria
Novella and the abolition of the guild of the *popolo minuto* (August
31, 1378) through the restoration of the oligarchy and the reconsolida-
tion of patrician power, around 1383.

When the patterns of intermarriage are compared for the three
periods within the mid-Trecento sample (Table 1.5), certain differences
appear over time. The extent of endogamy within each of the geographi-

Table 1.4
Gonfaloni *and Parishes of Florence*

S. Spirito		
	Scala	S. Niccolò, S. Giorgio, S. Gregorio, S. Lucia de'Bardi, S. Maria sopr'Arno, S. Felicità
	Nicchio	S. Felicità, S. Iacopo sopr'Arno, S. Spirito
	Ferza	S. Felice in Piazza, S. Pier Gattolino
	Drago	S. Frediano, S. Maria in Verzaia
S. Croce		
	Caro	S. Piero Scheraggio, S. Romolo, S. Stefano al Ponte, S. Cecilia, Orsanmichele
	Bue	S. Simone, S. Apollinare, S. Firenze, S. Croce
	Leon Nero	S. Romeo, S. Iacopo fra le Fosse, S. Croce
	Ruote	S. Procolo, S. Stefano alla Badia, S. Martino
S. Maria Novella		
	Vipera	SS. Apostoli, S. Maria sopra Porta
	Unicorno	S. Lucia Ognissanti, S. Trinità
	Leon Rosso	S. Pancrazio, S. Paolo, S. Miniato fra le Torri, S. Maria degli Ughi, S. Andrea
	Leon Bianco	S. Maria Novella, S. Michele Berteldi, S. Donato de' Vecchietti, S. Piero Buonconsiglio
S. Giovanni		
	Leon d'Ora	S. Lorenzo, S. Marco, S. Iacopo in Campo Corbolini, S. Maria del Fiore
	Drago	S. Maria Maggiore, S. Salvatore, S. Maria del Fiore, S. Leo, S. Maria Nipotecosa, S. Cristofano, S. Marco, S. Rufillo, S. Michele Berteldi
	Chiavi	S. Piero Maggiore, S. Proccolo, S. Ambrogio, S. Bartolommeo al Corso
	Vaio	S. Michele Visdomini, S. Piero Celoro, S. Maria degli Alberighi, S. Maria Nipotecosa, S. Benedetto, S. Michele in Palchetto, S. Margherita de'Ricci, S. Maria in Campo, S. Procolo, S. Bartolommeo al Corso

cal categories, the parish *a*, the *gonfalone b*, the cluster *d*, and the quarter *c*, declined from the 8-year period preceding the Black Death to the period preceding the Revolt of the Ciompi; while the patterns of cross-quarter *e* and cross-cluster *f* exogamy increased by 13 and 9%, respectively; and intermarriage between the city population and the *contado* almost doubled from 7 to 13% (see Table 1.4 and the Appendixes C.1, C.2, and C.3). Then, from this period, which precedes the Revolt of the Ciompi to the period of the last years of the government of the Arti Minori, 1380–1383, the patterns of endogamy contracted slightly. Intermarriage within the parish returned to the levels of the pre–Black Death population (36% endogamy); on the other hand, the contraction in the patterns of endogamy beyond the smaller units of neighborhood association—the parish and the *gonfalone*—was not as striking. While endogamy within the quarter (*a* + *b* + *c*) increased from 48 to 57%, intermarriage within the ecological clusters (*a* + *d*) dropped from 46 to 45%. In the last period of analysis, the patterns of intermarriage beyond the parish thus resembled more closely the 1350–1378 period than the period preceding the Black Death. Despite these fluctuations, the shifts in the patterns of endogamy over the middle and late Trecento were not critical. For the whole period, 1340–1383, the rates of endogamy exceeded those of the middle period, 1348–1378, only by negligible differences: 2% for the parish; .54% for the *gonfalone b*; .41% for the cluster *d*; 1.14% for the quarter *c*; and 1.90% for the city, *a* + *b* + *c* + *d or a* + *d* + *f*.

Let us now turn to the sample of marital relations for the latter half of the fifteenth and the early sixteenth centuries. This sample represents extremely well the population distribution within the city walls. We find roughly the same population ratios for the various parishes of the city and geographical clusters of parishes when these units are compared with the frequencies of fathers identified by parish in the baptismal register of Florence (see Table 1.6).[53] The distribution of contracts over the period 1450–1530, however, does not represent equally well all parts of this 80-year spectrum. The contracts cluster significantly in the middle years; 77% were redacted between 1461 and 1499, and less than 10% pertain to the sixteenth century (see Appendix D.1). When we consider, however, only those marriages that can be utilized in the study of urban Florence, the distribution of relationships over the 80

---

53. Archivio dell'Opera del Duomo, *Registro delle fedi di battesimo*, 1451–1526.

Table 1.5

Marriage Endogamies for the Fourteenth Century by Period

Period	Endogamies				Exogamies			Total[b]
	Parish (a)	Gonfalone (b)	Quarter (c)	Cluster (d)	Cross-quarter (e)	Cross-cluster (f)	Contado[a] (g)	
1340–1349								
Women	35	12	20	21	27	38	8	102
Men	35	12	20	21	27	38	6	100
Total	70	24	40	42	54	76	14	202
	34.65%	11.88%	19.80%	20.79%	26.73%	37.62%	6.94%	
Cumulative		94	134	112				
		46.53%	66.34%	55.45%				
1350–1379								
Women	116	23	60	54	164	193	75	438
Men	116	23	60	54	164	193	29	392
Total	232	46	120	108	328	386	104	830
	27.95%	5.54%	14.46%	13.01%	39.52%	46.51%	12.53%	
Cumulative		278	398	386				
		33.49%	47.95%	46.51%				
1380–1383								
Women	104	17	41	41	89	106	48	299
Men	104	17	41	41	89	106	32	283
Total	208	34	82	82	178	212	80	582
	35.74%	5.84%	14.09%	14.09%	30.58%	36.43%	13.75%	
Cumulative		242	324	290				
		41.58%	55.67%	49.83%				

[a] *Contado*, here, is an abbreviation. All spouses from beyond the city walls who married into the city (whether they resided in an adjacent suburban parish or in a foreign country) are included in g.

[b] $a + b + c + e + f + g = $ Total and $a + d + f + g = $ Total).

34

years changes radically. These differences in distribution result from a slight difference in the selection procedure between the fourteenth century sample and that of the late fifteenth and early sixteenth centuries.

When I compiled the fourteenth-century sample, the unit for analysis was the city of Florence. Notaries were selected who resided and worked primarily within the city walls of Florence. For the fifteenth-century sample (the first sample compiled in this study) on the other hand, I selected notaries from the Pieve of S. Giovanni. This district included, in addition to the city of Florence, the rural belt surrounding Florence extending south as far as the village of Cintoia (which lies in the Potesteria of Galluzzo), southeast of Monte Ripaldi, west to Nuovoli and east to S. Martino a Mensola, near Settignano.[54] In our sample the rural suburbs are represented in large part by the contracts found in the protocols of Ser Antonio Naldi, who worked through the parishes surrounding the village of Legnaia (just beyond the Gate of S. Frediano) during the years 1461–1497.[55] From Ser Antonio's contracts, we have collected no less than 640 separate marital relationships. As a result, when we consider only those relationships in which at least one spouse resided in the city of Florence, the middle years, instead of being over-selected, become for the purposes of this study underrepresented. We find 335 marriages for the last 16 years of Cosimo's rule (1450–1465), 241 marriages for the period 1466–1489 roughly covering the rule of Lorenzo, and 347 marriages for the period 1490–1530.

Finally, the question arises: Should we consider the 80-year period, 1450–1530, as a single period for analysis? The 80 years were originally selected on the basis of demographic characteristics. According to the baptismal records of Florence, these 80 years show remarkable consistency: steady population growth until the plagues and political disorders at the end of the 1520s.[56] But beyond the demographic continuum other social phenomena might impinge, such as changes in the organization of neighborhoods or the social networks of association among the popular classes. We have, therefore, divided this sample into three subsets that correspond roughly with the major historical and political changes over the 80-year period: (*a*) the last 16 years of Cosimo

---

54. Cf. *La Tavola antica di tutti popoli*, in *Delizie degli Eruditi Toscani*, edited by Frater Idelfonso di San Luigi, Vol. XIII (Florence, 1780), pp. 207–288.

55. *Notarile Antecosimo N* 19 (1461–1497), 4 vols.

56. Marco Lastri, *Richerche sull'antica e moderna popolazione della citta di Firenze* (Florence, 1775).

Table 1.6
Relative Population Sizes of Parish Clusters, 1450–1530 [a]

Area	Number found in Notarile	Ratio	Number found in baptismal register	Ratio	Frequency expected	Chi-square
S. Frediano	125	.14	147	.11	99.7	6.42
Other parishes in cluster	115	.13	222	.17	150.6	8.42
Total cluster	140	.27	369	.28	250.3	.42
S. Niccolò	40	.04	46	.03	31.2	2.48
Other parishes in cluster	11	.01	22	.02	14.9	1.02
Total cluster	51	.05	68	.05	46.1	.11
S. Lucia Ognissanti	75	.08	90	.07	61.0	4.25
Other parishes in cluster	68	.08	120	.09	81.4	2.21
Total cluster	143	.16	211	.16	143.1	.00
S. Ambrogio	71	.08	103	.08	69.9	.02
Other parishes in cluster	131	.15	186	.14	126.1	.19
Total cluster	202	.23	289	.22	196.0	.18
S. Lorenzo	153	.17	226	.17	153.3	.00
Other parishes in cluster	7	.01	15	.01	10.2	1.00
Total cluster	160	.18	241	.18	163.5	.07
Central city cluster	104	.11	149	.11	101.1	.08
Total	900	1.00	1327	1.00		

[a] a = the frequency of appearances of the wife's parish; b = the ratio of a to the total number of appearances of parishes (identified for wives) within the city; c = the number of births identified by parish for twelve 1-month periods selected between 1451 and 1530: January 1451, January 1456, January 1461, January 1466, January 1471, January 1476, January 1481, January 1486 (males), January 1496 (females), January 1506 (males), January 1516 (females), January 1526 (males); d = the ratio of c to the total number of births within the city parishes. According to a chi-square test for signifiance $\chi^2 = \Sigma$ $[(f_o - f_e)^2/f_e]$, where f_o = frequency observed and f_e = frequency expected, the differences in the frequencies of appearance for the parishes considered individually are significant between the two samples ($\chi^2 = 26.09$ at 10 degrees of freedom). When the clusters are compared, however, the differences are highly insignificant ($\chi^2 = 1.00$ at df = 5).

de'Medici (1450–1465);[57] (*b*) the period of Lorenzo (1466–1489);[58] and (*c*) the period extending from Savonarolian fervor to the fall of the Florentine Republic (1490–1530).[59]

When patterns of endogamy are considered between these three periods, the most substantial variation occurs in the parish endogamies *a* between the first period of our analysis, 1450–1466 and the period of Lorenzo. (See Table 1.7 and Appendixes D.2, D.3, and D.4.) Parish endogamy decreases from 36% to 30%. This change, however, by a standard error of a proportion test is not significant.[60] In the ensuing period (1490–1530) moreover, the ratio of parish endogamy returns to the 1450–1465 level, 34%. Thus, for purposes of the marriage endogamies within various geographical divisions of the city of Florence and for evaluating the networks of social interaction reflected by these ratios of endogamy, we can reasonably consider the 80 years, 1450–1530, as a single period for analysis.

The most serious problem for the analysis of the later sample arises not from the selection process nor from problems of periodization but, instead, from the character of notarial redaction during the Quattrocento and early Cinquecento. Not all of the marriages found for the later period provide information which would demonstrate a relationship between the residences or geographical origins of the spouses. Unlike the fourteenth-century data, moreover, the omission of this information is not generally distributed through the population. We lose 27% of the marriages in the fifteenth century when we consider only those marriages which reflect a geographical relationship. This 27% loss, however, is disproportionately absorbed by the patriciate of Florence. Generally, by the middle of the fifteenth century, the notary no longer identified the rich and the powerful by his or her parish of residence. They were simply called *cives Florentinis* ('citizens of Florence'). Nineteen percent of the population found in the marriage contracts had family names, but less than 38% of these relationships (thus, a 62% loss) could be used in our analysis. Even this figure is deceptive. Among those bearing family names and identified by parish, we find predomi-

---

57. Actually, Cosimo de'Medici died on August 1, 1464.

58. Lorenzo's period as the effective head of state stretches from 1469 to 1492.

59. The Republic of Florence falls in August, 1530.

60. Significance is here tested by the standard error of a proportion: $z = (p - \pi)/[\pi(1 - \pi/N]^{1/2}$ where p = the proportion observed, π = the hypothesized value of the *population* proportion, and N = the number of persons in the sample. To calculate z; the 1450–1465 and the 1466–1489 samples were considered as two subsets of a single population, the hypothesized proportion (π) is then computed as the mean proportion of the two subsets for any category of endogamy: $p = .3574$; $\pi = .3277$; $N = 931$, $z = 1.93$.

nantly names that are obscure to the student of Florentine history— patronymics that had recently been converted into family names. During the fifteenth and early sixteenth centuries the notary rarely identified by parish spouses from the most notable Florentine families (the Medici, Strozzi, Bardi, Soderini, Tornabuoni, Pitti, Alberti, etc.).

Keeping in mind these characteristics of the data, let us now compare the aggregate statistics on marriage endogamies for the Trecento and Quattrocento.[61] From the results in Table 1.8 we do not find any striking changes. Perhaps this is as one should expect in an era before the massive dislocation of place of residence and place of work created by the Industrial Revolution and extending through the revolution in transportation of the late nineteenth century.[62] Basically, we find the residents of Florence bunched fairly closely together within the parish communities when we view their social relations through the networks of consanguinity. Around a third of the population in both periods of our analysis chose to marry someone who resided within the same parish. Let us remember that although several of the parishes possessed populations of over 5000, there were over 50 parishes in fourteenth and fifteenth century Florence, many of which encircled tiny communities.

Beyond this basic category of social exchange—the parish—we find no other clear focus of social (or at least marital) interaction. Marriage within the next ring of endogamy—the *gonfalone*—was particularly weak. And the *gonfalone* (with the exceptions of Leon d'Oro, Drago Verde (S. Spirito), and possibly, Leon Bianco) was at least twice the population and territory of any parish within its jurisdiction. Within the central city, moreover, the territory and population of the *gonfalone* was often 5 to 10 times greater than any of its constituent parishes. In both periods only 6% married outside their parishes and into the ring enclosed by the confines of the *gonfalone b*. The selection of a spouse even within the ring outside of the parish and within the confines of the quarter $(b + c)$—an area that was usually four times the size of the *gonfalone* and at least seven times that of the parish (with the exception of four or five large parishes)—was not so common. In fact, for the later period, it would have been almost as likely (according to

61. For this comparison, the business of Ser Naldo d'Antonio has been extracted. Nonetheless, (because of differences in the selection procedures between the two samples described above) the late fifteenth-century sample is still biased towards an overstatement of intermarriage between city and *contado*.

62. For generalizations on the sociological character of the preindustrial city, see Lewis Mumford, *The City of History: Its Origins, Its Transformations, and Its Prospects* (New York, 1961); Gideon Sjoberg, *The Preindustrial City: Past and Present* (New York, 1960); and Sam Bass Warner, Jr., *The Private City: Philadelphia in Three Periods of Its Growth* (Philadelphia, 1968).

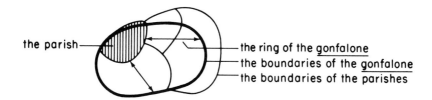

the parish — the ring of the gonfalone
— the boundaries of the gonfalone
— the boundaries of the parishes

these statistics) for a spouse to arrange a lifetime commitment with a partner who resided outside the city at the time of marriage as it would have been for him or her to find a spouse from the community within the quarter but outside the parish. Nineteen percent married within the ring of the quarter $(b + c)$, while 16% married beyond the city walls (g).

The comparison between the endogamies within the parishes and endogamies within those rings just beyond the parish, the *gonfalone*, the geographical cluster, or even the much larger area of the quarter suggests that there probably were not other nodes of interaction smaller than the parish (such as a cluster of houses, a street corner, a neighborhood tavern) that generally exerted a pull or provided a focus for marital interaction stronger than or equal to that of the parish church and its community. Otherwise, we would have expected a much more gradual tapering off of geographical endogamies through the administrative and ecological rings of the city; instead, the ratios of endogamy drop radically from the parish to the larger district of the *gonfalone*.

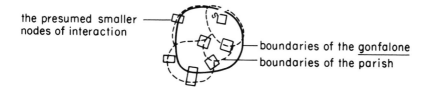

the presumed smaller nodes of interaction
— boundaries of the gonfalone
— boundaries of the parish

Finally, these patterns of social interaction persist over time, from the insurrectionary days of the Ciompi through the period of social peace during the latter part of Cosimo de'Medici's rule. The most substantial difference between the two periods concerns those who sought a spouse who resided at the time of marriage beyond the city walls. Twelve percent married outside the city during the Trecento, while 16% of the marriage relations during the Quattrocento crossed the city walls. Yet, this difference might exaggerate real changes in immigration through marriage between the periods. As we mentioned

Table 1.7
Marriage Endogamies for the Fifteenth Century

Period	Endogamies				Exogamies			Total
	Parish (a)	Gonfalone (b)	Quarter (c)	Cluster (d)	Cross-quarter (e)	Cross-cluster (f)	Contado (g)	
1450–1465								
Women	104	17	41	41	89	106	48	299
Men	104	17	41	41	89	106	32	283
Total	208	34	82	82	178	212	80	582
	35.74%	4.84%	14.09%	14.09%	30.58%	36.43%	13.75%	
Cumulative		242	324	290				
		41.58%	55.67%	49.83%				
1466–1489								
Women	52	11	18	18	66	77	23	170
Men	52	11	18	18	66	77	32	179
Total	104	22	36	36	132	154	55	349
	29.80%	6.30%	10.32%	10.32%	37.82%	44.13%	15.76%	
Cumulative		126	162	140				
		36.10%	46.42%	40.11%				
1490–1530								
Women	97	17	35	31	81	102	38	268
Men	97	17	35	31	81	102	67	297
Total	194	34	70	62	162	204	105	565
	34.34%	6.02%	12.93%	10.98%	28.67%	36.11%	18.58%	
Cumulative		228	298	256				
		40.35%	52.74%	45.31%				

Table 1.8
Comparison of Total Marriage Endogamies, 1340–1383 and 1450–1530

Period	Endogamies				Exogamies			Total
	Parish (a)	Gonfalone (b)	Quarter (c)	Cluster (d)	Cross-quarter (e)	Cross-cluster (f)	Contado (g)	
1340–1383	510 31.60%	104 6.44%	242 14.99%	232 14.37%	560 34.70%	674 41.76%	198 12.27%	1614
Cumulative Totals		614 38.04%	856 53.04%	742 45.97%				
1450–1530	506 33.86%	90 6.02%	188 12.57%	180 12.03%	472 31.55%	570 38.10%	240 16.04%	1496
Cumulative Totals		596 39.84%	784 52.41%	686 45.86%				

41

earlier, for the Quattrocento sample, I selected notaries who normally worked in the rural suburbs of Florence as well as notaries from the city. The additional contracts provided by these rural notaries (even after the omission of the marriage records redacted by Ser Antonio Naldi) would overstate somewhat (in comparison to the earlier period) the interrelation between city and *contado*. In the later period we can observe partially those city spouses who went to a rural parish to celebrate their marriage or contract their dowry as well as those *contadini* who travelled to an urban parish for these agreements and rituals. For the earlier period, on the other hand, we see only the *contadini* who came to the city. Second, because notaries in the Quattrocento did not identify their clients quite as often by a parochial residence as their predecessors had done during the previous century, it would be more likely in the Quattrocento than in the Trecento to interpret a typonymic of a city resident as the place of residence at the time of marriage.

Beyond these statistics on the intermarriage between spouses of the city and the *contado,* we do not, however, find a single significant difference in any of the rings of marriage endogamy between the fourteenth and fifteenth centuries.[63] But could these aggregate figures obscure important differences between various classes in Florentine society and possibly important changes in social structure and consciousness between the two centuries? Let us remember that the fourteenth-century sample contains a greater percentage of observations of the marital behavior of the wealthy. Because of changes in notarial practice, the patriciate of fifteenth- and early sixteenth-century Florence hardly enter into our analysis. We might indeed expect the marriage patterns of the patriciate to be different from those of the *popolo minuto*. Since they comprised a much smaller proportion of the population, we might expect them to seek marriage partners over a larger geography. We need now to cut cross sections through the aggregate statistics. We will begin by trying to separate out for analysis the patriciate, or the wealthy and powerful of Florence, for the two periods of our study.

---

63. Standard error of a proportion test: $p = 31.60$, $\pi = .3273$, $N = 3110$, $z = 1.35$, which is insignificant at 0.05.

Chapter 2

The Patriciate

*T*o cut beneath the patterns that the aggregate marriage statistics reveal and investigate possible changes within patrician communities—their networks of casual association—we must first explore the theoretical question: How do we define the Florentine ruling classes in the fourteenth and fifteenth centuries? Then, from the scraps of evidence contained in the notarial contracts, we must proceed to the operational difficulties of actually delineating the contours which best demarcate our theoretical notions of the patriciate, in order to compare the two centuries. Unlike the results of the previous chapter, this chapter will reveal a remarkable shift in social structure between the fourteenth and fifteenth centuries.

The fifteenth-century sample may reasonably be assumed to represent the world of the *popolo minuto* and the burgeoning middle classes of Florence—laborers, artisans, petty shopkeepers, and even some major guildsmen. However, because of changes in notarial conventions, the effect on our aggregate statistics of the marriage behavior of the Florentine patriciate is minimal. In comparison, the fourteenth-century sample represents more closely a true cross section of Florentine society. For the fourteenth-century sample, 58% of those marriage relations in which at least one spouse bore a family name could be used in our analysis to show a linkage between the residences of spouses. In the fifteenth century, less than 38% of these relations could be considered to demonstrate a relationship between either occupations or residences. As we have argued, moreover, those who bore family names and were at the same time identified as belonging to a particular parish church (*de populo de . . .*) in our fifteenth-century sample, usually were not members of the prominent families of Florence, but instead appear to have been *novi cives* bearing family names of recent origin, in many instances a patronymic which by the sleight of the notary's pen had been converted from the genitive to the ablative. Members of those prominent families well known to the student of Florentine history—degli Serragli, Bardi, Peruzzi, Capponi, Altoviti, etc.—were almost never designated by a parish church. In the notarial books of the fifteenth century, they were simply referred to as *de Florentia* and, more often, as *cives Florentini.*

Dowry size more clearly indicates the change in notarial practice between the fourteenth and the fifteenth centuries concerning the identification of the upper classes. During the period 1340–1383, 16.77% of the population exchanged a dowry of 400 florins or more; a corresponding percentage of the fifteenth-century population (16.99%) is found to have payed dowries of 600 florins or greater. In the fourteenth-century population with dowries reflecting an elite status, 81 of 109 relationships (or 74%) could be used in our analysis to show a connection between the residences of the spouses. The number representing an equivalent status in the fifteenth century falls drastically to four relations or 6.77% of these marriages.

Were the circles of *parenti* carved out by the marriage contracts of the patriciate similar to those of the *popolo minuto* or the city population in general? We might speculate that, because of their smaller numbers, the patriciate would have had to go farther afield in the selection of their wives or husbands. If this were the case, the aggregate results of the geographic endogamies for the fourteenth century would overstate the extent of general exogamy in comparison with our sample from the late fifteenth century. Were the networks of *parenti* of the patriciate stable over the two centuries of our analysis? Did their patterns of intermarriage covary with those of the general population or with those of the *popolo minuto*? Before we can investigate further the sociology of the working and artisan classes, we must attempt to construct samples of more similar populations. The first step in this analysis will be to isolate, as best the notaries' practices permit, the Florentine patriciate or upper classes from the general analysis of marriage patterns.

How do we distinguish the Florentine patriciate? Unlike the patriciate of Venice, which was a firmly established set of families, the patriciate of late medieval and Renaissance Florence was not legally defined. Even in the broader social sense its contours were not well defined. In the late fifteenth century, the eclectic, Benedetto Dei, attempted to compile a list of the 200 elite families of Florence similar to the fixed number of families in the Venetian patriciate. The list, however, was never completed; only 150 families could be so designated.[1] Unlike the signorial governments of other central and northern

1. Guido Pampaloni, "Fermenti di riforme democratiche nella Firenze medicea del quattrocento," *Archivio Storico Italiano* (1961), cxlx, 48–49.

Italian city–states, the government of Florence, the group selected as eligible for holding office, was not coterminous with the social elite or patriciate of Florence; instead, the *reggimento* and the patriciate were overlapping sets. [2] Moreover, in a curious fashion, during the rule of the Medici the *reggimento* became more broadly based socially as the government became more despotic, as social structure became more polarized, and as the patriciate became a more separate caste. The governmental strategies of the fifteenth-century Medici were such that there was thus an inverse relationship between changes in the *reggimento* and the patriciate.[3]

These theoretical problems in defining the Florentine patriciate lead to other operational problems; from the fourteenth to the fifteenth century, moreover, this problem changes in nature. From a social perspective the family name is the best indication of patriciate status that can be supplied by the notary—but as we have already seen, the significance of the family name shifts from the late fourteenth through the late fifteenth century. In the fourteenth century, these names most certainly identified an individual as a part of a *consorteria*—a family clan with a consciousness of itself as well as with recognition by society as a corporate identity, even though, by the beginning of the fourteenth century, this recognition no longer carried a juridical significance.[4] As we have said, the number of individuals in our documents who bore family names may understate the actual size of patriciate society. Whereas only 12% of the individuals in the fourteenth century possessed family names, in the fifteenth century the number increases to 19%.

As well as the appearance of patronymics recently converted into family names during the fifteenth century, there is the problem of increasing numbers of *poveri vergnonosi* or *popolani grassi* who had fallen from the station in life that their family name formerly conveyed.[5] In our fifteenth-century records we find spouses who must have been victims of this social phenomenon. Members of prominent Florentine families in our later sample exchanged pitiful sums for dowries. For instance, in 1496, a member of the Strozzi family, a certain Nicolai di Filippo,

2. Dale Kent, "The Florentine *Reggimento* in the Fifteenth Century," *The Renaissance Quarterly* (1975), XXVIII, pp. 575–630.

3. A. Molho, "Politics and the Ruling Class in Early Renaissance Florence," *Nuova Rivista Storia* (1968), LII, pp. 401–420.

4. On the significance of the *consorteria* and the family clan, see again F. W. Kent, *Household and Lineage in Renaissance Florence: The Family Life of the Capponi, Ginori and Rucellai* (Princeton, 1977); and Jacques Heers, *Le clan familial au moyen âge* (Paris, 1974).

5. Richard Trexler, "Charity and the Defense of Urban Elites in the Italian Communes," in *The Rich, the Well-Born, and the Powerful*, edited by F. C. Jaher (Urbana, 1973), pp. 64–109; and Gene Brucker, *The Civic World of Early Renaissance Florence* (Princeton, 1977), p. 406.

gave his daughter a dowry of 60 florins and a trousseau worth 50 lire to marry Paolo di Guglielmo di Paolo di Bernardo degli Altoviti.[6] A certain Alessandra, the daughter of a weaver who bore the prominent Florentine name, degli Asini, presented in 1504 a dowry of 50 florins to the wool carder, Piero di Iacopo di Piero.[7] The confraternity of silk weavers and spinners, Santa Croce, moreover, contributed 25 *libbra* towards this worker's dowry. Finally, in 1472 we find a member of the important Trecento banking family of the de'Bardi making a dowry payment that would not have been uncommon for a peasant marriage, 25 florins, in the marriage of his daughter to a washer of woolen cloths *(lava panni)*.[8] Were these spouses who bore prestigious Florentine family names all actual biological members of disenfranchised branches of the aforementioned *stirpe* who had fallen on hard times during the late Quattrocento because of political or economic misfortunes? In most cases they probably were. But it is possible that some of these de'Bardi and degli Asini were instead descendents of men and women who had been servants of these patrician families. After a servant or slave was emancipated from duty, it was still common for them to be identified by the name of the household in which they had served.[9]

Beyond these examples of members from the well-known families of Florence exchanging meager dowries, we find many more Florentines with obscure family names, probably recently acquired during the fifteenth century, transacting mediocre dowries. The family name during the fifteenth century characterized all members of the Florentine elite; it had at the same time penetrated little by little into other sectors of society as well. Not only do we find *sottoposti* in the wool and silk industries occasionally identified by a family name; even peasant families in the rural suburbs came to be so identified during the course of the fifteenth century. In the parish of S. Piero Monticelli, the rural parish just beyond the porta of S. Frediano, the notarial business of Nardo di Antonio (1461–1497) frequently mentions members of the Orlandi family. For the most part they are identified as tillers of the soil or sharecroppers *(laboratores terrae)*, and they offered their daughters dowries from 25 *libbra* to 50 florins.

6. N(otarile) A(nte)c(osimo), M 115 (1494–1498), 59v.
7. NAC, G 122 (1495–1506), 89v–90r.
8. NAC, L 140 (1463–1501), 190v–191r.
9. In the baptismal records and the *Notarile*, servants and slaves were commonly identified by the names of their masters; see, for instance, *Registro delle fedi di battesimo*, I (1450–1460), November 3, 1453; January 20, 1454; October 14, 1454; October 28, 1454; February 27, 1459; December 22, 1459; March 20, 1460; May 12, 1460; August 13, 1460; and NAC D 98 (1466–89), 150v; G 237 (1491–99), 128v; L 21 (1524–43), 94r; L 140 (1500–1517), 48r; M 275 (1492–1504), 4v; M 393 (1495–1512), 97v; M 604 (1453–1465), 3r; R 31 (1492–1508), 35r.

In contrast, we do not find any individuals in our fourteenth-century sample with family names who gave a dowry in lire, and there was only one marriage involving a spouse with a family name in which the dowry fell into the lowest quartile of all dowries. In conclusion, the appearance of a family name during the second half of the fourteenth century probably did mean that an individual was of the Florentine elite. In the fifteenth century, on the other hand, the proliferation and trickling down of these names through society means that such an appearance is a less precise indicator of elite status.

The problem, however, of comparing the marriage patterns of those who bore family names in the fourteenth century with those of the fifteenth century does not end here. The difficulty is exacerbated by changes in notarial practices. In the fourteenth century, notaries identified those of patrician status—members of the *ottimati* families such as the Alberti, Albizzi, Ricci, Frescobaldi—by parish with almost the same regularity with which they identified by parish *sottoposti* of the wool industry or those who exchanged nominal dowries in lire. In the fifteenth century, on the other hand, the preponderance of those bearing family names were not identified by a parish church. Of those fifteenth-century marriages for which we know the amount of the dowry, there were 218 marriage relations in which at least one spouse possessed a family name; of these only 22 comprised the parochial residences of both spouses and could therefore be utilized in our analysis of geographical endogamies. These relations, moreover, are not representative of the set of marriages in which we find a spouse with a family name. The median dowry payment of all those marriages in which there was an individual with a family name was 508 florins—a respectable sum for fifteenth-century marriages, certainly beyond the expectations of wool workers and small artisans and even most shopkeepers. Around this amount, just beneath the lower limits of the largest dowries, we begin to find with regularity the names of the prominent Florentine families: the Pitti, Adimari, Acciaiolo, Antinori. On the other hand, the 22 marriage relations for which we find the parochial residences of both spouses reflect a very different social composition. The median dowry payment for this group was 70 florins, a payment that falls slightly below the upper half of the population found in our records exchanging dowries; it was a sum which was not beyond the expectations of well-to-do artisans or even certain *sottoposti*. Thus, the group of Florentines who bore a family name and who were also identified by a parish church in our fifteenth-century sample (both those exchanging dowries and those for whom this information is missing) hardly represents the elite of Quattrocento Florence, although members of the elite might be discovered intermingled within this group.

Another means of identifying members of the upper classes might be by profession. Except for the *magnati* (who by the middle of the fifteenth century had for the most part, at least within the city, purchased *popolo* status and no longer suffered the more stringent regulations and juridical penalties of the nobility), all of the Florentine patriciate were members of a guild.[10] But these prominent members of the *popolani grassi*, from families such as the Strozzi, Rucellai, and Tornabuoni, were almost never identified by a profession in any of the documents which we have considered in this study—the *estimi, catasti, notarile,* criminal sentences, and baptismal register—unless they were *giudici* ('lawyers'), *notai* ('notaries'), or *medici* ('doctors'). What then did it mean if an individual was identified by an occupation that belonged to the *arti maggiori,* one of the upper seven guilds? In some sense these men, even if they represented only the lower echelons of the major guilds, were a part of elite society in Florence. For instance, only they, could hold office or be represented in the *mercanzia* (the merchant's court).[11]

Moreover, in the fifteenth century, the dowries exchanged by members of the upper guilds did not vary nearly as radically as those exchanged by individuals possessing family names. Most of these members of the *arti maggiori* presented dowries within the middle range of between 100 and 700 florins—an amount that was beyond the expectations of the ordinary laborer or artisan and yet beneath the great dowries of the important political marriages which linked together families such as the Stozzi, Medici, and Soderini. Of 56 marriage relations in which at least one spouse was identified by a profession belonging to one of the major guilds, only three exceeded a 1000 florins and only one was a bequest presented in lire. The median dowry of these marriages was 300 florins, the twenty-fourth percentile of the largest dowries.[12] When we consider only those marriages from which a geographical relationship between parishes can be observed, the figure falls to 200 florins or the twenty-eighth percentile of the largest dowries. Thus, unlike the marriages involving persons with family names, we do not find an extreme deviation between the total population of marriages involving major guildsmen and the subset of those identified by parish. Those

---

10. The criminal archives of the Podestà, the Capitano del Popolo and the Esceutore degli Ordinamenti di Giustizia singled out individuals as *Magnates et Potentes.* The courts meted out special and exorbitant penalties against the distinguished violators of the *popolani* and the civil peace of Florence.

11. Niccolò Rodolico, *La Democrazia Fiorentina nel suo tramonto* (1378–1382) (Bologna, 1905), p. 229; and G. Bonolis, *La Giuridizione della Mercanzia in Firenze nel secolo XIV* (Florence, 1901).

12. See pages 125–126.

identified by a major guild profession must have been active businessmen and manufacturers; they were not, however, the merchant princes of the Florentine economy or even those who partook regularly in international commerce. In fact, we do not find individuals identified as merchants of the Calimala or *cambiatori* ('bankers') in the *Notarile*. It is possible that the distinction by profession within the major guilds might be a means for isolating and comparing at least the lower echelons of the patriciate—shopkeepers and petty industrialists—during the fourteenth and fifteenth centuries. Unfortunately, the meager sample of those identified by profession during the fourteenth century does not permit us to draw a significant comparison.

Finally, a significant proportion of the marriage relations in both the fourteenth- and fifteenth-century samples included the amount of dowry promised or actually transacted. It could be argued that the amount of dowry would be as good or even better an indicator of status than the tax assessments or calculations of wealth found in the tax surveys—the *estimi* and the *catasti*. Whereas political favoritism and corruption might affect one's tax assessment greatly (especially in the period of the *estimi*),[13] the dowry payment was a matter of honor.[14] Although there may at times have been some trade-off between new commercial money and old family distinction, the dowries in both of our periods of study do not indicate this to have been a general tendency in the determination of the dowry payment. It is true that Lorenzo de'Medici, the richest as well as politically the most powerful man in late Quattrocento Florence, did not endow his daughter Lorenza with the largest dowry of our fifteenth century sample. But, certainly, he could have negotiated her marriage to Iacopo di Giovanni d'Alamanno di Messer Iacopo Salviati or to anyone else in late Quattrocento Florentine society for far less than the 2,000 florins—one of four largest dowries in our sample—which Iacopo Salviati received.[15] More importantly, during the fourteenth century some of the largest dowry payments in our sample were given by fathers who were not identified

---

13. On political favoritism and the calculation of tax assessments, see Giovanni di Pagolo Morelli, *Ricordi*, edited by V. Branca (Florence, 1956), pp. 256–257; on changes in the reliability of tax assessments from the Trecento *estimi* to the Quattrocento *catasto*, see David Herlihy and Christiane Klapisch, *Les Toscans et leurs familles: Une étude du catasto florentin de 1427* (Paris, 1978), pp. 11–47.

14. A. Molho and Julius Kirshner, "The Dowry Fund and the Marriage Market in Early Quattrocento Florence," *Journal of Modern History*, 50 (1978), 403–406; and Kirshner, *Pursuing Honor While Avoiding Sin: The Monte delle doti*, Quaderni di "Studi Senesi", edited by Domenico Maffei, n. 41 (Milan, 1978).

15. NAC, M 530, 72r, September 13, 1481; in our sample, there are two dowry bequeaths of 3,000 florins.

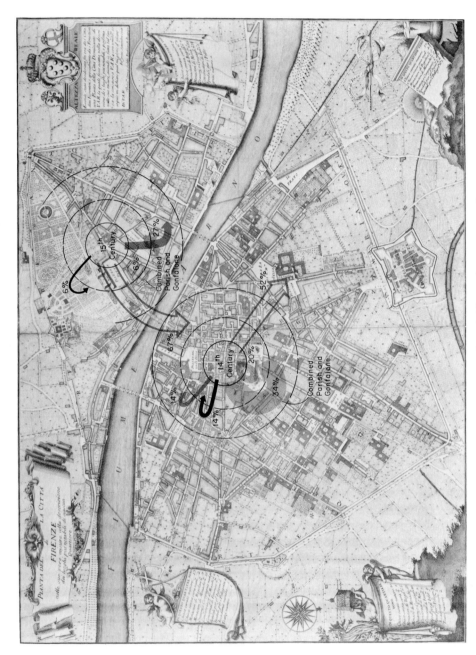

Figure 2.1. *The ideal typical parish in the fourteenth and fifteenth centuries: the patriciate.*

by a family name; these do not reflect an exchange of new wealth for old family distinction, however. Among the extraordinary dowries of 800 florins or more (the upper 2.6 percentile during the fourteenth century) we do not find women of apparently new mercantile wealth marrying into the old families or vice versa; instead the recipients of these dowries appear to have come from similar families, perhaps with wealth but without old family lineage. In late fourteenth-century Florence there appears to have been more room for the successful *novi cives* in patrician society; the most successful apparently either did not need to or could not intermarry with the old *consorterie*.

In comparing the fourteenth- and fifteenth-century patriciates according to dowry amount, however, we again experience difficulties. If we agree that inclusion in the upper sixteenth or seventeenth percentile of dowry payments would roughly distinguish a spouse of patrician status in both periods of our analysis, the fourteenth century might produce an adequate size sample—81 marriages. On the other hand, the fifteenth-century sample, as we have mentioned, shows only nine marriages or 18 separate statistics for observing the patterns of patriciate endogamy.

In Table 2.1 and Appendixes E.1–E.7, we have drawn various rings which comprise portions of Florentine patriciate society. In summary, there are three means at our disposal for isolating the patriciate from the rest of society: (*a*) the presence of a family name; (*b*) membership in a profession belonging to one of the upper guilds; and (*c*) the amount of dowry. Each presents problems. First, the significance of the family name shifts in importance from the fourteenth to the fifteenth century. But, more importantly, those marriages involving at least one spouse with a family name that can be used in our analysis of geographical endogamies are biased severely towards the poorer, less prestigious members of this group in the fifteenth-century sample. For the same reason—the tendency of fifteenth-century notaries to identify the elite simply as citizens of Florence and not as members of a certain "*popolo*"—we cannot observe from the *Notarile* alone the geographical relationships between those who exchanged dowries of upper-class status.

The fifteenth-century notaries did provide, however, information for isolating at least the lower reaches of the Florentine patriciate—the professions of the spouses or their fathers. But in the fourteenth century, notaries were not wont to include this information. Because of these changes in notarial practices, our estimations of patriciate society are more precise for the fourteenth century than for the fifteenth century. For the fourteenth century, we have composed groups of marriage endogamies which reflect four graduations of patriciate society: first, those with dowries greater than or equal to 200 florins and less than 400

Table 2.1
Summary of Marriage Endogamies of the Florentine Elite for the Fourteenth and Fifteenth Centuries

Sample	Endogamies				Exogamies			Total
	Parish (a)	Gonfalone (b)	Quarter (c)	Cluster (d)	Cross-quarter (e)	Cross-cluster (f)	Contado (g)	
Fourteenth century								
200–400 Florins	22 .2716	2 .0247 .2963	10 .1235 .4197	15 .1852 .4568	44 .5432	41 .5061	3 .0370	81
400 Florins +	28 .1818	13 .0844 .2662	26 .1688 .4351	27 .1753 .3571	85 .5519	97 .6299	2 .0130	154
Family names	20 .1942	8 .0777 .2718	22 .2136 .4854	16 .1553 .3495	52 .5049	66 .6408	1 .0098	103
Family names and 400 Florins +	10 .2000	7 .1400 .3400	7 .1400 .5800	5 .1000 .4400	26 .5200	35 .7000	0	50
Fifteenth century								
Family names	22 .1618	8 .0588 .2206	22 .1618 .3824	13 .0956 .2574	68 .5000	85 .6250	16 .1176	136
Major guilds	8 .1356	6 .1017 .2373	4 .0678 .3051	10 .1695 .3051	32 .5424	32 .5424	9 .1525	59
Tratte		4 .0606	18 .2727	44 .6667				66

florins (roughly the population between the upper twenty-fifth percentile and the upper seventeenth percentile of largest dowries); second,
those with dowries of 400 florins or more (roughly the upper seventeenth percentile of largest dowries); third, those who had family
names, and finally, a subset of the latter two samples—those who had
family names and who also exchanged dowries of 400 florins or more.

Because of the changes in notarial conventions, the means for identifying the patriciate of the fifteenth century must be different. For the
most general definition of the patriciate, we will include all those marriages in which at least one spouse possessed a family name. The second
tier is composed of those who were members of a major guild profession.
To study the real elite of Florentine society we must, however, go beyond the materials provided in the *Notarile*. For this population, we
have first considered those nine marriage relationships in which 600
florins or more (the upper 16.99 percentile) were exchanged, and in
which both spouses were identified by a parish. Secondly, we have included those marriages in which both spouses bore a family name and
in which a dowry of 600 florins or more was exchanged. Almost none
of these individuals are identified by a parish; all are simply called
cives florentini. To unravel the networks of association among these
ottimati we have created a sample by linking these individuals to lists
found in the *Archivio della Repubblica* called the *Tratte*.

Registers 39 and 1093 of the *Tratte* are lists of the dates of birth of
the group of Florentines who might become eligible for holding an
elected office in the Communal government. These lists, which were
first compiled in 1429 and continue through the fifteenth century,
have recently been processed into machine-readable language by Professor David Herlihy. Of those marriages in which both spouses or the
fathers of both spouses could be traced, a large proportion is represented
by the notarial business of Niccolò Michelozzi, the son of the architect,
who was a personal secretary to Lorenzo de'Medici. His protocol, which
runs from 1468 to 1515, contains 57 patriciate marriages and engagements. The majority of these marriages were celebrated at the Medici
palace and were witnessed by Lorenzo. In several instances Lorenzo
even provided the dowry. We find the state, in effect, taking an active
role in the structuring of marriage relations, which were, at the same
time political alliances.[16] From these 57 marriages we were able to link
both spouses in the *Tratte* for another ten *ottimati* marriages. Combined
with other linkages we now have a sample of elite marriages from the

---

16. Christiane Klapisch, "Zacharie, ou le père évincé: Les rites nuptiaux toscans entre
Giotto et le concile de Trente," *Annales: E.S.C.*, 34 (1979), 1225.

Table 2.2
Patriciate Marriages from the Fifteenth-Century Sample Located in the Tratte (n. 39 and n. 1093)

Notarial Reference	Year	Dowry	Marriage Partners	District [a]
F 498 (1499–1465)	118r 14510126	777F	Brigida di Bardo di M. Alessandro Bardi	1:1
			Iacopo di Alamanno di M. Iacopo Salviati	2:4
G 617 (1463–1465)	40r 14631003	1100F	Gostanza di fu Agnolo di Domenico Busini	2:3
			Francesco di fu Giovanni di Bartolommeo Morelli (S. Iacopo tra le Fossi)	2:3
G 617 (1463–1465)	94r 14640209	1800F	Nanna di fu Antonio di M. Lodovico della Casa	4:1
			Piero di Bernardo di Piero Vespucci	3:2
G 617 (1463–1465)	204v 14650512	1400F	Caterina di Bernardo di Lapo Niccolini	2:4
			Francesco di fu Luca di M. Maso degli Albizzi	4:3
G 363 (1476–1483)	234r 14840104	1150F	Lisabetta di Giorgio di Niccolo Ridolfi	1:3
			Andrea di fu Bese di Giovanni Ardinghelli	3:2
N 3 (1487–1489)	24r 14870822	1000F	Lionarda di fu Ghezzo di Agnolo della Casa	4:2
			Antonio di fu M. Alessandro Alessandri (S. Piero (Maggiore)	4:3
G 618 (1476–1478)	133v 14770428	1400F	Maria di Lotto di Duccino Rinuccini	2:2
			Filippo di fu Dominico di Giovanni Giugni	2:4
L 139 (1461–1469)	94v 14660126	800F	Casa di fu Pagnolo di Niccolo di Pagnolo Benci	4:2
			Arrigo di fu Bastiano di Iacopo Guasconi	4:1
L 139 (1477–1482)	107r 14800526	800F	Dionora di fu Andrea di Remigio Bucelli	2:1
			Antonio di fu Spadino Spadini	4:3
P 71 (1476–1482)	7v 14760618	750F	Tita di Girolamo di Solette di Pera Baldovinetti	3:1
			Lorenzo di fu Fede di Giovanni Ridolfi (S. Lorenzo)	4:1
M 530 (1468–1515)	15v 14720501	1500F	Cassandra di Francesco di fu Niccolo di Ugolino Martelli	4:1
			Benedetto di Tanai di Francesco Nerli	1:2
M 530 (1468–1515)	24r 14730214	1300F	Lucrezia di fu Benedetto di Francesco degli Strozzi	3:3
			Pacchino di fu Bernardo degli Adimari	4:4

Source	Folio/Date	Amount	Name	Ratio
M 530 (1468–1515)	24v 14730220	1200F	Gostanza di Ruberto di fu Francesco Biagio Leoni	2:4
			Francesco di fu Gherrardo Gherrardi	2:4
M 530 (1468–1515)	42v 14741221	1200F	Ginevra di Tommaso di fu Luigi di M. Lorenzo Ridolfi	1:3
			Tommaso di Federigo Federighi	3:3
M 530 (1468–1515)	45r 14750722	1500F	Lucrezia di fu M. Luca Buonacorso Pitti	1:3
			Piero di fu Bernardo di Bernardo Tornabuoni	3:4
M 530 (1468–1515)	47v 14751006	1000F	Maddalena di Niccolo di fu Francesco di M. Simone Tornabuoni	3:4
			Giuliano di fu Piero Simone Orlandini	2:3
M 530 (1468–1515)	70r 14810517	1000F	Lucrezia del Magnifico Lorenzo di Piero di Cosimo de'Medici	4:1
			Lorenzo di Lotto Salviati	2:4
M 530 (1468–1515)	71r 14810903	1000F	Lisabetta di Ristori di Antonio Serristori	2:3
			Bartolommeo di Lutozzo Nasi	1:1
M 530 (1468–1515)	72r 14810903	2000F	Lucrezia del Magnifico Lorenzo di Piero di Cosimo de'Medici	4:1
			Iacopo di fu Giovanni di Alamanno di M. Iacopo Salviati	2:4
M 530 (1468–1515)	73r 14811006	1000F	Alessandra di Niccolo di Ugolino di Niccolo Martelli	4:1
			Neri di Piero di Neri di M. Donato Acciaiuoli	3:1
M 530 (1460–1515)	74r 14830423	1000F	Ginerva di Bernardo di Giovanni Iacobi	2:3
			Guglielmo di fu Bernardo degli Adimari	4:4
M 530 (1460–1515)	76r 14840207	1500F	Lucrezia di Niccolo di Sandro Biliotti	1:2
			Antonio di fu Iacopo di Pagnozzo Ridolfi	1:3
M 530 (1460–1515)	77r 14861023	1800F	Beatrice di Giovanni di fu Adovardo Portinari	4:4
			Antonio di fu Inghilese Ridolfi	1:2
M 530 (1468–1515)	77v 14930511		Contissima di fu Lorenzo di Piero di Cosimo de'Medici	4:1
			Piero di Niccolo di Luigi di M. Lorenzo Ridolfi	1:3

Table 2.2 (Continued)

Notarial Reference	Year	Dowry	Marriage Partners	District [a]
			Dowries of 600 florins or greater with indications of parish for both spouses	
M 144 (1491–1497)	137r 14960708	1000F	Casa di Ferovanni di fu Malapaglio Cicciouili (S. Trinità)	2:2
M 646 (1460–1469)	164v 14631201	800F	Raffaello di Guaspare di fu Agnolo di Francesco (S. Felice in Piazza)	1:3
			Ginevra di Maestro Antonio di fu Bartolommeo di Giovanni Squarcialupi (S. Lorenzo)	4:1
			Giovanfrancesco di Nofri di Agnolo del Brutto di Bonamico *linaiolo* (S. Piero Maggiore)	4:3
M 646 (1460–1469)	421v 14660615	700F	Alessandra di Bartolommeo di Domenico (S. Maria del Fiore)	4:2
			Piero di fu Andretto *Merciaio* (S. Piero Maggiore)	4:3
P 71 (1500–1512)	157r 15120718	1000F	Piera Maria di Francesco Ghivetti (S. Michele Visdomini)	4:4
			Batista di Batista da Silvonica (S. Piero Maggiore)	4:3
P 128 (1452–1462)	2v 14510403	1500F	Piera di fu Lorenzo Gherrardo Buondelmonte (S. Stefano al Ponte)	2:1
			Luigi di fu Carlo di Gaylordo Bonamici (S. Apollinare)	2:2
P 128 (1452–1462)	460r 14610407	1000F	Gostanza di Ser Giuliano di fu Giovanni Lanfredini *Notaio* (S. Frediano)	1:4
			Signorino di Andrea di Signorino di Marco di Signorino (S. Pancrazio)	2:3
B2331 (1481–1489)	33r 14820713	650F	Caterina di fu Bernardo di Domenico Dei (S. Felice in Piazza)	1:3
			Dominico di Giorgio di Iacopo di Giorgio Aldobrandini (S. Lorenzo)	4:1
M 604 (1453–1465)	218r 14610710	600F	Papa di Giovanni di fu Lotto *Rigattiere* (S. Lorenzo)	4:1
			Matteo di fu Stefano di Iacopo di Bonino *Cartolaio* (S. Paolo)	2:3
P 218 (1452–1462)	365v 14600425	700F	Bartolommea di Sasso d'Antonio di Martino di Sasso (S. Frediano)	1:4
			Ser Bartolommeo d'Antonio di Ser Bartolommeo d'Orso *Notaio* (S. Paolo)	2:3

[a] The numbers in the far right column correspond to the quarter and *gonfalone* of the spouse or to the father of the spouse. They are the following: Quartiere di S. Spirito—Scala (1:1), Nicchio (1:2), Ferza (1:3), Drago (1:4); Quartiere di S. Croce—Carro (2:1), Bue (2:2), Leon Nero (2:3), Ruote (2:4); Quartiere di S. Maria Novella—Vipera (3:1), Unicorno (3:2), Leon Rosso (3:3), Leon Bianco (3:4); and Quartiere di S. Giovanni—Leon d'Oro (4:1), Drago (4:2), Chiavi (4:3), Viao (4:4).

late fifteenth century of 33 marriages or 66 statistics of social interaction. Unfortunately, we can observe parish endogamy only for those spouses who were actually identified by parish in our original sample; the *Tratte* identifies those eligible for office by the secular jurisdictions of the *gonfalone* and the quarter (see Table 2.2 and Appendix E.7).

Because of the differences in the graduations between the groups in each of the centuries, the various tiers of the fourteenth-century sample are not really equivalent to those of the fifteenth century. Instead, for the fourteenth century we have one criterion for estimation of the lower extension of patriciate society—those who exchanged dowries of 200 florin or more and less than 400 florins. For the fifteenth century, there are two criteria for examining a comparable portion of patrician society—those with family names and those with major guild occupations. On the other hand, for a more precise picture of patriciate society as a whole, we have three methods of estimation for the fourteenth century—the exchange of dowries of 400 florins or more, those with family names, and those with both family names and dowries of 400 florins or more. For a picture of patrician society or the ruling class in the fifteenth century we have only one means for estimation available—the composite set compiled from the *Tratte* and the *Notarile*.[17]

When we consider the patterns of endogamy for the various levels of patriciate society, we find tendencies which are the opposite of those revealed when the aggregate populations were considered (see Summary and Table 2.1 and Appendixes E.1–E.7). Concerning the lower reaches of the Florentine elite, intermarriage within each of the geographical units—(*a*) the parish, (*b*) the *gonfalone*, (*c*) the quarter and (*d*) the cluster—is less in the fifteenth century than it was for the fourteenth century. When we compare spouses with dowries of 200 florins or more and less than 400 florins in the fourteenth century with spouses with family names in the fifteenth century, endogamy within (*a*) the parish falls by more than 40% and the decline of intermarriage within (*d*) the

---

17. I realize that this discussion of the definitions of various rings and divisions of the Florentine patriciate reifies the notion of class. Definitions according to dowry or occupation objectify a reality that is the ensemble created by the social relations of production and power relations within the structure of the state. The demarcations drawn above, nonetheless, are the best approximations of social strata that the documentation permits. They approximate, but certainly are not synonymous with, definitions of class based on social relations and power relations. My objectification of class is similar to the relation which prices bear to exchange value. Prices are an objectification of exchange value, but at the same time are determined by exchange value. And it is data on prices (not exchange value) which Marxists and non-Marxists alike, in their empirical work, are forced to analyze. For a criticism of the objectification of class in the works of sociologists and political scientists, see E. P. Thompson, *The Making of the English Working Class* (London, 1963), pp. 9–16.

cluster is even greater.[18] When the more precise criterion of status in the lower echelons of elite society of Quattrocento Florence, identification by major guild profession, is compared with the fourteenth century group, the differences in endogamy are more accentuated. For all the geographical units, the intermarriage among major guildsmen of the fifteenth century is less than that of the fifteenth-century group who bore family names and were also identified by parish. As a result, intermarriage within (a) the parish between members of the lower echelons of patrician society in the fourteenth century is more than double that of the fifteenth-century major guildsmen, and endogamy within the cluster is more than two-and-a-half times greater in the fourteenth than in the fifteenth century.[19]

When we shift our attention to the narrower and more precise estimations of patrician society—estimations which more reasonably correspond to groups of the ruling class—the differences between the fourteenth and fifteenth centuries are more striking. First, within the fourteenth century, endogamy within the parish does decline from the lower reaches of patrician society to the ruling class. But the (b) *gonfalone* might be a better unit for comparison between these various levels of society, since a greater proportion of the patriciate resided in those 34 tiny parishes tightly bunched together within and around the street patterns of the old Roman city. When we look more carefully at our tables, indeed, we find in the central city lower rates of endogamy within the parish but higher rates within the *gonfalone* than we find for other areas of the city. If the *gonfalone*, then, is considered as the basic unit of analysis for comparing rates of endogamy across the social structure of patrician society, we do not find striking changes for the fourteenth century. Endogamy among the aggregate population within (b) the *gonfalone* registers at 33%; moving upward from the lower reaches of the patriciate through three tiers of the ruling class in Trecento Florence, intermarriage changes insignificantly from 30% to 27% to 27% again, until, at the highest level of society captured by our analysis, the curve turns upward to 34%, a figure almost as high as that for the population as a whole. Endogamy within the *gonfalone* for the fifteenth century, however, does not show the same continuity through these various levels of social structure. From the intermarriage within the *gonfalone* of 44% for the aggregate population, the rate diminishes by half to 22% of those bearing family

18. Standard error of a proportion test: p = .2716, π = .2167, N = 217; z = 1.963, which is significant at .05.

19. Standard error of a proportion test: p = .2716, π = .2036, N = 140; z = 2.00.

names; then, from the lower echelons of patrician society signified by those with major guild professions to the sample of the Quattrocento ruling class, endogamy within the smallest secular unit of geography diminishes from 24% to a mere 6%.[20] (See Figure 2.1.)

Thus, intermarriage within the *gonfalone* for the general population (see Table 1.8) was 6.57 times greater than it was for the ruling elite of Quattrocento Florence. Indeed, at the level of society of such families as the Rucellai, the Medici, the Strozzi, there seem to have been unconscious rules of geographical exogamy at play during the late fifteenth century. For the 18 observations of intermarriage where there is an indication of the link between parishes, we do not find a single intermarriage within the parish. This fact and the marriage endogamies in general for this group of Quattrocento *dirigenti* contrast fundamentally with the marriage patterns of similar groupings for the fourteenth century, in which 20% married within the parish and 34% within the *gonfalone*.[21] In the fourteenth century a greater proportion of the patriciate married within the *gonfalone* than the proportion of the fifteenth century ruling class marrying within (*c*) the quarter—a geographical unit which was generally four times the population and size of the *gonfalone*, across the Florentine landscape.

Perhaps the changes in notarial practice from the fourteenth to the fifteenth century which made it so difficult to estimate the geographical marriage patterns of the Quattrocento Florentine elite—that is, the strong tendency of the notaries rarely to identify members of the *ottimati* by their parish of residence but, instead, simply as *cives Florentini*—was not an accident or an arbitrary change in notarial style. Indeed, the change reflects a certain recognition on the part of the notary and a self-consciousness on the part of the patricians themselves of those very changes in the structure of patrician society which our statistics on marriage patterns underlie. The networks of association, at least those carved out by our analysis of marital relations, do not distinguish the fourteenth century patriciate radically from the general population. The same was not true for fifteenth century social structure. The Quattrocento patriciate was distinguished sharply from the rest of society, both by general notarial custom and by the changes reflected in our statistics. Even though the palaces of particular *consorterie* may

---

20. Endogamy within the *gonfalone* among the scrutinized patriciate of the late fifteenth century, despite the small sample size, was significantly less than it was for the general population of the fifteenth century or for the lower echelons, measured by those bearing family names; standard error of a proportion test: $p = .2206$ (those with family names, fifteenth century), $\pi = .1406$, $N = 202$; $z = 3.27$.

21. Standard error of a proportion test: $p = .34$, $\pi = .2003$, $N = 116$; $z = 3.76$.

have remained clustered around certain streets and *piazze*,[22] the Quattrocento patriciate no longer saw themselves primarily as members of a
particular parish community; they assumed, rather, a city-wide identification of themselves. The vast majority (*67%*) sought to extend
their kin networks even beyond the quarter (see *e*).[23]

What do these changes imply about the development of the patriciate
as a class from the fall of the Ciompi to the eve of the Principality in
Florence? We must proceed here with caution. So much more work
must be carried out in the *Archivio di Stato* which will reflect on this
problem: networks of associations disclosed by changes in business associations, executors of wills, relationships among litigants in the civil
and criminal courts, and membership in religious confraternities.[24] The
study, moreover, of the class division between the *popolani grassi* and
the *magnati*—so much the subject of debate for historians of the late
Dugento and early Trecento—has not been extended through the late
fourteenth and fifteenth centuries.[25] Even if there was not a clear economic distinction dividing these two groups in Florentine society, certainly the tensions between them did not cease to be a major source of
conflict during the Trecento. The criminal archives of the middle and
late Trecento—the Podestà, the Capitano, and the Esecutore—are filled

22. See Dale Kent, *The Rise of the Medici: Faction in Florence, 1426–1434* (Oxford, 1978),
pp. 61–62; F. W. Kent, *Household and Lineage*, p. 227. For examples of the movement of
families during the fifteenth century from their traditional neighborhood niches of power and
influence, see D. Kent, *The Rise of the Medici*, p. 66; and F. W. Kent, *Household and Lineage*,
p. 190. For a different impression of the social organization of the fifteenth century Florentine
patriciate from the one which we have drawn above, see *Household and Lineage*, pp. 16 and
228, "Each family came from a distinct part of Florence, a social, political and psychological
fact which would have seemed important to Florentines and ought not to be lost on us. . .
The physical environment of family life had not in fact changed very drastically between the
thirteenth and the fifteenth centuries." For a counter interpretation, see Richard Goldthwaite,
Private Wealth in Renaissance Florence: A Study of Four Families (Princeton, 1968); and
concerning palaces and the environment of family life of the patriciate, see Isabella Hyman,
*Fifteenth Century Florentine Studies: The Palazzo Medici and a Ledger for the Church of
San Lorenzo* (New York, 1977) pp. 42, 171, 191, and 199, "The development of the palace
courtyard after the 1450s made the traditional family loggia redundant."

23. Corresponding to these quantitative changes, there were qualitative changes in the
marriage ceremonies themselves. From a public neighborhood festivity celebrated in front of
the bride's parish church, increasingly during the Quattrocento patrician marriages became
private affairs, confined to the *palazzo* of the groom's *parentele*. See Christiane Klapisch,
"Zacharie ou le père évincé: Les rites nuptiaux toscans entre Giotto et le concile de Trente,"
Annales: E.S.C., 34 (1979), 1216–1243.

24. For an analysis of the networks among members of religious confraternities, see the
forthcoming work of Ronald Weissman, *Florentine Confraternities, 1200–1600* (New York,
1981).

25. For studies on the *magnati* in the Dugento and early Trecento, see Gaetano Salvemini,
Magnati e popolani in Firenze dal 1280 al 1295 (Florence, 1899); Nicola Ottokar, *Il Comune
di Firenze alla fine del Dugento* (Florence, 1926); and more recently, Sarah R. Blanshei,
Perugia, 1260–1340: Conflict and Change in a Medieval Italian Urban Society, Transactions
of the American Philosophical Society, Vol. 66, part 2 (Philadelphia, 1976), and S. Raveggi,

with the collective violence of the *magnati* against *popolani*. We find bands of *magnati* roaming through the countryside of Florence, pillaging, burning fields, killing animals, kidnapping and murdering men, and raping women.[26] In the criminal sentences of the middle of the Quattrocento we cease to find the crimes of these *magnates et potentes* singled out for special prosecution by the medieval tribunals. The criminal archives leave us the distinct impression that the nature of political conflict within the patriciate had changed. No longer do conflicts over castles, property, and honor seem to have been a yearly or even monthly occurrence between neighboring *magnati, popolani,* and the Florentine Commune.[27] Although usually these conflicts were waged in the country-side, occasionally they errupted in the city during the middle and late Trecento.[28] In addition, in the Trecento though not during the Quattrocento we find in the criminal archives evidence of the cleavages that cut across the patriciate geographically. We find, for the earlier period, members of the powerful *popolani grassi* families involved in neighborhood brawls assisted by blacksmiths or other artisans of their quarter.[29]

The changes in literary themes, historiography, and political thought give a layer of flesh to the structural changes which our statistics have plotted. From the *Chronica de Origine Civitatis* composed in the latter part of the twelfth century through the chronicle traditions of Malispini, Dino Compagni, Giovanni Villani, and Dante's *Divine Comedy*, the cycle of factional rifts, supposedly originating from the irreconcilable races which inhabited the city—the Fiesolani of Etruscan blood and the true Florentines of Roman blood—was a principal theme of early Florentine literature.[30]

M. Tarassi, D. Medici, and P. Parenti, *Ghibellini, Guelfi e Popolo Grassi: i detentori del potere politico a Firenze nella seconda metà del Dugento* (Florence, 1978).

26. A(tti del) P(odestà) 127, fol. 2r, 17r, 35r, 167r, 212v, 303r, 312v, 347v, 387r, 394r; A(tti del) C(apitano del) P(opolo) n. 19, fol. 2r, 17r, 21r, 26v, 33r, 35r; ACP, n. 11, fol. 1r, 11r, 11r, 12r, 13v, 15r–16v, 17r, 17v, 20r, 27v, 33r, 36v; AP, n. 116, 105r, 120v, 283r, 331v; ACP, n. 42, fol. 17v; ACP, n. 43, fol. 3r–v, 5r; ACP, n. 62, 1r, 7r, 15r; ACP, n. 63, fol. 5r; AP, n. 3297, fol. 27r; A(tti dell') E(secutore degli) O(rdinamenti di) G(iustizia), n. 56, fol. 1r, 28v; AEOG, n. 870, fol. 11r.

27. See, for instance, Marvin Becker, "The Florentine Territorial State and Civic Humanism in the Early Renaissance," in *Florentine Studies*, edited by N. Rubinstein (London, 1968), pp. 112–113.

28. AP n. 127, fol. 45r, 271r, 302r, 354r; AP, n. 2732, fol. 297r, 411v; ACP, n. 11, fol. 27r.

29. ACP n. 26, fol. 3r, 23r, 26v–27r; ACP n. 28, fol. 38v; ACP n. 30, fol. 22r; AP 127 fol. 85r; ACP n. 19, 38r. See, moreover, Marchionne di Coppo Stefani, *Cronica fiorentina*, edited by N. Rodolico in Rerum Italicarum Scriptores, new ed., Vol. 30, part 1 (Città di Castello, 1903-1955), p. 245.

30. Nicolai Rubinstein, "The Beginning of Political Thought in Florence: A Study in Medieval Historiography," *Journal of the Warburg and Courtauld Institutes*, Vol. V (1942), 198-227.

And notice how the Florentines are always at war and that there is dissension among them; there is no reason to be astonished, since they are born and reared from two peoples so contrary and inimical and different in customs as were the virtuous, noble Romans and the Fiesolani, rough and ready for war.[31]

In the Quattrocento, Renaissance culture, political ideology, and the conceptualization of the city and her citizens experienced a transformation. The theme is no longer the irreconcilable struggle between groups or races within the city; the perimeters of conflict have expanded. Now, the humanist ideologues begin to see Florence as a whole, the unity of the city as the defender of Republican liberty surrounded by an encroaching sea of despotism.[32] In the *Laudatio Florentinae Urbis*, Leonardo Bruni applauds Florence's physical and social harmony, praising her citizens for those very qualities which her Dugento and Trecento *literati* found racially and historically impossible for the Arno city ever to obtain: unity, a harmony of diversities, stability, a cooperative and agreeable spirit.[33]

We might argue along with Professor Hans Baron that the changes in political ideology and humanist culture were the results of changes in the diplomatic and power structure of Italy. But why was Florence so resilient; why did the Florentines not succumb like Bologna? The answer may lie, at least in part, in the nature of changes internal to the polity of Florence, the development of the patriciate as a single, self-conscious class after the fall of the Ciompi and the government of the *Arti Minori*. Although Leonardo Bruni's *Laudatio Florentinae Urbis*, which praises the city's remarkable geographical and aesthetic harmony and unity, may have been written purely for political or rhetorical

---

31. G. Villani, *Cronica*, IV, 7, *"E nota, perchè i Fiorentini sono sempre in querre e in dissensione tra loro, che non è da maravigliare, essendo stratti e nati di due popoli cosi contrarii e nemici e diversi di costumi, come furono gli nobili Romani virtudosi, e Fiesolani ruddi e aspri di guerre."*

32. Hans Baron, *The Crisis of the Early Italian Renaissance: Civic Humanism and Republican Liberty in an Age of Classicism and Tyranny*, 2 vols. (Princeton, 1955).

33. Leonardo Bruni, *Laudatio Florentinae Urbis*, edited by H. Baron in *From Petrarch to Leonardo Bruni: Studies in Humanistic and Political Literature* (Chicago, 1968), p. 233, *"Ut enim non nullos filios vedimus tantam habere cum parentibus similitudinem ut in ipso aspectu manifestissime cognoscantur, ita huic nobilissime atque inclite urbi tanta cum suis civibus convenientia est ut neque eos alibi quam in illa habitasse nec ipsam alios quam huius modi habitatores habuisse summa ratione factum videatur. Nam quemadmodum ipsi cives naturali quodam ingenio, prudentia, lautitia et magnificentia ceteris hominibus plurimum prestant, sic et urbs prudentissime sita ceteras omnes urbes splendore et ornatu et munditia superat.*

Principio igitur, quod prudentie maxime est: nichil ad ostentationem facere nec periculosam et inanem iactantiam sequi potius quam tranquillam stabilemque commoditatem, hoc Florentiam quidem cernimus observasse." And *ibid*, pp. 258–259, *"Sed cum foris hec civitas admirabilis est, tum vero disciplina institutisque domesticis. Nusquam tantus ordo rerum, nusquam tanta ele-*

reasons, its spirit (especially in contrast to the Dugento and Trecento conceptualizations of the city) nonetheless expressed a certain socio-logical truth—at least concerning a particular class.[34] By the fifteenth century the Florentine ruling class emerged from the vestiges of tower family formation and parochial solidarities which had persisted through the fourteenth century. They developed a certain city-wide solidarity and class unity that they had probably never known in their previous history, and certainly which they did not possess during those turbulent years of Ricci and Albizzi factionalism. As Professor Brucker has argued, this earlier lack of unity may explain (at least in part) the success of the *popolo minuto* during the summer of 1378.[35] We must now ask how well Bruni's portrayal of Florence pertained to the popu-lation as a whole and to the *popolo minuto* in particular.

---

gantia, nusquam tanta concinnitas. Quemadmodum enim in cordis convenientia est, ad quam, cum intense fuerint, una ex diversis tonis fit armonia, qua nichil auribus iocundius est neque suavius, eodem modo hec prudentissima civitas ita omnes sui partes moderata est ut inde summa quedam rei publice sibi ipsi consentanea resultet, que mentes atque oculos hominum sua con-venientia delectet."

See, moreover, Brucker, *The Civic World*, pp. 284 and 302. For other texts of Leonardo Bruni and Poggio Braccioloini which support a new ideology of equality among citizens and which rigoursly attack cleavages within that class based on privilege and status, see N. Rubinstein, "Florentine Constitutionalism and Medici Ascendancy in the Fifteenth Century," in *Florentine Studies*, edited by Rubinstein (London, 1968), p. 449.

34. Whether Leonardo Bruni's perception of the city, its constitution, and population rep-resented a permanent change in the ideology and consciousness of the Renaissance patriciate in Florence might be questioned. The appearance of Matteo Palmieri's *Della vita civile* in the 1430s revived at least for the moment the old themes and fears of factionalism and disunity. See Quentin Skinner, *The Foundations of Modern Political Thought* (Cambridge, 1978), Vol. I, p. 73.

35. Brucker, *Florentine Politics and Society, 1343–1578* (Princeton, 1962), p. 390, "The regime fell through its failure to resolve the internal conflicts and disorders of its members." See also, Victor Rutenburg, *Popolo e movimenti popolari nell'Italia del'300 e '400* (Bologna, 1971; Moscow, 1958), pp. 162–185. For manifestations of cultural and ideological fragmentation that may have created a crisis in the confidence of the ruling classes in the period immediately preceding the Revolt of the Ciompi, see Millard Meiss, *Painting in Florence and Siena after the Black Death* (Princeton, 1951), pp. 93ff.

The rise of party politics in the 1420s, moreover, may have been a force in the dissolution of the particularistic factionalism characteristic of medieval Florentine politics. These new political associations of the Medici and their opponents overshadowed older corporate forms of alliance—the guilds, the *gonfalones*, the Parta Guelfa—and may have contributed to the development of the Renaissance patriciate as a city-wide organization. (See, Becker, "The Florentine Territorial State," 109–140; Brucker, *The Civic World*, pp. 506–507; and John Na-jemy, "Guild Republicanism in Trecento Florence: The Successes and Ultimate Failure of Cor-porate Politics," *American Historical Review*, 84 (1979), 53–71. Unfortunately, Dale Kent, *The Rise of the Medici*, does not discuss the historical distinctiveness of party politics in the early fifteenth century; see, S. Cohn, Jr., review in *Renaissance Quarterly*, 33 (1980), 74–76.

Chapter 3

The *Popolo Minuto*

IN considering the laboring classes of Renaissance Florence we are once again confronted with the problems of defining class, both ideally or theoretically, and operationally. As with our study of the patriciate of Renaissance Florence, the problems and possibilities for demarcating the boundaries of the *popolo minuto* differ over the two periods of observation. Despite these difficulties, it will be found that the laboring classes of the fourteenth and fifteenth centuries were not a static force. The contours cast by their casual interactions and the conclusions to be drawn concerning their social organization and consciousness change from the Trecento through the Quattrocento as radically as the changes which have been observed in the communities of the Florentine ruling elite. The changes implied by these statistics are commensurate with other scraps of evidence pertaining to Renaissance popular culture. From the Trecento, when numerous forms of popular religiosity occurred outside the church and its formal hierarchies, to the era of the rule of the Medici, the religious experience of the laboring classes seems to have entered a less agitated period. Processions which enlisted mass participation were not so spontaneous as they had been during the period of the Ciompi. Except for the years of Savonarola's prestige in Florence, the Commune and the Medici initiated, orchestrated, and controlled popular and religious processions for their own purposes, and religious heresy all but disappeared.

In first defining and then distinguishing the *popolo minuto* from the general population, the theoretical problems are not quite so severe as those encountered with the patriciate. In Trecento or Quattrocento Florence, citizens of Florence most certainly had notions, despite juridical demarcations or social registers, of who constituted the elite of Florence. But this awareness in both centuries must have remained somewhat amorphous. In some contexts, the successful artisan who became inscribed in the registers of the *Tratte* might be looked upon by his co-workers as a member of the Florentine ruling elite. In other contexts, only members of those well-founded *consorterie* who happened to be in favor with the ruling regime could in any meaningful way be considered part of the Florentine patriciate. In still other contexts, it was only certain branches among these old families—the Rucellai, the Frescobaldi, the Soderini—who were known to have special stature, whose words in the *Consulte e Pratiche* meant more than others and would sway patrician opinion.[1]

To be sure, there were similar gradations in that portion of the population, comprising probably half of it, that histories have called the *popolo minuto*.[2] In the fourteenth century there were families of tailors whose dowries could match those of certain branches of the degli Serragli or members of other old Florentine lineages.[3] And on the other end of this spectrum were the recently arrived immigrants: In the fourteenth century they came mainly from the surrounding countryside of Florence; in the fifteenth, more originated from foreign places,

---

1. For discussions on the definition of the ruling elite in Renaissance Florence, see Dale Kent, "The Florentine *Reggimento* in the Fifteenth Century," *Renaissance Quarterly*, Vol. XXVIII (1975), 575–638; Anthony Molho, "Politics and the Ruling Class in Early Renaissance Florence," *Nuova Rivista Storica*, LII (1968), 401–420; "The Florentine Oligarchy and the Balìa of the Late Trecento," *Speculum*, Vol. XLIII (1968), 23–51; and Gene Brucker, *The Civic World of Renaissance Florence* (Princeton, 1977), pp. 248–253 and 264.

2. For a discussion of divisions within the *popolo minuto* and the wool workers, see Marvin Becker, "Florentine Politics and the Diffusion of Heresy in the Trecento: A Socioeconomic Inquiry," *Speculum*, 34 (1959), p. 67; Victor Rutenburg, *Popolo e movimenti popolari*, translated by G. Borghini (Bologna, 1971; Moscow, 1958), pp. 291–294; Brucker, "The Ciompi Revolution," in *Florentine Studies*, edited by N. Rubinstein (London, 1968), pp. 219–223; Gino Scaramella, *Firenze allo scoppio del Tumulto dei Ciompi* (Pisa, 1914), p. 15; and Niccolò Rodolico, *La democrazia fiorentina nel suo tramonto (1378–1382)* (Bologna, 1905), p. 199.

3. For instance, the tailor, Buoncorso del Mugellino di fu Bettino gave his daughter, Betta, on September 18, 1350, a dowry of 125 florins (Notarile Antecosimo C 600, 1345–1353, no pagination)—which during the late fourteenth century was just below the upper third of all dowry payments in our sample. Six years later, the tailor, Bonacorso, gave another daughter, Bilia, the same dowry payment for her marriage to the painter, Francesco di fu Bono (N(otarile) A(nte) C(osimo), C 601, 1353–1358, no pagination, February 18, 1350). On January 18, 1364, Bonacorso gave his grandchild, Iacopa, the daughter of his deceased son, Iacopo, a dowry of 150 florins (NAC, C 602, 135–163, no pagination). A year later, Agnola, another daughter of Bonacorso married the major guildsman, Adimaro, a druggist (NAC, C 603, 1363–1370, no pagination, February 8, 1365). Finally, in the following year, the tailor, Bonacorso, who had witnessed the marriage of his granddaughter 2 years previously, remarried and received a dowry of 200 florins (*ibid.*, no pagination, January 30, 1366). In contrast, we find Agnolo, a member of the old *magnati* family of the Serragli receiving a dowry of only 150 florins from the Beccuti family of the parish of S. Lorenzo (NAC M 272, 1384–1385, no pagination, April 14, 1385). On October 25, 1375, another member of an old *magnati* family, de'Rossi or de Rubeis, received a dowry of only 150 florins (NAC G 165, 1374–1376, 141r). And on November 23, 1379, Antonio di Guidetto de'Pazzi gave his daughter the undistinguished dowry of 130 florins (NAC C 335, 1378–1383, 20r).

from Ragusa in present-day Yugoslavia, from Cologne, Flanders, and Naples and other foreign city–states throughout the Italian peninsula. Many, such as the silk weavers from Flanders and Northern Germany, brought with them special skills, much sought after by the expanding industries of fifteenth-century Florence. But others, perhaps the vast bulk, lived in destitution, paying minimal taxes; very likely, they often remained unmarried and moved from *contado* village to working-class quarter, or from city to city in search of day labor. The many differences in livelihood, status, and relations to the means of production of this large working population called the *popolo minuto* certainly had its subjective ramifications in the psychology and political solidarities within this grouping.[4] Even at the pinnacle of its political awareness, we already see, tearing at the seams, its internal divisions; which, in large part, may have made it impossible for this grouping to realize a significant or sustained political awareness again in Florentine history before the Industrial Revolution. Nonetheless, this group—the *popolo minuto*—can be defined, and was defined by contemporaries, much more clearly than the amorphous patriciate or ruling elite of Florence. The *popolo minuto* (more accurately, the *Popolo di Dio*) was that group which had no corporate representation in the Florentine Commune. They were, in other words, those artisans and laborers who were, from the end of the thirteenth century to the creation of the five *universitates* during the period of the Principality, outside of the guild system, except for the 3 years of the Ciompi and the rule of the Arti Minori, 1378–1381.

The political successes of those years, the creation of the revolutionary guilds, which for a brief moment in Florentine history meant that almost the entire adult male population experienced corporate representation, delineated in a very clear and conscious manner the constituency of this grouping who in the documents were known as *"membrum Populi Dei."* A *Provvisione* of September 11, 1378, refers in its preamble to a constitution of August 28 (which does not survive) in which the *membrum Populi Dei* are defined and subdivided into the three newly created guilds. The *Ars Tintorum et Conciatorum et aliorum membrorum ipsi Arti connexorum*, the *Ars Farsettariorum, Cimatorum et aliorum membrorum ipsi Arti connexorum*, and finally the *Ars* called *Popoli minuti* which consisted of *Pectinatorum* ('wool carders'), *Schardisseriorum* ('wool skinners'), and *aliorum membrorum ipsi Arti connexorum*.[5]

From two documents uncovered in the Archivio di Stato by Niccolò

---

4. See note 1, this chapter.

5. Niccolò Rodolico, *La democrazia fiorentina nel suo tramonto (1378–1382)*, (Bologna, 1905), document no. 2, 445–452.

Rodolico at the beginning of the twentieth century, the occupational character and organization of the first two guilds are more precisely defined. In a petition presented to the Priores and approved by the Councils on September 22, 1378, the rights and privileges of the Arte dei Tintori and the Arte dei Farsettai were specified. The guild of the doublet-makers included in addition *cimatori* ('shearers'), *sartori* ('tailors'), *barberi* ('barbers'), *refaiuioli* ('threaders'), *cappellari* ('hatters'), *banderari* ('banner-makers'), and "others connected to this guild." The *Tintorum* ('dyers') guild also included *cardatores* ('carders'), those who make the instruments for carding—*facientes cardos, saponares* ('makers of soap'), the *cardaiuoli* or those who carded at another stage in production, *pettinagnoli* ('the combers'), the *tiratori* ('stretchers'), the *rimendatori* ('sewers of wool cloth'), the *tessentes drappos* ('weavers'), the *lavatores sucidi* ('cloth washers'), and "others who were connected to the guild." [6] The third guild of carders and skinners remains enigmatic.

Soon after the fall of the radical wing of the Ciompi, called the Otto di S. Maria Novella or *li Otto Santi de la Balia del popolo de Dio*, the third revolutionary guild, that of the *popolo minuto*, was dissolved.[7] Exactly which workers were included in this guild and which workers would have been placed outside any corporate affiliation after the fall of the Ciompi cannot be determined from the documentation. Apparently, the carders were immediately absorbed by the guild of the dyers. It is possible that the reconstitution of the guilds on September 22 was primarily a reorganization, which perhaps excluded only the *scardassieri* ('skinners').[8]

Thus, the problem of identifying the *popolo minuto* (which in the chronicles generally assumed the larger contours of the *Popolo di Dio* instead of being a reference simply to those belonging to the twenty-fourth guild of carders and skinners) seems rather straightforward. At least in the fourteenth century they included all the *sottoposti* in the wool and silk industries (and several collateral professions which were specified in the *Provvisioni* and records of the Mercanzia in 1378–1379).[9] But the *popolo minuto* as they conceived of themselves and as they were perceived by contemporary chroniclers, *litterati*, and patri-

---

6. *Ibid.*, document no. 2, 446, and document no. 3, 452–454.
7. *Ibid.*, document no. 1, 442.
8. *Ibid.*, document no. 2, 446.
9. Although the revolutionary provisions certainly pertained predominantly to wool workers, *tessente drappos* could have meant silk weavers as well as wool weavers, and *tintores* could equally well have been dyers of flax, silk, or wool.

cians cannot always be completely restricted to those occupations excluded from membership in the Arte della Lana and Por S. Maria.[10]
Although these workers composed a considerable portion of the Florentine work force—in 1338, a third and by the middle of the fifteenth
century, perhaps as much as one-half—there were still the marginal
populations of the unemployed and underemployed, as well as *discepoli*
and *sottoposti* of other guilds who effectively remained throughout their
lives outside the Florentine guild system and, therefore, without corporate representation in the Communal government. The largest group
was probably the numerous day-laborers in the building industry, the
manovali, who seldom in the *Notarile* were identified by profession.
Moreover, guild artisans who might have matriculated in a minor guild
such as those of the *muratori* ('the masons') or the *legnatori* ('the car-
penters') but who may have had to rely on casual employment, might
have considered themselves and, at times, would have been seen by their
contemporaries as a part of the urban poor, the *popolo minuto*. Despite
guild representation, these individuals were often effectively outside
the ranks of the Florentine citizenry and were recognized by the notary
as members of a parish but not as *cives Florentini*. Indeed, the subjective
definition of the *popolo minuto*, their self-conception, and the perception of them by contemporaries belonging to the Florentine citizenry
must have resembled the fluid and amorphous composition assumed by
the Parisian *sans-culottes* during the French Revolution—a large amalgam of wage earners, artisans, and even some petty shopkeepers. One
chronicler refers to this population of *"minutaglia"* as *"giente che
nacque ieri"* (people born yesterday) or as *"uomini senza nome e
famiglia"* (men without name and family), which might be interpreted
as those without family names.[11] Certainly, this last description would
comprise a considerable portion of the Florentine working population.
The occupational composition of the rank and file of those participating
in and arrested during the Revolt of the Ciompi and during those riots
of the preceding 30 years confirms this impression. Although the majority of those identified by profession were *sottoposti* of the wool

---

10. For a discussion of the terms *ciompi* and *popolo minuto* in the chronicle literature, see
Victor Rutenburg, *Popolo e movimenti popolari*, pp. 158–161. My reading of the chroniclers
differs from that of Rutenburg. He interprets the terms *ciompi* and *popolo minuto* as synonymous; both terms referred strictly to wage earners of the wool industry. I find, on the other
hand, that terms such as *popolo rozzo*, *popolo minuto*, *gente minuta*, *minutaglia*, usually conveyed broader and more amorphous connotations; they referred to the poor in general or the
mass of the Florentine population who were not citizens.
    11. *Cronaca Seconda d'Anonimo*, edited by G. Scaramella in Rerum Italicarum Scriptores,
new ed., t. XVIII, part 3, p. 121.

industry, they were allied with other artisans in the building industries and other trades.

Once we go beyond the strict definition of the *popolo minuto* or *Popolo di Dio* as those *sottoposti* in the wool and silk industries, the problems of identifying their class operationally, that is, identifying them in the documents, become more troublesome. Even if we restrict our definition to the *sottoposti,* those who were outside the guild structure, there remains the problem of identifying those who were *sottoposti* of various minor guilds. Exactly what does a mention in the notarial, tax, or baptismal records of a minor guild profession mean? Did it always imply that that individual was a matriculated member of the guild, or could it possibly mean that the individual simply practiced the trade and could have been practicing it as a *sottomaestri* ('journeyman'), or even as an apprentice? Only in the trade of masons did the notaries distinguish between *magistri* and *muratore.* But it would probably be incorrect to assume that those identified simply as *muratores* were not matriculated members of the guild. Because of the large percentage of those not identified by occupation even by the meticulous officials of the Catasto, or by certain notaries of the late fifteenth century and scribes of the baptismal register, it is probably safe to assume that the identification in the *Notarile* or baptismal register by a minor guild profession meant in fact that that individual was a matriculated member of the guild.

But if we make this assumption, the problem of characterizing even those identified by profession does not vanish. Individuals identified by certain occupations could have been separate members of various minor guilds; on the other hand, they may have practiced their livelihood outside the guild structure. Several *portatores* ('haulers') were important members of the guild of *muratores;* they were in fact wholesalers of raw materials for the building trades.[12] Yet, there were probably many more individuals in Florentine society described in the documents as *portatores* who were outside guild representation, who perhaps hauled water to the upper floors of working class tenements or goods on a non-contractual basis, who in other words comprised a portion of Florence's casual poor.

Similar to the irregularities between the fourteenth and fifteenth century samples which we found when comparing samples of patriciate society, differences in notarial customs from fourteenth to fifteenth century Florence compound the difficulties in the identification of the *popolo minuto.* This time, the fifteenth century sample proves to be

---

12. I would like to thank Professor Richard Goldthwaite for this information.

the better set for demarcation and identification. For the fifteenth century sample we can actually isolate a significant portion of the population which would fit the strict definition of the *Popolo di Dio* defined in the constitution, provisions, and petitions of 1378, that is, all those who were identified by *sottoposti* occupations in the wool and silk industries and certain other collateral occupations. For the fourteenth century, however, the notaries did not frequently identify their clients by occupation. They identified *sottoposti* in the wool industry by profession even less often than minor or major guildsmen. Among the *sottoposti* we find only *sartores* ('tailors') designated by occupation. Thus, to estimate a portion of the population which might represent the *popolo minuto* in our marriage sample, we must once again resort to the dowry price.[13] If we can trust Giovanni Villani's estimate that the wool industry alone provided subsistence for one-third of the Florentine population in 1338,[14] and if we estimate that another 10–15% of the population were either *discepoli* of other trades or workers who practiced crafts outside the guild structure, a dowry price which would delimit the lowest dowries for about 45% of the population might prove to be an effective gauge for estimating and isolating the Florentine *popolo minuto*.[15] In the fourteenth century, those spouses who exchanged dowries equal to 50 florins or less would correspond to 44.62% of our sample.[16]

A considerable proportion of this population (91.03%) expressed or paid their marriage gifts in lire. In the period 1340 to 1383 the ratio between these silver coins and the gold florins was not stable. During our period, the lire inflated from 3 lire per florin to 3 lire, 10 soldi or 3.5 lire per gold florin. The exchange rates varied as follows: [17]

---

13. See Chapter 2, note 16.

14. G. Villani, *Cronica*, VI, p. 184; in Chapter one, moreover, it is shown that of those identified by profession in the fifteenth-century *Notarile* almost half were *sottoposti* in the wool or silk industries.

15. Another component of the *popolo minuto* are those *miserabili*, who were outside the skilled work force of Florence, the structurally unemployable and transient day laborers. These individuals, so difficult to trace through the medieval and Renaissance sources, in many cases probably did not marry or rear children; in other cases, they may have contracted marriages which escaped the notaries' purview; see C. Paoli, *Mercato, scritta e denaro di Dio* (Florence, 1895).

16. See pp. 125–126.

17. G. F. Pagnini della Ventura, *Della decima e di varie altre gravezze imposte dal Comme di Frenze della moneta e della mercatura de'Fiorentini fino al secolo XVI* (Lisbon, Lucca, 1765), Vol. I, Table IV; more detailed information on the fluctuations of the rates of exchange between lire and florins can be found in Charles de la Roncière, *Florence: Centre économique régional au XIVe siecle*, Vol. II (Aix-en-Provence, 1977), pp. 505–547; and M. Bernocchi and R. Fantappie, *Le Monte della Repubblica di Firenze*, Vol. IV (Florence, 1974). For our purposes the tables of Pagnini provide sufficient detail.

1331	Fiorino stretto	3.——.——	
1345	Florin del Suggello	3. 2.——	
1347	Florin del Suggello	3. 8.——	
1352	Florin del Suggello	3. 7. 6	
1353	Florin del Suggello	3. 8. 6	
1356	Florin del Suggello	3.10.——	
1375	Fiorino nuovo	3.10.——	
1378	Fiorino nuovo	3. 8.——	
1380	Fiorino nuovastro	3.10.——	

To simplify the conversions, we have estimated the rate for the entire period as 3.3 lire or 3 lire and 6 soldi per florin.

For the fifteenth century, those who exchanged dowries equal to 70 florins or less demarcate a corresponding proportion of the population (44.46%). Again, many of the dowries exchanged by this portion of the population were expressed in lire, but in the latter half of the fifteenth century, the proportion declined considerably, to less than half (46%). The lire during 80 years of our analysis was inflated in relation to the florin at an even steeper rate than it had been during the period of the Ciompi. From 4 lire, 5 soldi per florin at the beginning of our period the price of the florin rose to 7 lire, 2 soldi during the first decade of the sixteenth century.[18]

1448	Fiorino del VIII Sigillo	4. 5.——	
1460	Fiorino del IX Sigillo	4. 6.——	
1461	Fiorino a peso Pisano		
1462	Fiorino a peso Pisano	4. 7.——	
1464	Fiorino largo	5. 6.——	
1471	Fiorino largo	5. 8.——	
1475	Fiorino largo	5. 8.——	
1480	Fiorino largo	5.11.——	
1485	Fiorino largo	5.11. 4	
1495	Fiorino largo	5.11. 4	
1501	Fiorino d'Oro largo	5.11. 4	grossi
		7.——.——	neri
1503	Fiorino d'Oro largo	7.——.——	neri
1508	Fiorino d'Oro largo	7. 2.——	

Since we find in the notarial documents of the latter part of the fifteenth century various sorts of florins in use, even after the introduction of

---

18. Pagnini, *Della decima*, Vol. I, Table IV.

more valuable florins (and often the type of florin which was exchanged is not specified), we have not tried to average these exchange rates over time; rather, we have used a conservative rate of conversion of 4.5 lire or 4 lire and 10 soldi per florin for the whole period.

In conclusion, for the period of the Ciompi, we can estimate and delineate the bounds of the *popolo minuto* by means of the dowry.[19] These means certainly will exclude from our analysis certain wealthy, unusual or prestigious artisans who were in fact *sottoposti* or wage earners in the wool industry; on the other hand, other artisans who could have been matriculated members of the minor guilds enter the analysis as a part of the *popolo minuto*. Although the use of the dowry to identify the *popolo minuto* only roughly corresponds to the constitutional definition found in the documents of 1378 or to its objective definition in terms of the social relations of production, these means will perhaps better identify the *popolo minuto* in its subjective sense: that more amorphous class, which corresponded roughly to the poorest half of working Florentine men and women and which Charles de la Roncière has argued forcefully conceived of itself on the eve of the Ciompi in religious, social, and political terms as "the poor." [20]

For the fifteenth century, we can create six subsets of the *popolo minuto* through a consideration of the information on occupation and dowry payment that is supplied: (*a*) a combined definition based on dowry and occupation—1. those workers who either exchanged a dowry of more than or equal to 70 florins or for whom a dowry exchange was not found, and 2. those workers who were identified by an occupation which in 1378 became a part of one of the three revolutionary guilds; [21] (*b*) the poor: those who exchanged dowries of less than or equal to 70 florins and who practiced trades which were not under the supervision of the wool or silk industries or who were not identified by profession; (*c*) those *sottoposti* who exchanged dowries of less than or equal to 70 florins; (*d*) all those who were identified as *sottoposti* by occupation (sets *a* and *c*, combined; (*e*) all those who exchanged dowries of less than or equal to 70 florins (sets *b* and *c*); and (*f*) the combined *popolo minuto* or any marriage which involved a *sottoposto(a)* or a dowry transaction of less than or equal to 70 florins (sets *a*, *b*, and *c*). We thus find the following configuration of subsets:

---

19. See Chapter 2, note 16.

20. "Pauvres et Pauvreté à Florence au XIVe siècle," in *Etudes sur l'histoire de la Pauvreté (moyen âge–XVIe siècle)*, edited by M. Mollat, Vol. II (Paris, 1974), pp. 661–745.

21. Predominantly, these occupations were under the jurisdiction of either the wool or silk guilds; hence, in the pages which follow, we will refer to these workers as *sottoposti*.

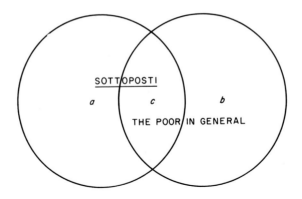

Basically, the six sets above have been formed from two different notions of the Florentine *popolo minuto:* first, the *popolo minuto* in its strictly juridical sense, the wage earners or *sottoposti* of the wool and silk industries and other collateral professions; and second, those spouses who exchanged dowries of 70 florins or less, whom we will identify as the poor in general.

Let us begin our analysis by considering the more complex data from the fifteenth century. The various rates of endogamy and exogamy present some interesting variations. (see Table 3.1 and Appendixes F.2–F.4) First, the poor in general (those spouses who exchanged dowries within the lowest forty-fifth percentile of all dowries regardless of occupation, set *e* above) married slightly more often within the confines of the parish (53%) than those workers in the wool and silk industries (47%). When the larger rings of endogamy are considered (the quarter and the cluster), however, the intermarriage of the *sottoposti* (set *d*) exceeds that of the general poor by 8.38% and 6.84%, respectively; endogamy in the quarter and within the cluster, in other words, varies from 60% to 65% in the quarter and from 57% to 61% in the cluster. Thus, from the population of *sottoposti* to that of the general poor, intermarriage beyond the parish varies from 8% to 19% when the quarter is considered, and from 5% to 15% when we consider the geographical cluster.

This inverse in the endogamy ratios between the general poor and the *sottoposti* is more surprising when we consider the variations in the residential patterns of the two groups. The *sottoposti,* slightly more frequently than the general poor, tended to reside in the large (both in terms of area and population) parishes of S. Maria in Verzaia, S. Frediano, S. Lorenzo, and S. Ambrogio, which covered a vast portion of the city's periphery between the city and the ring of streets that in the late thirteenth century delineated the radius of concentrated urban building. (see Figures 3.1, 3.2, and 3.3 and Chapter 4, note 32) Thus, if factors of demography and distance were the only forces at play, we would expect the opposite phenomenon; that is, the *sottoposti* should have had a slightly higher rate of parish endogamy than that of the poor in general, and the rate of endogamy beyond the parish within the cluster or quarter should have been slightly higher among the poor in general than among the *sottoposti*. Our statistics suggest that in the fifteenth century the shape of the communities of wool and silk workers outlined through the networks of marital relationships was slightly different from that of the poor in general. There was a tendency for the *sottoposti* to form more ties which extended into communities beyond the parish and within either the *gonfalone*, the quarter, or the geographical cluster.

The social ties of the poor in general, on the other hand, if they were not focused within the parish, were more likely than those of the *sottoposti* to extend beyond the boundaries of the largest geographical units—the quarter and the cluster—and to cut across the city's geography or even beyond the city walls. Of those with dowries of 70 florins or less twice (18%) the proportionally number contracted marriages with spouses who resided beyond the city walls at the time of marriage, as compared with the *sottoposti* (9%). If we then consider only those who married within the city, the difference in inner parish marriages between the *sottoposti* and the poor in general becomes accentuated. This difference is significant. Of these *sottoposti*, 51% compared with 64% of those exchanging dowries of 70 florins or less, found spouses within their parish—an increase by 25%.[22] We must remember that this difference occurs despite the fact that a greater proportion of *sottoposti* than the poor in general lived in the larger and more populous parishes. Evidently, in the interlacing of the communities of the *popolo minuto*, channels other than the parish, such as the place of work or even occupational identification, must have been more important among *sottoposti* than they were for the poor in general, and this despite the absence of formal working-man's associations.[23]

When attention is focused on fifteenth century wool and silk workers, moreover, we find a difference in the marriage patterns between the poorer workers, that is those workers who exchanged dowries of 70 florins or less (*b*), and those workers for whom we do not find a dowry

---

22. Standard error of a proportion test: $p = .6395$, $\pi = .5752$, $N = 630$, $z = 3.26$; 51.09% was derived by dividing the parish column by the Total column or by 458; similarly, 63.95% was derived by dividing the parish column by 162.

23. See the forthcoming volume by Richard Trexler, *Public Life in Renaissance Florence* (New York, 1980); and note Chapter 1, note 28.

Table 3.1

Summary of Marriage Endogamies of the Florentine Popolo Minuto for the Fourteenth and Fifteenth Centuries [a]

Sample	Endogamies				Exogamies			Total
	Parish	Gonfalone	Quarter	Cluster	Cross-quarter	Cross-cluster	Contado	
Fourteenth century Dowries ≤ 50 florins	128 30.92%	22 5.31% 150 36.23%	76 18.36% 226 54.59%	72 17.39% 200 48.31%	130 31.40%	156 37.68%	58 14.01%	414
Fifteenth century (a) *Sottoposti* without an indication of dowry or with dowries ≥ 70 florins	162 43.32%	42 11.23% 204 54.55%	44 11.76% 248 66.31%	68 18.18% 230 61.50%	96 25.67%	114 30.48%	20 5.35%	374
(b) Non-*sottoposti* with dowries ≤ 70 florins	38 46.91%	2 2.47% 40 49.38%	6 7.41% 46 56.39%	4 4.94% 42 51.85%	12 14.81%	16 19.75%	23 28.40%	81

(c) *Sottoposti* with dowries ⩽ 70 florins	72 56.25%	6 4.69%	78 60.94%	2 1.56%	80 62.50%	6 4.69%	78 60.94%	34 26.56%	36 28.13%	14 10.94%	128
(d) *Sottoposti*	234 46.61%	48 9.56%	282 56.18%	46 9.16%	328 65.34%	74 14.74%	308 61.35%	130 25.90%	150 29.88%	44 8.76%	502
(e) All dowries ⩽ 70 florins	110 56.63%	8 3.83%	118 56.46%	8 3.83%	126 60.29%	10 4.78%	120 57.42%	46 22.01%	52 24.88%	37 17.70%	209
(f) Combined *popolo minuto, sottoposti* and those with dowries ⩽ 70 florins	272 46.66%	50 8.58%	322 55.23%	52 8.92%	374 64.15%	78 13.38%	350 60.03%	142 24.36%	166 28.47%	67 11.49%	583

a For clusters, see Table 3:3

contract or who exchanged dowries of more than 70 florins (*a*). For those richer workers, intermarriage within the parish dropped to the lowest percentage of any of our subsets of the *popolo minuto* (43%), while the parish endogamy of the other half of these workers—those who exchanged dowries of 70 florins or less—climbed to the highest figure among our subsets (56%). The differentials in the rates of endogamy within those rings outside the parish and within the *gonfalone,* quarter, and cluster, on the other hand, show the same inverse in tendencies for inner-parish marriage that have just been observed in the differences between the poor and all *sottoposti.* Again, the differences within the ranks of the *sottoposti* reflect the extremes of all our estimates of the population of the *popolo minuto.* Nearly four times as many of the more wealthy wool and silk workers as compared with their poorer confrères (23% as opposed to 6%) married within neighborhoods which cut across parish boundaries (the *gonfalone* and the quarter). Finally, we find a greater percentage of poorer workers marrying spouses beyond the city walls (the *contado*)—11% as compared to 5%. Thus, the differential in intra-parish marriage between the richer and poorer workers who found spouses then residing in the city becomes stronger. Of these poorer workers, 63% married within the parish, while only 46% of the richer *sottoposti* did the same.[24]

To conclude: the contours of the communities traced out by the marital relationships of various subsets of the fifteenth century *popolo minuto* reflect some curious differences. First, the neighborhoods of wool and silk workers, although largely delimited by the exigencies of parish geography, tended, more than those of other *popolo minuti* who were defined by paltry dowries, to circumvent the draw of parish magnetism and to reach into areas of the *gonfalone,* the quarter, and the geographical cluster in the formation of their social networks and communities. In other words, even though those exchanging dowries of 70 florins or less more often married within their parishes, when they did not do so, they were in fact more likely than *sottoposti* to extend and diffuse their kinship ties across the city, beyond the quarter or geographical cluster, or even beyond the city walls. Secondly, when the richer *sottoposti* are distinguished from their less prestigious co-workers, similar patterns of endogamies and exogamies become even sharper. The poorer workers married more often within the parish but less often in the secular and geographical rings of the *gonfalone,* quarter, and cluster. Similarly, a greater proportion of the poorer workers married outside the city. The communities of the poorer workers and the poor

---

24. The denominators for these computations were 354 and 114, respectively.

in general, in other words, if not narrowly focused within the bounds of the parish, tended to be more diffuse than similar communities of the richer workers and artisans.

We find, therefore, from the differentials of rates of endogamy among various subsets of the fifteenth century *popolo minuto* that a strict sense of arithmetic distances is not the best grid for understanding the marriage relationships.[25] That portion of the population which married farthest afield and which most frequently married beyond the city walls, at the same time married most consistently within the confines of the narrowest unit of our geographical investigation—the parish. More importantly, the marriage records provide us with some clues about the nature of the communities and social associations of that population on which the sources otherwise shed so little light—the *popolo minuto*. The implications about the consciousness and the political consequences of these community structures, forged in large part through the magnetism of the urban parish church, will be surveyed in subsequent chapters.

Let us now turn our attention to the *popolo minuto* of the fourteenth century. Unlike the *popolo minuto* of the fifteenth century, we do not find in the period of the Ciompi a striking difference between the *popolo minuto* and the general population (see Table 3.2). Endogamy within the parish is almost identical for both populations; the intermarriage of the general population within the parish in fact even slightly exceeds by around one-half of a percentile point the endogamy of the *popolo minuto* (see Appendix F.1.). The same pattern holds within the *gonfalone*. Within this geographical ring, 6.44% of the general population married, while only 5.33% of the *popolo minuto* did the same. Moreover, when we compare the networks of *parenti* among the fourteenth century patriciate with the Trecento *popolo minuto*, again we do not find wide discrepancies (see Chapter 2, p. 52). Only endogamy within the parish differs substantially, and then only when the higher levels of patriciate society are compared with the poor. When endogamy within the more standardized secular geography of the *gonfalone*—the district that we have argued is better suited for the comparison of various social strata with one another—is considered, no substantial difference whatsoever can be found between the highest strata of patrician society, those with family names and dowries of 400 florins or more (34%), and the *popolo minuto* (36%). And when the quarter is considered, intermar-

---

25. For studies which consider patterns of marriage endogamy strictly according to concentric circles of distances varying from a central place, see *Annales de démographie historique*, 7 (1970).

Table 3.2
Comparison of the Marriage Endogamies of the Total Population and the Popolo Minuto, 1340–1383

	Endogamies				Exogamies			
	Parish (a)	Gonfalone (b)	Quarter (c)	Cluster (d)	Cross-quarter (e)	Cross-cluster (f)	Contado (g)	Total
Aggregate	510 31.60%	104 6.44%	242 14.99%	232 14.37%	560 34.70%	674 41.76%	198 12.27%	1614
Cumulative totals		614 38.04%	856 53.04%	742 45.97%				
Popolo minuto	128 30.92%	22 5.31%	76 18.36%	72 17.39%	130 31.40%	156 37.68%	58 14.01%	414
Cumulative totals		150 36.23%	226 54.59%	200 48.31%				

riage between members of the elite families of fourteenth century Florence (58%) even exceeded that of the *popolo minuto* (49%).

Thus, we do not find the wide discrepancies in the marriage behavior or networks of association between classes in the fourteenth century that our statistics for fifteenth-century society reveal. When rates of endogamy are compared between the fifteenth century *popolo minuto* and the ruling elite of fifteenth-century Florence, nearly 11 times the number of artisans and laborers married within the *gonfalone* as did members of the patriciate (64% as opposed to 6%).

There was a significant bifurcation in fifteenth-century society. As the *popolo minuto* concentrated their social networks around the numerous parochial communities, the patriciate seems to have adopted rules of exogamy. Their relationships extended across the city; we do not find them any longer identified (either by the notary or as defined by our statistical analysis) by the parish communities, or even by the larger secular units of the *gonfalone* or quarter. Only half the proportion of members of the ruling elite (27%) married within the quarter as compared to the proportion of fifteenth century *popoli minuti* who married within a parish (47% to 56%)—and a quarter such as S. Giovanni contained at least 25 different parishes.

Despite the substantial differences in class structure between the two periods of our analysis, was there a significant change in the sociology of the *popolo minuto* itself from the period of the Ciompi to the period of the Medici? For this comparison, we will consider, not the fifteenth century population that reflected the most dramatic rates of marriage endogamies (the poorer laborers in the wool and silk industries) but rather that more amorphous population which more closely coincides with the structural dimensions of a fluid class of laborers and poorer artisans—those who were juridically locked out of corporate identification with the citizenry of Florence. We will consider, in other words, the broadest representation of the *popolo minuto* for the fifteenth century available, those with dowries of 70 florins or less, regardless of profession, plus all *sottoposti* of the wool and silk manufacturers, regardless of the amount of dowry exchanged (set *f*).

Indeed, the difference between the fourteenth- and fifteenth-century populations of the *Popolo di Dio* were significant. The proportion of those marrying within the confines of the parish community increased by 50% from 31% to 47%.[26] Yet, as with the differentials that were observed between rich and poor artisans and laborers in the fifteenth

---

26. By a standard error of a proportion test, this difference is highly significant: $p = .3092$, $\pi = .3879, N = 997, z = 5.10$.

century, those rings beyond the parish—the *gonfalone,* the quarter, and the geographical cluster—were more important as foci of popular neighborhoods and social associations in the fourteenth century than they were in the period of the Medici. In the fourteenth century, 24% of the *popolo minuto* married within the ring of *gonfalone* and quarter around the parish and 18% within the ring inside the cluster, while in the fifteenth century 18% married within the quarter ring and 13% within the ring of the cluster. Again, the comparisons of intermarriage between various groups show that distance was not always the factor which distinguished marriage patterns of these groups; rather, we find that neighborhoods were defined by various structures. (See Figures 3.1–3.3.)

In the fourteenth century, the influences of the parish church did not have the same magnetism in shaping the social relationship and kinship networks of the *popolo minuto* which it later came to play during the latter part of the fifteenth century. Certain reflections and consequences of these changes in the social structure of the *popolo minuto* have long been known to historians of the Ciompi and the religious movements of late medieval and Renaissance Florence. In the latter half of the Trecento, we find competing forms of religious experience, from processions to secret societies of noble youth [27] to heretical movements (the Fraticelli). As a result, according to the chronicler Stefani, when mass was heard there was never more than 1% of the parish community present.[28] Rodolico, Becker, la Roncière, and Trexler have shown us that there was indeed a Ciompi religion, that of the spiritual Franciscans, who defied the hierarchy of parochial organization.[29] On the other hand, for the fifteenth century (at least before the popularity of Savonarola), the most significant fact about religion in Florence was the almost complete absence of heretics and heretical movements. From 1389 to 1498 only one heretic was burnt at the stake in Florence.[30]

With the decline in official religion and the rise of other competing forms of spiritual awareness, meeting places other than the parish—the work place, the neighborhood tavern—appear to have exerted a stronger pull and must have been more important foci in the daily lives of laborers and artisans than they were a century later. For the mid-

---

27. Marchionne di Coppo Stefani, *Cronaca Fiorentina,* edited by N. Rodolico, in Rerum Italicarum Scriptores, new ed., Vol. XXX, part I (Città di Castello, 1903–1955), p. 296.

28. Ibid., pp. 295–296.

29. Rodolico, *La Democrazia fiorentina,* pp. 50–81; Becker, "Florentine Politics and the Diffusion of Heresy in the Trecento: A Socioeconomic Inquiry," *Speculum,* 34 (1959), 60–75; la Roncière, "Pauvres et Pauvreté," pp. 661–745; see, moreover, Millard Meiss, *Painting in Florence and Siena after the Black Death* (Princeton, 1951), pp. 87 ff.

30. Brucker, *Renaissance Florence* (New York, 1969), p. 207.

Figure 3.1. *The ideal typical parish in the fourteenth and fifteenth centuries:* the popolo minuto.

Figure 3.2. *Endogamy among the* popolo minuto, *1340–1383.*

Figure 3.3. *Endogamy among the* popolo minuto, *1450–1530.*

Table 3.3
A Code Sheet of the Popoli *within the City of Florence* [a]

I.   Cluster of S. Frediano
.01   S. Frediano   S.S. Drago
.02   S. Maria in Verzaia   S.S. Drago
.03   S. Pier Gattolino   S.S. Ferza
.04   S. Iacopo sopr'Arno   S.S. Nicchio
.05   S. Felicità   S.S. Nicchio, (Scala)
.06   S. Felice ia Piazza   S.S. Ferza
.07   S. Spirito   S.S. Nicchio

II.   Cluster of S. Niccolò
.10   S. Niccolò   S.S. Scala
.11   S. Gregorio   S.S. Scala
.12   S. Giorgio   S.S. Scala
.13   S. Lucia dei Bardi (Magnoli)   S.S. Scala
.14   S. Maria sopr'Arno   S.S. Scala

III. Cluster of S. Lucia Ognissanti
.20   S. Lucia Ognissanti   S.M.N. Unicorno
.21   S. Maria Novella   S.M.N. L.Bianco
.22   S. Paolo   S.M.N. L.Rosso
.23   S. Pancrazio   S.M.N. L.Rosso
.24   S. Trinità   S.M.N. Unicorno
.25   Ognissanti S.M.N.

IV.   Cluster of S. Lorenzo
.30   S. Lorenzo   S.I. L. d'oro
.31   S. Iacopo in Campo Corbolini   S.I. Chiavi
.32   S. Marco   S.I. Drago

V.   Cluster of S. Ambrogio–S. Piero Maggiore
.40   S. Ambrogio   S.I. Chiavi
.41   S. Pier Maggiore   S.I. Chiavi
.42   S. Michele Visdomini   S.I. Vaio
.43   S. Simone   S.C. Bue
.44   S. Remigio (S. Romeo)   S.C. L.Nero
.45   S. Iacopo tra|le |Fossi   S.C. L.Nero
.46   S. Croce   S.C. L.Nero, Bue

VI.   The Central City Cluster
.50   S. Maria del Fiore   S.I. L.d'oro, Drago (S. Reparata)
.51   S. Maria Maggiore   S.I. Drago
.52   S. Rufillo   S.I. Drago
.53   S. Michlele Berteldi S.M.N. L.Bianco, S.I. Drago
.54   S. Leo   S.I. Drago
.55   S. Donato dei Vecchietti   S.M.N. L. Bianco
.56   S. S. Tommaso   S.I. Drago
.57   S. Pier Buonconsiglio   S.M.N. L.Bianco
.58   S. Maria in Campidoglio   S.I. Chiavi
.59   S. Miniato fra le Torri   S.M.N. L.Rosso
.60   S. Andrea   S.M.N. L.Rosso

Table 3.3 (*Continued*)

.61   Orsanmichele   S.C. Carro
.62   S. Biagio (S. Maria sopra Porta)   S.M.N. Vipera
.63   SS Apostoli   S.M.N. Vipera
.64   S. Stefano al Ponte   S.C. Carro
.65   S. Piero Scheraggio   S.C. Carro
.66   S. Cecilia   S.C. Carro
.67   S. Romolo   S.C. Carro
.68   S. Firenze   S.C. Bue
.69   S. Appellinare   S.C. Bue
.70   Badia (S. Stefano alla Badia) S.C. Ruote
.71   S. Procolo   S.C. Ruota, S.I. Chiavi, Vaio
.72   S. Margherita dei Ricci   S.I., Vaio
.73   S. Bartolommeo al Corso   S.I. Chiavi, Vaio
.74   S. Maria Nipotecosa   S.I., Drago, Vaio
.75   S. Michele delle Trombe   S.I., Vaio (in Palchetta; S. Elisabetta)
.76   S. Maria degli Alberighi   S.I. Vaio
.77   S. Maria in Campo   S.I. Vaio
.78   S. Benedetto   S.I., Vaio
.79   S. Cristofano degli Adimari   S.I., Drago
.80   S. Maria degli Ughi   S.M.N. L.Rosso
.81   S. Piero Celoro   S.I., Vaio
.82   S. Salvatore   S.I., Drago
.83   S. Martino   S.C. Ruote

ª S.S. = S. Spirito; S.M.N. = S. Maria Novella; S.I. = S. Giovanni;
S.C. = S. Croce; L. = Leon.

Trecento, in fact, the chronicler Stefani draws our attention to the tension between the geographical ambit (in this case, the *gonfalone*) and other competing bonds of association.[31] He describes with some disdain the effervescence of popular culture following the Duke of Athens' assumption of power. Spontaneous festivals and dancing and singing, according to the chronicler, spread through working class and artisan neighborhoods. There was one in S. Ambrogio, another from the corner of la Macina extending to Belletri and finally to Ognissanti; another

---

31. For discussions of various forms of community ties and association and the relationship between geography and social bonds, see Karl Marx, *Grundrisse,* transl. Martin Nicolaus (New York, 1973), pp. 83, 471–479, and 485–490; Ferdinand Tönnies, *Community and Society,* transl. C. Loomis (East Lansing, 1957); C. Tilly, L. Tilly, and R. Tilly, *The Rebellious Century, 1830–1930* (Cambridge, Mass., 1975), pp. 4–13; and C. Tilly, "How Protest Modernized in France, 1845–1855," in *The Dimensions of Quantitative Research,* edited by Aydelotte, Bogue and Fogel (Princeton, 1972), pp. 192–256, "Collective Violence in European Perspective," in *Violence in America: Historical and Comparative Perspectives,* ed. H. Graham and T. Gurr (Beverly Hills, 1979), and "Hauptformen kollektiver Aktion in Westeuropa, 1500–1975," in *Geschichte und Gesellschaft* (1977), Heft 2, *Sozialer Protest,* ed. Richard Tilly (Göttingen, 1977), pp. 154–163.

occurred in Borgo S. Paolo; another in S. Frediano; another in S. Giorgio; and another in Via Larga.[32] Stefani laments that this "magnification of the *gente minuta* and the wool workers" even corrupted Florence's ancient festival of S. Giovanni. Whereas, in the past the *gonfaloni* organized the festival, now each guild put on the festival "for itself," and common *sottoposti* as well as the signores participated. Stefani concludes that this corruption of the ancient customs went against "all human and divine reason." [33]

In the same rubric Stefani gives another clue about another possible node of communication and association within the *popolo minuto* during the revolutionary period preceding the Ciompi. He explains the origins of the word "Ciompi":

And among other things which disgraced the city even more was a term, which the *popolo minuto* took from the French, courtiers and soldiers. In French they are accustomed to saying "comrade"; and just in speaking to their comrades, they go willingly to the taverns. And the *gente minuta* make use of wine and the tavern. It was fashionable to go there together to drink. And the French would say "Compar, allois a boier (Comrade, let's get a drink)." And the *popolo rozzo* would garble the French, saying, "Ciompo, Ciompo" and suddenly they were all Ciompi, that is, comrades. And thus the Florentine (citizen) saw the French and the signores along with the small and the vile, servants and soldiers alike using his city, disgracing the good and ancient customs. And he would say all day long,

---

32. For the identification of these places, see *Stradario storico e amministrativo della città e del comune di Firenze* (Florence, 1913).

33. Stefani, *Cronaca fiorentina*, 202, rubric 575,

Come fece fare molte belle feste in più dì specialmente per S. Giovanni . . . Nel detto anno il Duca per le feste, che sono di maggio fece fare sei brigate nelle quali fece signori, e vestire il fece a divisa, e diè loro per ispese danari e doni di vino e da mangiare; ma furono tutte queste brigate di gente minuta; il quali danzando, ballando, sonando andavano per la città. L'una fu a S. Ambruogio; l'altra fu da il canto la Macina giuso per Belletri insono a Ognissanti; l'altra in borgo S. Paolo; l'altra nella via Larga, dagli Spadai infino al canto alle Rondine, la via del Cocomero e de' Servi su a Monte Loro. La festa di S. Goivanni fece fare per arti e non per gonfaloni, e ciascuna arte per sè; poi tutti i certi ordinati e palii, li quali avea da 'signori e comuni sottoposti al Comune, e poi a lui bracchi e sparvieri. Questa fu onorevole festa ed offerta e bella, perocchè tutte queste cose ragunò in sulla piazza di S. Croce, e poi le condusse in sulla piazza del suo palagio, e andarono a S. Giovanni. Onde li cittadini, che si ricordarono delle offerta co' gonfaloni, e veggendo magnificare la gente minuta e scardassieri ed inalzargli, sdegnarono forte di ciò, perchè era fuori d'ogni umana e divina ragione. Lo palio di S. Giovanni fece foderare di vaio e molto riccamente ed onorevolmente addobbare d'ogni cosa. Parendo tante cose sconce nella nostra città farsi per lo signore, abbandonando gli antichi cittadini, e riducendosi e magnificandosi con gli minuti uomini.

"The small do not rob the commune; they rob only the big ones so." Such
disgrace! Night and day they ponder how to become free.[34]

Here, we find the word "Ciompo" used not exclusively as synonymous
with wool workers (a meaning which it later assumed), but instead
it refers to the "vile" in general and possibly to those French courtiers
and soldiers (at least initially) who were accustomed to drinking together with the *popolo rozzo.* The term, in Stefani's etymology, conveys
a social and political connotation—the sense of association, itself. The
relationship becomes the thing; the act of association makes the Ciompi.
And we find the tavern right at the center of the interaction in which
the *gente minuta* met, drank and became comrades, that is, Ciompi. It
is interesting here to note that after wool combers and wool skinners,
tavernkeepers were one of the most often cited of the professions found
in the lists of condemned Ciompi insurrectionists of the middle and late
Trecento.[35] They must have been important *link-men* in the formation
of revolutionary ties among members of the *popolo minuto* and with
others sympathetic to their struggle. Similar to eighteenth- and nineteenth-century English society, the tavern in late Trecento Florence
was the antipode of the parish church, and it was the tavern where the
laboring classes could forge their own plebeian culture.[36,37]

---

34. Stefani, *Cronaca fiorentina,* 203,

> Ed infra l'altre cose che piu avieno a sdegno, si era un vocabolo, lo quale avieno preso
> i Franceschi e i cortigiani e i soldati, perocchè in francesco s'accorda il nome di dire
> compare, quasi nel parlare loro compar, e vanno volentieri alle taverne, e la gente
> minuta usano il vino e la taverna; usavano insieme a bere, e dicea il Francesco: Compar,
> allois a boier: Compare andiamo a bere. E il popolo rozzo di vocabolo francesco diceano:
> Ciompo, andiamo a bere; e così diceano: Ciompo, Ciompo; e quasi erano tutti ciompi,
> cioè compari. E così veggendo il Fiorentino usare la sua città a Franceschi, 'Signori,
> con vili e minuti e i famigli ed i soldati il simile, ed buoni ed antichi sdegnare, e
> dicesi tutto dì: "Il piccolo non ha rubato il Comune, ma li grossi si," sdegnati, di e
> notte pensavano come potessero essere liberi.

35. Moreover, Brucker, *The Civic World,* 327, maintains that the "desperate workers" in
plotting the abortive insurrection of 1411 met in taverns to share their grievances.
36. Certainly, Paolo da Certaldo, the moralist of the merchant class in late Trecento
Florence, saw the tavern and the church on opposite ends of the moral spectrum:

> Molto ti guarda de l'usanze de le taverne: non l'usare. Usa la chiesa i dì de le feste; e
> gli altri dì, quando puoi con giusto modo lasciare la bottega o 'l fondaco, anche usa la
> chiesa.

(Libro di buoni costumi, edited by Alfred Schiaffini (Florence, 1945), 96.
37. For an analysis of a comparative situation, see E. P. Thompson, "Patrician Society,
Plebeian Culture," *Journal of Social History,* 7 (1974), pp. 382–405.

Finally, unlike the patterns of endogamy cast by the differentials between the richer and poorer *sottoposti,* we find a greater proportion of the fourteenth-century *popolo minuto* marrying outside the city (14%) than we find for their great-grandchildren during the Quattrocento (12%). This discrepancy, however, hardly affects the difference in parish endogamy between the two populations when only those marrying within the city are considered. Intra-parish marriage for the fourteenth century becomes 36% and 53% for the period of the Medici.[38] But before we proceed to analyze the political implications and consequences of the changes in social structure of the *popolo minuto*—the disappearance of the vibrant Trecento popular culture beyond the borders of the parish church and the retreat of the *popolo minuto* in the fifteenth century into parochial identifications and associations—let us first consider more closely the structural changes which have been sketched out above. Can we rest assured with these statistics? Could there have been other structural changes, such as immigration or a change in the population densities of certain parishes or a fundamental change in the social and economic composition of the city's neighborhoods, which might explain the observed changes in parish endogamies?

38. The denominators for these computations were 356 and 516, respectively.

Chapter 4

Immigration

STRUCTURAL dimensions of the data presented can now be considered. The statistics will be examined to discover whether there were qualitative changes in the nature of immigration and if there were fundamental transformations in the neighborhood organization or ecology of the Arno city that may have been influencing factors in the observed shifts in parish and neighborhood endogamies. Did the flow of workers and artisans from the countryside and foreign places change in quantity or character over the period of our analysis? Were there changes in urban geography over these two centuries which might in part account for the higher parochialism of laborers in the fifteenth century, or even overturn our earlier conclusions? Were there other changes in the social distances between classes in this Renaissance city?

Let us begin with a consideration of changes in immigration. The raw results seem quite inconsequential; as noted in the previous chapter, migration to the city through marriage among the *popolo minuto* decreased from the fourteenth to the fifteenth century by 2.5 percentile points, which was less than a 20% decline. When the sex ratios of these immigrants are considered, however, these rates become some of the most significant statistics our inquiry has uncovered thus far. There is a complete reversal in the percentages of men, as compared with women, who married into the city between the two sample periods. (see Appendixes F.1, F.2, F.3, and F.4.)

In the fourteenth century, 76% of immigrants through marriage were men; whereas in the fifteenth century, the majority of those from beyond the city walls establishing city residence through marriage were women (67%).[1] This higher ratio of women to men, moreover, in-

---

1. For the fifteenth century these figures were derived from the sex ratios found in column g, Appendix F.2, plus those in Table F.3.

creases as we descend the social scale through the various fifteenth century *popolo minuto* subsets. From the "*sottoposti* as a whole" category (Appendix F.2), 64% of the immigrants were women, while 74% of the immigrants among those who exchanged dowries of 70 florins or less were women. When the *sottoposti* of the wool and silk industries are separated into subgroups of richer and poorer workers (Appendix F.4), the differences in the sex ratios are striking. Among the richer workers, only slightly more women than men contracted relations with spouses from the surrounding countryside and points beyond (52%). From the poorer group, however, we do not find even a single man making his way into the city through marriage, while 20% of the women in this sample resided beyond the city walls and found husbands who were Florentine residents.

How do we interpret these statistics? Might they reflect an improvement in the status of women from the fourteenth to the fifteenth centuries? The variation among subsets of the *popolo minuto* of the fifteenth century indeed suggests that there was a negative correlation between the number of women immigrants and prestige or price of the dowry. Women from the countryside tended to marry into the bottom layers of urban society. There is a substantial difference between the average dowries of those peasants residing in the surrounding countryside of Florence during the fifteenth century and the dowries of urban workers and artisans. Unlike those of the urban *popolo minuto* during the fifteenth century, the majority of peasant dowries were exchanged (or at least expressed) in lire; moreover, the amount clustered within the range from 25 lire to 30 florins. Finally, in the fifteenth century sample there is a distinct trade-off between occupational status and city residence when the marriage patterns of fifteenth century notaries are observed. In all but one instance of notaries marrying downward out of the major guilds and into the ranks of the minor guildsmen and their families, it was the daughters of country notaries who married urban shopkeepers or artisans.

When the social mobility of women through marriage during the period of the Ciompi is considered, the sex ratios of immigrants remain enigmatic. Women in fifteenth century Florentine society definitely married downward. This phenomenon has been studied most thoroughly at the top of society. Anthony Molho and Julius Kirshner,[2] David Herlihy and Christiane Klapisch,[3] and Richard Trexler[4] have demon-

---

2. "The Dowry Fund and the Marriage Market in Early Quattrocento Florence," *Journal of Modern History*, 50 (1978), pp. 403–438.
3. *Les Toscans et leurs familles: Une étude du catasto florentin de 1427* (Paris, 1978), p. 418.
4. "Le célibat à la fin du moyen âge: Les religieuses de Florence," *Annales, E.S.C.*, 27 (1972), pp. 1348–1349.

strated—from changes in the differentials of age at marriage, from information contained in the *Monte delle Doti,* and from the striking growth in the building and patronage of and enrollments in nunneries during the latter part of the fifteenth and in the early sixteenth centuries—that women fared less favorably than previously on the marriage market. More and more nubile women either could not find adequate relationships, remained celibate, and entered monastic institutions.

The marriage data for the fourteenth century, however, do not support that conclusion. First, within the ranks of the patriciate, we find only a slight tendency for women of prestigious birth to marry downward. When all marriages in which one spouse possessed a family name are considered, 32 (30%) married a partner who also possessed a family name; 33 (or 31%) of husbands married women from families undistinguished by a family name in the *Notarile;* and 43 women (or 40%) apparently married downward. When looking below the levels of the *ottimati,* considering the scraps of information concerning occupational intermarriage during the mid-Trecento, the statistics do not suggest that women married downward. Of the women in our sample, two from families of major guildsmen married husbands who were major guildsmen, and two married into families of minor guildsmen. The daughter of a silk merchant married an innkeeper and the daughter of a wool manufacturer married a *fornaio* ('baker'). From the families of minor guildsmen, 10 women married minor guildsmen, and 3 married downward occupationally. Of these, one, the daughter of a *biadaiolo* or grain dealer married a *portatore* ('carrier of goods')—who possibly was a member of the guild whose goods he carried. Another, the daughter of a cobbler, married a tailor; the third, the daughter of a *pianellaio* ('slipper-maker'), married a tailor. Finally, among three families of *sottoposti,* all of whom were tailors, we find striking upward mobility among the women; two married into the ranks of the major guildsmen. In one case the husband was a notary; in the other, he was a goldsmith—a separate *membrum* of the Arte di Por S. Maria. In the third instance, a tailor's daughter married a *dipintore.* He could possibly have been a member of Por S. Maria, but probably was a common house painter and thus, like the tailor, locked out of corporate recognition by the Commune.

To summarize, we do not find a clear tendency for these women to marry downward. The majority (65%) married into professions which were of the same corporate status; five married occupationally downward and four married upward. But we find the most striking marital upward mobility among the daughters of *sottoposti,* who thus broke into the families of the major guildsmen (Table 4.1).

Table 4.1
Occupational Intermarriage—
1340–1383

Wives	Husbands
rigattiere	lanaiolo, linainolo
notaio	notaio
lanaiolo	fornaio
setaiolo	setaiolo, albergatore
beccaio	beccaio, beccaio, beccaio
calzolaio	sarto
fabbro	fornaio
legnaiolo	coreggiaio
muratore	fornaciaio, orafo
bastiere	linaiolo
pianellaio	sarto
sarto	notaio, orafo, dipintore
biadaiolo	ferratore, portatore

Thus the change in the social status of women in the marriage market runs in a contradictory direction to the facts on immigration. All other factors being equal, the selection of a spouse from the countryside must have been an unfavorable marriage from the perspective of the city dweller. In both periods and across social classes, residency in the city of Florence carried a certain prestige. For the urban laborer or small artisan, it meant a form of livelihood that was more lucrative than the toil of the *mezzadro* or, in many cases, than that of the small peasant proprietor. In the Catasti of 1427, 1457, and 1480 we find, in fact, many *sottoposti* in the wool and silk industries who owned their own homes or strips of arable land and who, in many instances, leased other holdings in the city and in the countryside. From the standpoint of the country artisan, marriage into an urban family of *arti minori* often proved an opportunity for him to become a part (in a corporate sense) of the Commune of Florence. And for the *ottimati*, it could prove a means for direct involvement in the affairs of the Florentine state, and for gain from its fiscal and financial opportunities. By 1427, liquid capital (shares in the *Monte*), industrial production, administrative activities, general wealth, and even landed wealth had become heavily concentrated within the city of Florence.[5]

Perhaps the change in the sex ratios of immigrants through marriage into the city of Florence had little to do with changes within the city;

---

5. D. Herlihy, "The Distribution of Wealth in a Renaissance Community: Florence 1427," in *Towns in Societies*, edited by Abrams and Wrigley (Cambridge, 1978), pp. 131–157; and Herlihy and Klapisch, *Les Toscans et leur familles*, pp. 241–267.

its causes might have arisen from structural changes in the countryside: the expansion of the *podere*—the rational enclosed farm—and the spread of a new form of peasant exploitation, the *mezzadria,* which became the dominant mode of land tenure and agricultural exploitation by the sixteenth century in Tuscany.[6] In a recent comparative investigation of geographic mobility, Emmanuel Todd finds clear differences in the eighteenth century between an area of Artois (the Longuenesse) that was dominated by large farms and wage labor, and the peasant communities of Pratolino on the outskirts of Florence, where the *mezzadria* was the dominant form of agricultural exploitation. Although the economy of the eighteenth-century Longuenesse certainly does not correspond to the social and agrarian relationships found in the fourteenth-century *contado* of Florence, Todd's comparison does illuminate certain characteristics of the *mezzadria* that probably characterized this land tenure institution in Tuscany from the fifteenth century through the eighteenth century.

Todd found that adolescent and nubile men of the Artois left their parents' homes to work on large estates in neighboring villages, where they later married and established households. The curve of male mobility thus climbs rapidly during the adolescent years, and peaks during the early twenties. Afterward, through young adulthood and middle age, the curve declines rapidly; the new households were extremely stable.[7] In contrast, in Pratolino a similar peak in the mobility of men at the age of marriage is not found; instead, mobility was stable throughout the life cycle. Todd explains the contrast by differences in the type of mobility. In the Longuenesse mobility was individual, whereas in Pratolino it was group mobility. Because of short agrarian leases, the *frérèches* or large extended family of the *mezzadria* moved from place to place through its life cycle, as a unit.

The picture for women, on the other hand, is completely different. In order to avoid incest, women in Pratolino left their families around the age of marriage to find husbands in neighboring villages.[8] In contrast to the Longuenesse, the marriage pattern in the villages of Pratolino was patrilocal. Only women, the old, and those of illegitimate birth escaped the tight control of these strong patrilineal families.[9] Thus, with the spread of the *mezzadria* during the fifteenth century, many more women than men would have been freed for migration into the cities as well as to other families in the countryside.

---

6. Emmanuel Todd, "Mobilité, géographique et cycle de vie en Artois et en Toscane au XVIIIᵉ siècle," *Annales E.S.C.,* 30 (1975), 741.

7. *Ibid.,* E. Todd, pp. 730–731.

8. *Ibid.,* E. Todd, pp. 734–735.

9. *Ibid.,* E. Todd, p. 734.

The growth of the *mezzadria,* however, does not entirely explain the divergences in sex ratios of immigrants from the period of the Ciompi through the period of the Republic. When we separate the rural immigrants from the *contado* of Florence from all other immigrants (those originating from the subject cities, from other Italian city–states, and from places outside Italy), we find differences between the two centuries in sources of immigration to the city of Florence. Of those who married into urban families of the *popolo minuto* in the fourteenth century, only three (two men and a woman or 5%) came from places beyond the rural belt of Florence. In the fifteenth century, the proportion from foreign cities—Genoa, Padau, Bologna, Milan—climbed to nearly a quarter of the immigrants. Although the sex ratio of immigrants from the countryside was low (i.e., 46% were men), the abundance of women over men from foreign cities contributed in the fifteenth century to the excess of female migrants to the city. There were 10 women and 6 men, or a sex ratio of 60.

If we go beyond these meager statistics and consider immigration for all the marriages in our sample, it becomes clear that, from the fourteenth centry through the fifteenth century, Florence relied increasingly on foreign places (both foreign city–states in Italy and foreign countries) instead of the *contado* for its labor force supply and for the resurgence in population growth (Table 4.2). To compile these statistics we will not only consider immigrants through marriage, we will utilize all the place names supplied by the notaries. There are certain dangers in doing this. It is not always possible to know from a phrase such as *"de Bononia"* or *"de Colonia"* whether the spouse, his or her father, or even a great-grandfather originated from Bologna or Cologne. In some cases, no doubt, the place name had become a family name. But in most cases, the notary made it clear that the person from a foreign place or *contado* village was a newcomer to the urban parish in which he or she resided at the time of the document's redaction. Before the phrase *"de populo de Sancti Laurenti or Sancti Fridiani,"* the notary inserted the phrase *"ad presens"* or *"ad hodie"* or *"moratur."*

In the late fifteenth century, the composition of immigrants was substantially different from that of the fourteenth century, not only among those who married into the city, but also among all those identified in the marriage records by a foreign place. Of those who married or had previously settled in Florence, more than twice as many immigrants (40%) in the fifteenth century as in the fourteenth (16%) originated from places foreign to the territory of Florence. When these immigrants are divided into those who came from places outside present-day Italy

Table 4.2
Foreigners to Florence

Immigrants from beyond the Present Boundaries of Italy

Fourteenth Century		Fifteenth Century	
Germany	3	Germany	90
France	2	France	7
Balkans	2	Flanders	6
Total	7	Balkans	6
		Ragusa	7
		Spain	3
		Luxemburg	1
		Sweden	1
		Britain	1
		Picardy	1
		Hungary	1
		Corsica	1
		Scotland	1
		Total	126

From other Italian city–states

Within fifteenth *territorio* (those places incorporated after 1340)

Prato	8	Prato	8
Arezzo	3	Pisa	6
Pisa	3	Arezzo	4
S. Gimignano	2	Cortona	3
Volterra	1	Volterra	2
Total	17	S. Gimignano	1
		Total	24

Within Tuscany

Lucca	4	Lucca	3
Siena	3	Siena	3
Total	7	Montepulciano	1
		Massa	1
		Orbetello	1
		Piombino	1
		Total	10

Outside Tuscany

Perugia	2	Genoa	31
Bologna	2	Milan	16
Genoa	2	Bologna	12
Faenza	2	Parma	5
Rome	1	Reggio	4
Trent	1	Lombardy	4

Table 4.2 (*Continued*)

Fourteenth Century		Fifteenth Century	
Mantua	1	Padua	3
Treviso	1	Como	3
Bergamo	1	Cremona	2
Gubbio	1	Modena	2
Piedmont	1	Ferrara	2
Ascoli	1	Verona	2
Grand total	16	Venice	2
		Foligno	2
Total	40	Mantua	2
		Brescia	2
		Puglia	2
		Bari	1
		Ancona	1
		Naples	1
		Pavia	1
		Piedmont	1
		La Spezia	1
		Piacenza	1
		Trent	1
		Perugia	1
		Urbino	1
		Turin	1
		Gubbio	1
		Aquila	1
		Crema	1
		Asti	1
		Friuli	1
		Rome	1
		Imola	1
		Total	114
		Grand total	148

and those arriving from other "Italian" city–states, the differences in the patterns of immigration appear even more sharply.

In the fourteenth-century sample, only seven persons (2%) trickled into Florence from places beyond the Alps: two Germans, two Frenchmen, a Greek, and a woman from Asia Minor *(de Darimaccia)*. In contrast, during the late fifteenth century almost equal numbers of immigrants came from distant foreign countries as originated from other Italian city–states: 19% and 20%. The preponderance of these foreigners (72%) were German, variously identified as from *Allamagna bassa* or *alta*. Occasionally they were identified by German cities such as Cologne *(Colonia)*. When we fix our attention on the migrants from other Italian city–states, the fourteenth and fifteenth centuries do not appear at first to be different. In the fifteenth century, 20% of the foreigners in the sample were other Italians, while in the fourteenth century, 14% arrived from these foreign city–states.

A closer look at these immigrants (Figures 4.1 and 4.2), however, reveals some interesting differences in the composition of these statistics. For the fourteenth century there is no clustering in places of origin of these immigrants. They sprinkle the map of Italy, with some concentration in the central region. During the fifteenth century, on the other hand, larger concentrations of immigrants arrived from the large seafaring and manufacturing cities in the north. More than half of these Italian immigrants (53%) came from three cities alone: Genoa (28%), Milan (14%), and Bologna (11%). In addition to differences in clustering and concentration of the immigrants, there are differences in the distances travelled. In the fourteenth century, more than half of these immigrants (59%) came from places within present-day Tuscany. Seventy-one percent of these places, moreover, were cities that by the middle of the fifteenth century had become incorporated into the district of Florence (Volterra 1361; Arezzo, 1384; S. Gimignano, 1348–1354; Prato, 1351; Pisa, 1408; Cortona, 1411).

If the unit of analysis, the territory of Florence, is limited to that area under Florentine sovereignty at the beginning of 1340, we must add to the fifteenth-century set of incoming foreigners to Florence another 24 individuals. Thus, 44% of the immigrants were foreigners to Florence, and 24% came from other Italian city–states. The development of a regional economy during the fifteenth century and the political incorporation of the Tuscan city–states listed above must have meant easier flow for persons as well as for materials from the outlying area of Florence's Quattrocento *territorio* into the city.[10] Yet, as a proportion of total immigrants, persons from these places beyond the traditional *contado* of Florence, but within the Quattrocento *territorio*, played a less significant role than they had during the previous century. In the fourteenth century, over one-third of all foreign immigrants originated from these city–states that were later incorporated into the territory of Florence; whereas, during the late fifteenth century, these towns comprised the places of origin of only 9% of those foreigners living in the city of Florence at the time of their marriage.

---

10. See Herlihy, *Medieval and Renaissance Pistoia: The Social History of an Italian Town, 1200–1430* (New Haven, 1967), pp. 155–179; and Herlihy and Klapisch, *Les Toscans et leurs familles*, pp. 291–300.

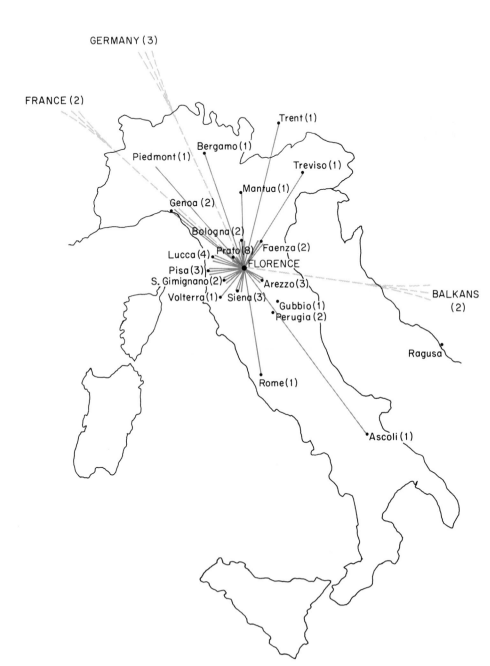

GERMANY (3)

FRANCE (2)

Trent (1)

Bergamo (1)

Piedmont (1)

Treviso (1)

Mantua (1)

Genoa (2)

Bologna (2)

Faenza (2)

Lucca (4)   Prato (8)

Pisa (3)   FLORENCE

S. Gimignano (2)   Arezzo (3)

Volterra (1)   Siena (3)

Gubbio (1)

Perugia (2)

BALKANS
(2)

Ragusa

Rome (1)

Ascoli (1)

Figure 4.1. *Patterns of immigration, 1340–1383.*

100

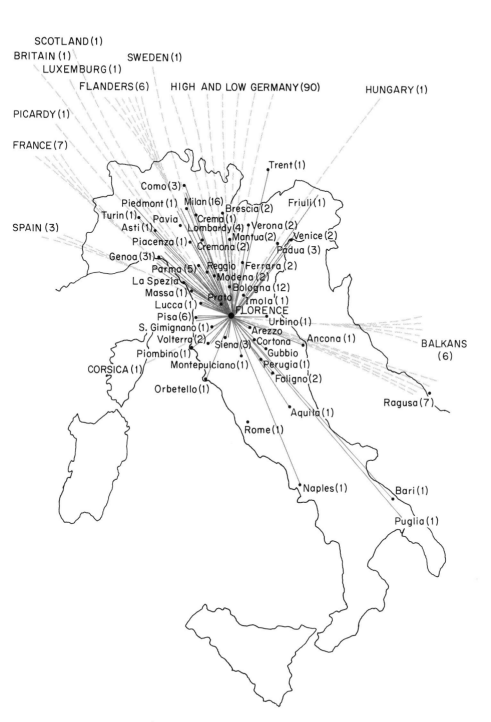

SCOTLAND (1)
BRITAIN (1)
LUXEMBURG (1)
SWEDEN (1)
FLANDERS (6)   HIGH AND LOW GERMANY (90)   HUNGARY (1)
PICARDY (1)
FRANCE (7)

Trent (1)
Como (3)
Piedmont (1) Milan (16) Brescia (2)   Friuli (1)
Turin (1)   Pavia   Crema (1)
Asti (1)   Lombardy (4) Verona (2)
SPAIN (3)
Piacenza (1)   Cremona (2)   Mantua (2)   Venice (2)
Genoa (31)   Padua (3)
Parma (5)   Reggio   Ferrara (2)
La Spezia   Modena (2)
Massa (1)   Bologna (12)
Lucca (1)   Prato   Imola (1)
Pisa (6)   FLORENCE
S. Gimignano (1)   Urbino (1)
Volterra (2)   Arezzo   Ancona (1)
Piombino (1)   Siena (3) Cortona
CORSICA (1)   Montepulciano (1) Gubbio   BALKANS
Perugia (1)   (6)
Orbetello (1)   Foligno (2)
Ragusa (7)
Aquila (1)
Rome (1)

Naples (1)   Bari (1)

Puglia (1)

Figure 4.2. *Patterns of immigration, 1450–1530.*

101

How to explain these differences in the composition of the active population of Florence between the late fourteenth and fifteenth centuries? First, the development and extension of *mezzadria* through various regions of Tuscany during the fifteenth century created an agrarian work force in which men were less likely to leave the land and immigrate to the city. Thus, for renewed growth, Florence had to attract a greater proportion of its immigrants (especially members of the male work force) from other urban centers beyond the traditional *contado*. Second, during the late fifteenth and early sixteenth centuries the growing number of Florentine slaves and domestic servants [11] came predominantly from places beyond the boundaries of the Italian-speaking population. Some were captured and traded from the Balkans and Eastern Europe: Ragusa (on the coast of present-day Yugoslavia), Albania, and Schiavonia. Of the seven individuals from Ragusa in our fifteenth-century sample, for instance, all were women and most were former slaves or domestic servants.[12] But the greater proportion of the new immigrants of the late fifteenth century did not originate from the east; instead, they came from the northwest, from France, Flanders, and primarily Germany. Their attraction to Florence in the fifteenth century may have resulted from social, political, and economic changes in Northern Europe that must remain beyond the scope of this analysis.

Perhaps there was a further dimension to the *Ballungen* (the concentrated exodus of villagers into larger villages and towns) and the deserted small towns and villages throughout Germany following the Black Death and recurrent plagues of the fifteenth century.[13] Besides immigrating to the larger towns and the emerging financial and manufacturing centers of Nuremburg, Augsburg, Cologne, etc., many of these rural migrants journeyed further south to the northern Italian cities in search of work. But, from our statistics, we find a considerable number migrating from the larger urban locations, such as Cologne. There appears to have been a series of waves in the migration and redistribution of population during the fifteenth century.

The influx of Germans and other northern Europeans, however, must be explained in part by changes in the Florentine economy. From its inception, the silk industry in fourteenth-century Florence had to rely

---

11. Herlihy and Klapisch, *Les Toscans et leurs familles,* p. 520; and A. Zanelli, *Le shiave orientali a Firenze nei secoli 14° e 15°* (Florence, 1885).

12. NAC F 498 (1441–146), 392r; G 238 (1517–1529), 17v; L 341 (1466–1475), no pagination, January 16, 1474; L. 139 (1477–1482), 129r; N 19 (1461–1469), 230r; N 61 (1497–1520), 82r; O 7 (1514–1518), 140r.

13. W. Abel, *Agrarkrisen und Agrarkonjunktur in Mitteleuropa vom 13. bis zum 19. Jahrhundert* (Berlin, 1935).

on foreign labor; these workers migrated from Lucca.[14] During the fifteenth century, when the industry grew rapidly (approaching the wool industry in importance by the end of the century), members of Por S. Maria were forced to search further afield for skilled labor. During the 1430s and 1440s the Commune issued several provisions designed to attract German silk weavers.[15] Of those of German and Flemish descent in our fifteenth-century sample who were identified by a profession, 69% were silk workers—32 of them weavers, and two spinners. Next in importance were wool weavers (18%); then there were four cobblers, a *cappellaio* or hatter, and a carpenter.

The preponderance of silk weavers among these distant migrants may help, moreover, to explain the shift in the sex ratios of those migrants marrying into the ranks of the Florentine *popolo minuto*. Silk production relied more than the wool industry on lighter tasks, such as weaving and spinning, which could be performed by women and children in the home. The more strenuous steps of production usually performed under managerial scrutiny in wool production—the tasks of those workers who in large part filled the ranks of the Trecento Ciompi, the *pettinatori, cardaiuoli, cardatori, scardassieri, purgatori,* and *battilana*—were not necessary to silk production, nor were there comparable tasks.[16] Perhaps as a result, Professor Jordan Goodman has found that, according to a survey of 1663, 84% of the silk workers in Florence were women.[17] But the seventeenth-century Florentine silk industry had a different character from its Renaissance ancestor. Instead of manufacturing the fine and expensive embroideries which Renaissance Florentine artists and artisans had designed for aristocratic consumption in northern Europe, by the seventeenth century Florence had lost these markets and were producing the lowest quality silk cloth for the less prestigious European markets.

From our statistics it appears, however, that the majority (71%) of those silk weavers attracted from northern Europe and marrying in Florence were men.[18] The dramatic changes in the sex ratios of Florentine

---

14. Robert Davidsohn, *Storia di Firenze,* Vol. 6, transl. G. B. Klein (Florence, 1973), pp. 155–158.

15. Curt Gutkind, *Cosimo de'Medici il Vecchio* (Florence, 1940), p. 8.

16. In the seventeenth century (when a census of the work force in the silk industry first appears), winding and weaving comprised 85% of the labor force; see Jordan Goodman, "The Florentine Silk Industry in the 17th Century," Unpublished dissertation, University of London, 1977, p. 32.

17. *Ibid.,* Jordan Goodman, p. 71

18. Indeed, Carlo Cipolla, *Before the Industrial Revolution* (London, 1976), pp. 71 and 124, finds that 83% of the weavers in the wool industry in 1627 were women. There are no figures for the sex ratio of the industry as a whole.

immigrants from the late fourteenth century to the late fifteenth century
at this point in research, must rest primarily on changes outside of Florence
and its urban economy. The supply of males (of marital age) to the
Florentine work force was greatly curtailed by changes which were occurring throughout the Tuscan countryside: the development of the
mezzadria and its strong patrilineal family group customs.

We must now inquire: Just what is the significance of the changes
in migratory patterns to the particular problems at hand—the changes
in patterns of intra-city endogamies and the possible political and social
implications of these changes? Our statistics suggest that the conclusions which Niccolò Rodolico derived over 70 years ago without
statistical analysis must be modified.[19] Behind the politicization of the
Florentine work force which culminated in the Revolt of the Ciompi,
Rodolico saw the force of the Black Death and its demographic consequences. To recoup its losses, Florence, more than ever before in its
history, was forced to rely on the influx of *contadini* from neighboring
parishes. The minor guilds temporarily lifted their monetary and family
prerequisites for matriculation.[20] Remarkable social as well as geographical mobility were the consequences. And Rodolico interprets the
new energy streaming from the countryside as the force and muscle
behind the Ciompi; at the same time, the urban environment and work
force politicized immigrants from the countryside.

> My research ends with the years of the Government of the *Arti Minori*.
> In recapitulation, I will say briefly that there are two facts especially
> worthy of mentioning: the immigration of laborers into the city and the
> rather sensitive oscillations in population changes; they produced new needs
> and new energies, which produced activities fecund in wealth and in
> liberty. From one side, immigration transformed that characteristic atavism
> of the rural populations into a disorderly spirit of agitation. After com-
> ing in contact with the urban population they lent their exalted zeal and
> muscle in the insurrections. . . .[21]

To be sure, importance must be placed on the demographic conditions
of the middle and late Trecento and their relation to the social and
political development of the *popolo minuto*. But the simple correlation
between demographic conditions and political activity and popular consciousness which Rodolico then foists onto social history in the period
of the Medicean Principality must be questioned.[22] Certainly, for the

---

19. Rodolico, *La Democrazia fiorentina*, pp. 7–45.
20. *Ibid.*, Rodolico, p. 36.
21. *Ibid.*, Rodolico, p. 44; see also p. 36.
22. *Ibid.*, Rodolico, p. 45; *"Si confrontino le oscillazioni continue della popolazione fiorentina
del XIV secolo e lo spirito agitato che animava allora lo svolgimento della democrazia con la*

intervening period of the Medicean Republic, the relationship between these demographic facts and the politicization of the masses is not so simple. By the middle of the fifteenth century, by 1470 at the latest, there was, as indicated by the numbers baptized at the font of S. Giovanni, a significant resurgence of the Florentine population which continued steadily through the early years of the sixteenth century.[23] Our statistics on the magnitude of immigration through marriage, moreover, show little difference between the period of the Ciompi and the fifteenth century—a period for which the chroniclers leave us no evidence of popular insurrection. The immigration of the *popolo minuto* through marriage declined only slightly between the late fourteenth and the late fifteenth centuries, from 14% to 11% of all marriages.[24]

When the character of Florentine immigration, however, is considered more closely, we find important differences (beyond the simple fact of sheer magnitude) which may have had significant consequences on the political and social development of the *popolo minuto* during the late Quattrocento. These may contribute to an understanding of the changes in the patterns of popular communities outlined by our marriage statistics. First, the raw statistics on migration might alter the conclusions drawn in Chapter 3. It might be argued that the slightly greater immigration of *popolo minuto* to the city of Florence during the late Trecento would exaggerate the sense of city-wide identification of these groups as compared to the Quattrocento *popolo minuto*. If the last column of analysis (g) is lopped off and only those individuals residing within the city walls of Florence are considered, the parish endogamies between the fourteenth- and fifteenth-century *popolo minuto* move slightly closer together. Instead of 31%, 36% married within the parish during the late fourteenth century, and 53% instead of 47% found a fellow parishioner to marry in the late fifteenth century. This calculation would mark an increase in parish endogamy of 45%, instead of 49%, between the two centuries. The differences in community structure between the Trecento and Quattrocento would nonetheless, remain highly significant.

One might argue, on the other hand, that an increase in immigra-

---

popolazione stazionaria dei tempi decadente principato medico, quando alla torpida quiete politica non meno torpidamente pare corrisponda la vita fisiologica."

23. Marco Lastri, *Ricerche sull'antica e moderna popolazione della città di Firenze* (Florence, 1775).

24. Although migration through marriage is not the most precise measure of total immigration, it gives an estimate of the migratory patterns of the active population (in the sense of biological as well as material production); see *Annales de démographie historique*, Vol. 7 (1970), which is devoted to problems of migration and mobility.

tion might have had the opposite effect. That is, an increase in mobility would have effectively increased the size of the pool of eligible spouses and would thus have exaggerated actual intermarriage among the more stable residents. If it can be assumed that certain notarial practices did not change substantially between the late Trecento and Quattrocento, then we might be able to control for the effect of mobility on intra-parish marriages. As mentioned earlier, often the notary specified more than one place of origin or residence for an individual. Presumably, if a spouse had recently moved into a parish, he or she was characterized as *ad presens de popolo de* . . . and his or her former place of residence was registered. Usually this secondary place name or parish was a rural village or a foreign city or country; occasionally, it was another parish within the city walls of Florence.

If we then search through all those marriages among spouses of the same parish, we find a greater number in the fourteenth than in the fifteenth century of intra-parish marriages contracted between a permanent resident and a newcomer to the parish or between two newcomers. These relationships do not suggest the same parochialism in social networks as would the marriage between two native, long-standing residents of the same parish community. If we then exclude from the parish endogamies these relations involving newcomers, the parish endogamy of the fourteenth century diminishes from 31% to 25% (a decline of 19%), while that of the fifteenth century falls by only 4%, from 47% to 45%. Thus, when we control (as best our sources will permit) for the effect of mobility on the rate of parochial endogamy, we find that the differences between the fourteenth century and fifteenth century become slighly accentuated. Instead of an increase of 51% in marital parochialism, the difference between the two centuries climbs to 79%.

Second, the qualitative changes in Florentine immigration may have had a more profound effect on urban neighborhood endogamies than the slight shift in the magnitude of immigration between the two centuries. As we have seen, Florence in the fifteenth century relied much less on its surrounding countryside for its demographic buoyancy than it had done previously, during the Trecento. In the Quattrocento, within the *contado* of Florence, relatively fewer immigrants from the surrounding hamlets, parishes, and villages—places such as Calenzano, Signa, Campi, and Fiesole—came to Florence than from the larger towns on the periphery (Radda, Scarperia, Borgo S. Lorenzo, etc.). Indeed, it seems, in comparison to the fourteenth century, the closer the place to city walls of Florence, the less likelihood there was of interpenetration, migration, or the establishment of a household within the city of Florence.

A single statistic from the late fifteenth century is telling enough. The notary Ser Antonio Naldi, during the part of his career that now survives, 1461–1497, redacted over 600 marriages almost exclusively between peasants and small artisans and laborers.[25] Ser Antonio spent his normal work day within the villages and hamlets which extended westward from the Porta di San Frediano up the Arno through Legnaia to Brozzi, Campi, Signa, and often as far as Calenzano. Occasionally, his business penetrated the working class and artisan parishes of Santo Spirito. With the copious contracts of Ser Antonio and several other notaries (such as Ser Paolo di Lorenzo) [26] who worked in the same area from the beginning of our period, 1450 to 1473, we can analyze with some detail the peculiar parish of S. Maria in Verzaia.

As mentioned in the first chapter, the so-called third ring of city walls built during the second half of the thirteenth century cut this parish in two. Thus, unlike the other large parishes on the periphery of thirteenth-century Florence (S. Lorenzo, S. Niccolò, S. Lucia Ognissanti, S. Felice in Piazza, S. Michele Visdomini, S. Ambrogia, S. Piero Maggiore), which left only small portions of their territories in the *contado,* the rural part of S. Maria in Verzaia remained extensive.

By the middle of the fifteenth century, the social significance of the city walls is well illustrated by the rates of intermarriage within the total parish of S. Maria in Verzaia, and between its urban and rural halves, S. Maria in Verzaia *dentro le mura* and S. Maria in Verzaia *fuori le mura.* As we have seen, intermarriage within the urban half of S. Maria in Verzaia was one of the highest ratios of parish endogamy within the city. Of the total population, 46% married within the urban limits of this parish. For the rural half of S. Maria in Verzaia, we have even a larger number of statistics (88 individuals). The intermarriage rate within the rural suburb was significantly lower than that of their urban neighbors; only 28 (or 32%) married within S. Maria in Verzaia *fuori le mura.* Most found spouses in the neighboring villages spreading down the Arno Valley to the hamlets of Signa, Brozzi, and Campi. The most striking statistic, however, concerns intermarriage between the two halves of S. Maria. Despite the high urban intermarriage within the parish and a total endogamy of 39%, only four individuals, or 2%, found a spouse within the parish and across the city walls.

These statistics on migration, the changes from the late fourteenth century (when over 75% of the influx of immigrants originated from the *contado* of Florence) to the late fifteenth century, when the division

---

25. NAC N 19 (1461–1497), four protocols.
26. NAC P 128.

between city and contado became ossified into two very separate social realms, bear a curious relationship to the poetry and ideology of the Florentine patriciate. It is in the fourteenth century, when there was in fact a greater integration within the city of the rural populace, that we hear the most vituperous denunciations against the *contadini* of Florence, especially those who had immigrated to the city.

In a letter to Pino dei Rossi, Giovanni Boccaccio expresses his contempt of those recently arrived: "Those who have come from Capalle and those from Cilicciavole, or from Viminiccio, taking off from the trowel or the plough and integrated into our highest offices." [27] Filippo Villani describes them with equal distaste as "those recently arrived men from the *contado* and district of Florence." [28] In the later Renaissance, however, even in the lessons provided by Giovanni della Casa [29] to *contadini* on manners and courtesies, the mockery is more gentle; the threat from the peasant upstart is less evident; they are instead patronized and their simplicity even extolled in the pastoral lyricism of the late Quattrocento.[30]

By the fifteenth century, our statistics clearly show that migration from the countryside was no longer as great a threat to the existing structure of government and old family dominion, nor to the culture of patrician Florence. There was no longer quite the same possibility of upward mobility—the challenge in commerce as well as the challenge in constitutional politics. Nor was there the threat of integration and consolidation of these groups with the resident Florentine *popolo minuto* to provide the "muscle" for class insurrection, as Rodolico has claimed.

The words of advice of Giannozzo Alberti to his son Lionardo reflect a patrician consciousness of the peasantry which is different from the bitter but intimidated remarks of Boccaccio or Dante:

> My dear Lionardo. . . It is better to bear the weight of such villainous ingenuities. . . to teach the peasants to exercise some degree of diligence. Besides, if you don't have too great a number of peasants to deal with, their malice will not be insufferable, and if you are careful they will not

---

27. "*Venuti chi da Capalle e quale da Cilicciavole, o da Viminiccio, tolti dalla cazzuola o dall'aratro e sublimati al nostro magistrato maggiore.*" (Quoted from G. Boccaccio, *Lettere volgari* (Florence, 1834), 12 in Rodolico, *La democrazia fiorentina*, 36.)

28. *Uomini novellamente venuti dal contado e dal distretto di Firenze.*" (Quoted from F. Villani, *Cronica di Firenze* (Florence, 1826), Lib. X, Cap. 65 in Rodolico, *La democrazia fiorentina*, 36.)

29. G. della Casa, *Il Galateo* (Venice, 1558).

30. Molho, "Cosimo de'Medici: Pater Patriae or Padrino?" *Stanford Review* (19/9), pp. 12–13.

be able to cheat you much. You will even take much secret delight in their little tricks and laugh heartily at them.[31]

And after extolling farming as the most noble profession, Giannozzo continues:

> Consider, too, that you can retire to your farm and live there at peace, nurturing your little family, dealing by yourself with your own affairs, and on a holiday talking pleasantly in the shade about oxen and wool or about vines and seeds. You can live undisturbed by rumors and tales and by the wild strife that breaks out periodically in the city. You can be free of the suspicions, fears, slanders, injuries, feuds and other miseries which are too ugly to talk about and horrible even to remember. Among all the subjects discussed on the farm there is none which can fail to delight you. All are pleasant to talk of and are heard by willing ears. Everyone tells what he knows that is useful to agriculture. Everyone teaches and corrects you where you erred in some of your planting or in your manner of sowing. The cultivation and management of fields does not give rise to envy, hate and malevolence. . . Yes, by God a true paradise. And, what is more, you can in the enjoyment of your estate escape the violence, the riots, the storm of the city, the marketplace, and the town hall. On the farm you can hide yourself and avoid seeing all the stealing and crime, the vast numbers of depraved men who are always flitting past your eyes in the city. There they never cease to chirp in your ears, to scream and bellow in the streets hour after hour, like a dangerous and disgusting kind of beast.[32]

The tale of separation between city and *contado* which our marriage records narrate no doubt resulted largely from the economic and ecological changes of the late Trecento and early Quattrocento—the tremendous concentration of wealth in Florence at the expense of the *contado*.[33] These differences between *cittadini* and *contadini* were in part consciously orchestrated by the urban patriciate. From the 1420s onward the Commune imposed much more stringent requirements for citizenship.[34] And, in part, the separation of town and country (at least from the perspective of our marriage statistics) was the consequence of more subtle and less direct measures of the Florentine elites. The

---

31. Leon Battista Alberti, *The Family in Renaissance Florence (I Libri della famiglia)*, transl. Renée Neu Watkins (Columbia, S.C., 1969), p. 190.

32. *Ibid.*, Renée Neu Watkins, pp. 192–193.

33. See note 5, this chapter.

34. Julius Kirshner, "Paolo di Castro on *Cives Ex Privilegio*: A Controversy Over the Legal Qualification for Public Office," in *Renaissance Studies in Honor of Hans Baron*, edited by A. Molho and J. Tedeschi (Florence, 1971), p. 263.

financial advantages provided by the *Monte delle doti* (which received
investments predominantly from citizens of Florence) made the possibilities for upward mobility from the rural bourgeoisie to urban promi-
nence more remote.[35] Indeed, by the second half of the fifteenth
century, the patriciate of Florence was in a better position than it had
been in the Trecento "to laugh heartily" at "the little tricks" of the
peasantry. For, at least within the city walls, the urban elite was not
confronted with "too great a number to deal with." The chemistry of
rural muscle and urban working class and artisan consciousness, which,
according to Rodolico,[36] precipitated the Revolt of the Ciompi, was no
longer a possibility by the fifteenth century. This change in patrician
consciousness, however, should not suggest that the Florentine elite
was any less contemptuous of the peasantry in the time of Alberti than
they had been during the period of Dante or Boccaccio. If anything,
at the same time that the distinction *cittadino–popolo minuto* become
more rigid, our statistics imply that the sense of race—*cittadino* versus
contadino—was fortified.

Second, we find that those long-distance migrants who settled in
Florence during the late Quattrocento behaved differently from the
novi homines of the late Trecento. We find far fewer of these foreigners moving upward and successfully becoming integrated into the native
population, especially into its citizenry and government. To illustrate
the isolation of these new groups we will concentrate on the largest
portion of these foreigners, the Germans.

As we have seen, these immigrants were predominantly *sottoposti* in
the silk and wool industries. The notaries identified very few of them
as citizens of Florence, and they do not appear in the lists of those
eligible for office (the *tratte*) during the fifteenth and early sixteenth
centuries.[37] We find that 42 Germans, or 45%, married spouses who in
the records appear to have been natives to Florence.[38] At first sight, the
national endogamy may not seem so extraordinary. When the Germans,
however, are compared to other foreign immigrants in Florence, their
intermarriage seems striking indeed.

35. Kirshner and Molho, "The Dowry Fund," p. 436, "By transforming the communal
government into the guarantor of the matrimonial alliances engineered by members of the
Florentine ruling class, the dowry fund reflected, and at the same time sustained, the political
hegemony of that class."

36. Rodolico, *La democrazia fiorentina*, p. 44.

37. I would like to thank Stephen Epstein for this information; he is currently rendering
into machine readable language the lists for eligibility for office in the Commune of Florence
(the *Tratte* nos. 39, 40, and 1193).

38. For this analysis we have combined the High and Low Germans, and those from
Flanders.

Table 4.3
Residential Patterns of Germans

S. Frediano	18
S. Maria in Verzaia	13
S. Lorenzo	15
S. Iacopo in Campo Corbolini	7
S. Maria Maggiore	4
S. Michele Visdomini	2
S. Donato de'Vecchietti	1
S. Tommaso	1
S. Maria Novella	1
S. Niccolò	1
S. Felice in Piazza	1
S. Iacopo sopr'Arno	1

Of the other fifteenth-century foreigners (that is, those from beyond the present borders of Italy), we do not find a single one marrying a compatriot, and only seven (or 39%) of them married other foreigners; whereas 53% of the Germans married spouses who originated beyond the Alps. These statistics contrast even more sharply with those from the late fourteenth century. Of the seven foreigners to Italy, there were no marriages among themselves, and only one married a spouse who presumably was not a native Florentine. Moreover, the bulk of Trecento immigrants to Florence (who were mostly from the surrounding countryside and the neighboring city–states of central Italy) give the impression of a fluid integration with the native Florentine population quite different from the racial exclusion which the German weavers of the late fifteenth century must have experienced. Of all those identified by a parish or place name beyond the city walls of Florence, 248 persons, or 84%, of these fourteenth century immigrants married native Florentines.

When we consider the residential patterns of all those Germans identified by a parish, their racial exclusion and ghetto confinement become more graphic. Of these Germans, 82% are found concentrated in two working-class–artisan neighborhoods of late Quattrocento Florence. (see Table 4.3) First in importance was the community which stretched out around the piazza of S. Maria in Carmine (commonly called Camaldoli) and included portions of the adjacent parishes of S. Maria in Verzaia and S. Frediano. Second, there was the community of S. Lorenzo in the opposite, northwestern corner of the city, including the small parish of S. Iacopo in Campo Corbolini which was engulfed by the much larger parish of S. Lorenzo.

The social networks reflected by the marriages contracted among

Table 4.4
Patterns of Endogamy among Germans, 1450–1530

Parish	Endogamies				Exogamies			Total
	Parish (a)	Gonfalone (b)	Quarter (c)	Cluster (d)	Cross-quarter (e)	Cross-cluster (f)	Contado (g)	
S. Frediano	14	3	–	3	1	1	1	19
S. Felice in Piazza	–	–	1	1	1	1	–	2
S. Maria in Verzaia	14	3	1	4	2	2	–	20
S. Iacopo sopr'Arno	2	–	–	–	–	–	–	2
S. Niccolò	2	–	–	–	–	–	–	2
S. Lucia Ognissanti	–	–	–	–	1	1	–	1
S. Maria Novella	2	–	–	–	–	–	–	2
S. Lorenzo	6	2	1	2	3	4	–	12
S. Iacopo in Campo Corbolini	4	2	–	2	1	1	–	7
S. Michele Visdomini	2	–	1	–	–	1	–	3
S. Maria Maggiore	4	–	–	–	–	–	–	4
S. Leo	2	–	–	–	–	–	–	2
S. Donato de'Vecchietti	2	–	–	–	–	–	–	2
Total	52	10	4	12	10	12	1	77

those of German descent again reflect their isolation. More than any subgroup we have examined, these Germans married within the constricted geographies of the parish. There even seems to have been little mixing between the two German communities on opposite sides of the Arno; 68% married within their own parish, and 81% married within the confines of the *gonfalone* (see Table 4.4).

In conclusion, the qualitative shift in migration during the late fifteenth century away from a supply of native Tuscan-speaking *contadini* to the influx of foreigners into the Commune and territory of Florence, both from Italian city–states and countries beyond the Alps, beyond the linguistic confines of Romance tongues, brought certain social problems, heretofore uninvestigated by Florentine historians, to the Florentine landscape. We have seen in the case of the Germans, the largest single migratory group revealed in our statistics, that these immigrants were less able than the largely Tuscan immigrants of the previous century to integrate themselves successfully into the social world of the native Florentine *popolo minuto*. More than any other group which we have examined, their communities were strongly focused around constricted neighborhood centers scarcely reaching beyond the parish. In the isolation and fragmentation of the more torpid *popolo minuto* of the late fifteenth century, we find a national–racial dimension laced within the geographical divisions of the population of artisans and laborers as a whole. What were the social and political consequences of these new divisions within the laboring classes introduced during the course of the fifteenth century. How would these patterns of immigration and urban settlement affect the possibilities of the *popolo minuto* organizing itself and conceiving of itself as a class during the latter part of the fifteenth century?

Chapter 5

The Ecology
of the Renaissance City

*B*EFORE drawing conclusions from our marriage data on the sociology and political consciousness of the *popolo minuto* from the
period of the Ciompi through the rule of Cosimo de'Medici, let
us investigate more thoroughly the structure of the residential patterns
and ecology of urban Florence between these two centuries. So far in
our comparisons, we have assumed that the social and demographic
character of the parish neighborhoods remained roughly the same over
the period of our analysis. As noted in the first chapter, the basic units
of analysis—the parishes—varied widely in geographic territory and
in population size. They ranged in size from the parish of S. Lorenzo—
whose territory included almost the entire *gonfalone* of Leon d'Oro,
the largest *gonfalone* of the city, which contained one-seventh of the
city's population during the late fifteenth century—to the very small
parishes within the Roman walls, some of which possessed communities
covering only a street block or two with populations of less than 100
souls.

At this point, there are two problems. First, there is the problem of
evidence. The distribution of the Florentine population found in our
fourteenth-century sample must be compared with an independent
source. If, for example, a disproportionate number of marriages in our
sample were among residents of the tiny parishes of the central city,
then the parish endogamies reflected in our study of fourteenth-century
society would be overstated. Second, after controlling for sampling
bias, we should attempt to investigate whether there were significant
changes in the urban-ecological development of Renaissance Florence
from the Black Death to roughly the time of the death of Lorenzo. If
the structure of urban neighborhoods did change over time, how might
this have influenced the rates of endogamy found in our analysis?

First, an independent source must be found to uncover possible biases in our sample. Unfortunately, the baptismal records which we consulted for the fifteenth-century materials do not extend backwards into the Trecento. Nonetheless for the years 1351–1352 and 1355, the tax officials of Florence redacted an *estimo* or survey, which for our purposes—the estimation of various parish populations—is even more exacting than the otherwise more detailed tax surveys (the *catasti*) of the fifteenth century. The fiscal historian, Bernardino Barbadoro, has accumulated the data found in these two *estimi*, retaining the geographic organization found in the original documents.[1] These geographic zones were defined first, as the quarters of the city; then as the sixteen *gonfaloni*; beyond the *gonfalone* (unlike the later *catasti* of the fifteenth century), there were further analyses. These subdivisions, however, are by no means consistent from area to area. In the quarter of Santo Spirito, for instance, the *gonfalone* of Scala is divided into the various parishes found in that *gonfalone*. Ferza, S. Spirito, on the other hand, is separated into the parish of S. Pier Gattolino and then into the remaining streets of the *gonfalone*. From information contained in the tax-surveys and the baptismal records, it is clear that these streets comprised roughly the jurisdiction of the parish of S. Felice in Piazza, which is the only other parish church in Ferza, and is not mentioned elsewhere. For other sectors of the city, however, the detail is not as meticulous. For the quarter of S. Maria Novella, the tax officials mentioned only the parish of S. Lucia Ognissanti. Otherwise, the quarter is simply subdivided into its four *gonfaloni*.

Although the city cannot be divided according to ecological clusters as neatly as we have done from the baptismal records of the late Quattrocento, we have nonetheless been able to divide the city into three ecological zones which roughly fit the three rings of the city's development and which separate the large parishes of the periphery from the middle-size ones of the inner city, and these from the tiny parishes clustered within and around the Roman city walls.[2] As we have mentioned before, the parish jurisdictions did not always correspond to secular or to ecological divisions. The jurisdiction of the very large

---

1. Bernardino Barbadoro, "Finanza e demografia nei ruoli fiorentini d'imposta del 1352–1355," in *Atti del congresso internazionale per gli studi sulla popolazione,* Vol. II (Rome, 1933), pp. 615–645.

2. The streets which divide the perihery from the inner ring on the *Pianta della città di Firenze* (Florence, 1731) are as follows: from the Arno in the Quarter of S. Croce—Via del Fosso, Via de Benci, Via del Diluvio, Via del Fosso, Via dello Sprone, Via S. Egidio, Via de Cresci, Via de Pucci, Via de Calderai, Via delle Contonelle, Via del Melarancio, Piazza Vecchia, Piazza di S. Maria Novella, Via della Scala, Via delle Porcellane, Via Nuova; across the Arno, they are: Via de Guicciardini, Piazza de Pitti, Via Romana, Via S. Giovani, Via degli Serragli and Piazza Soderini.

parish of S. Lorenzo, for instance, extended from the Roman city walls and ran through the second ring of walls, where the church itself was located, then encompassed a vast area of the city's periphery within the last ring of walls and finally cut into the farm lands of the *contado*. For those parishes in which the actual church buildings lay within the inner ring but their jurisdictions extended well into the periphery, we have set the following rule: If such a parish extended across the third ring of city walls into the *contado*, it is considered part of the periphery and not within the inner ring. Certain exceptions will be made. The parishes of S. Felice in Piazza, S. Michele Visdomini, and S. Maria Novella all had negligible portions of territory within the *contado*, and we will consider them as a part of the inner ring. In the case of S. Maria Novella, the data contained in the *Estimo* of 1351–1352 and 1355 does not make it possible to separate this parish from its *gonfalone*, Leon Bianco. The boundaries of this *gonfalone* stretch curiously across all three ecological zones well into the northwest corner of the Roman walls, comprising the small parishes of S. Donato dei Vecchietti, S. Pier Buonconsiglio, and a portion of S. Michele Berteldi. S. Michele Visdomini similarly belonged to a *gonfalone* which for the most part contained territory and churches which were located within the Roman walls. Finally, we find references to S. Felice in Piazza *fuori le mura* only in the *catasti* of the fifteenth century. Given its position inside the arc of the parishes of S. Niccolò, S. Pier Gattolino, S. Maria in Verzaia, and S. Frediano, it is difficult to see how a continuous strip of land would have run from this church into the *contado*, except possibly through the property of the Pitti Palace.

Further problems arise in fitting the marriage materials divided by parish into the grid fixed by the possibilities of the Estimo del Sega. The small parishes of S. Procolo and S. Michele Berteldi both lie in more than a single *gonfalone*. In both cases, moreover, these *gonfaloni* possess territories on the borders of separate ecological rings. Thus, for purposes of our analysis, the entire parish (in both cases) will be considered within the Roman walls, a part of the central city. (see Figure 5.1)

If we then take the data on the distribution of the city's population from 1355, the date closest to the mid-point (1362) of our fourteenth century sample, we find in fact some discrepancies between the population distribution in our sample and the tax survey. (see Tables 5.1 and 5.2) We find that we have overselected marriages from those areas of large parishes on the periphery characterized by high rates of endogamy, and underselected areas within the inner ring and the central city. In our marriage sample, 51% of the individuals belonged to parishes on the periphery, as compared to 43% of the household heads

Table 5.1
Possible Units of Analysis: Estimo del Sega

Quartiere	1351–1352			
	Outer ring	Inter ring	Inter city	Total
S. Spirito	1775	950	—	2725
S. Croce	—	776	1071	1847
S. Maria Novella	447	1370	252	2069
S. Giovanni	2086	206	1022	3314
Total	4308	3302	2345	9955
Percentages	43.27	33.17	23.56	
	1355			
S. Spirito	1777	947	—	2724
S. Croce	—	765	1086	1851
S. Maria Novella	396	1393	239	2028
S. Giovanni	2070	206	1025	3301
Total	4243	3311	2350	9904
Percentages	42.84	33.43	23.73	

from the Estimo of 1355; while 31% in our sample came from those parishes of the inner ring (as opposed to 33% from the Estimo); and finally, 19% in our sample were residents of the central city (as compared with 24% from the tax survey).

If we can then assume that these biases in the geographical selections for the fourteenth century represented roughly all social groups equally, then we can derive more precise figures of parish endogamy for the

Table 5.2
Possible Units of Analysis: The Marriage Sample of 1343–1383

Quartiere	Outer ring	Inner ring	Inter city
S. Spirito	229	49	–
S. Croce	–	115	117
S. Maria Novella	110	233	12
S. Giovanni	342	19	122
	68	416	251
	.5052	.3086	.1862
Differences from Estimo 1355 [a]			
Estimo	42.84	33.43	23.73
Difference	+7.68	−2.57	−5.11
	+17.78%	−7.69%	−21.53%

[a] Overstatement (+), understatement (−).

popolo minuto by weighing the significance of each ecological ring by the percentages of over- or understatement in comparison to the Estimo of 1355. Thus, in comparison with the other rings, the number of individuals in the periphery should be reduced by 17.78%, while those of the inner city and central city should be increased by 7.69% and 21.53% respectively. When the data are weighted in this manner, we find that the parish endogamies for the entire city and the *popolo minuto* become slightly less than our raw results show. From the periphery to the parishes within the city walls there were in fact differences in the rates of parish endogamy. In the fourteenth century, 34% of the *popolo minuto* in those large parishes of the periphery married within their parishes; 34% contracted inner-parish marriages in the medium size parishes of the central city; while only 18% married spouses from the same parish within the old Roman city. (see Table 5.3) When the various ecological zones have been weighted accordingly, the total parish endogamy of the *popolo minuto* falls slightly, from 30.92% to 30.30% and from 25.12% to 24.64% when the scores adjusted for the effect of mobility are considered. Because of the very close correspondence of the distribution of population found in our fifteenth-century marriage sample and the estimates taken from the baptismal register, we can compare the adjusted endogamies for the late fourteenth century with the observed ones for the fifteenth century. It then appears that the differences between the late fourteenth and late fifteenth century parish endogamies are even more accentuated.

More importantly, we must now consider the relationship between changes in the residential structures of Florence during the two centuries and the endogamies of the *popolo minuto*. There were, in fact, critical changes in the concentrations of the *popolo minuto*. In the latter half of the Trecento, the residential patterns of those giving 50 florins or less were only barely distinguishable from those of the population as a whole. If we consider the Estimo of 1355 as our point of comparison, 43% of the total population lived in the large parishes of the outer rings of Florence, while 44% of the *popolo minuto* lived in these same parishes; 33% of the integral population as opposed to 39% of the *popolo minuto* lived in the inner ring; and 24% of the Florentine poulation lived in those parishes roughly within the street patterns of the Roman city, while 16% of the *popolo minuto* occupied the same neighborhoods. (see Table 5.4)

If the residential patterns of the Trecento *popolo minuto* are compared instead with the distribution of the total population found in our marriage records, we find, in fact, a smaller proportion of the artisan and laboring classes (44%) than that of the total population (51%) re-

Table 5.3
Parish Endogamies of the Popolo Minuto *by Ecological Ring, 1340–1383*

Parish	Parish Endogamy	Total	Parish	Parish Endogamy	Total
The peripheral ring					
S. Frediano	8	25	S. Lucia Ognissanti	16	35
S. Maria in Verzaia	—	4	S. Lorenzo	32	68
S. Pier Gattolino	2	17	S. Ambrogio	—	5
S. Niccolò	—	4	S. Pier Maggiore	4	20
S. Maria Novella	—	6			
			Total	62	184
				33.07%	
The inner ring					
S. Iacopo sopr'Arno	—	1	S. Pancrazio	16	38
S. Felicità	—	4	S. Michele Visdomini	—	1
S. Felice in Piazza	18	40	S. Simone	2	10
S. Spirito	—	1	S. Remigio	—	4
S. Giorgio	—	4	S. Iacopo tra le Fosse	2	9
S. Lucia de'Bardi	—	1	S. Trinità	4	14
S. Paolo	12	36			
			Total	54	163
				33.13%	
The central city					
S. Lucia de'Bardi	—	1	S. Cecilia	—	1
S. Maria Maggiore	2	8	S. Firenze	—	1
S. Michele Berteldi	2	8	S. Apollinaire	—	3
S. Leo	2	3	S. Stefano alla Badia	—	2
S. Donato de'Vecchietti	—	1	S. Procolo	—	2
S. Tommaso	—	3	S. Maria Nipotecosa	—	1
S. Pier Buonconsiglio	—	1	S. Maria degli Alberighi	2	2
S. Maria in Campidoglio	—	1	S. Maria degli Ughi	—	1
S. Miniato fra le Torri	—	1	S. Salvadore	—	1
Orsanmichele	—	1	S. Maria in Campo	—	1
S. Maria sopra Porta	2	4	S. Benedetto	—	1
S. Stefano	—	4	S. Pier Celoro	—	2
S. Piero Scheraggio	2	14			
			Total	12	67
				17.91%	

siding in those parishes of the city's periphery. In the parishes of the inner ring, the proportionate population of the *popolo minuto* bulges relative to the total population (39% compared to 31%), while in the central city, the proportion of the entire population exceeded that of the *popolo minuto* by a negligible difference (19% compared to 16%).

By the latter part of the fifteenth century, the residential structure of the city had changed. Of the total population (that is, of all those identified by a Florentine parish), 72% resided in those 11 parishes on the outer ring, 17% in the inner ring, and 11% in the central city (or that area roughly within the street patterns enclosed by the old Roman walls). The *popolo minuto,* moreover, was even more concentrated in those parishes on the city's periphery; 80% of them lived in these 11 parishes, while 12% lived in the inner ring and only 8% lived in the small parishes of the Roman city. Because of changes in notarial practices—the tendency to identify patricians (who lived predominantly in *palazzi* of the inner ring, via Maggio, via Larga, via Ghibellina, and the central city) less and less by parish during the Quattrocentro—the class segregation must have been more accentuated than our statistics reveal.[3]

We might try to control for the effect of these changes in urban

3. Our statistics largely confirm Professor Brucker's impressions, drawn predominantly from city views and certain building projects, such as the extensions of the Piazza Signoria and the Loggia dei Lanzi, *Renaissance Florence* (New York, 1971), pp. 8 and 23: "The transformation of the urban center into a more spacious area . . . gathered momentum in the fifteenth century and was a result not only of economic pressures but also changing values, both public and private." But in his chapter on urban geography there is a striking inconsistency between descriptions of "working-class neighborhoods" and "slum areas" and assertions that there existed "remarkable . . . social and economic heterogeneity" in every district and neighborhood: "Each prominent family was closely identified with a particular neighborhood . . . Then, as now, the ground floors of elegant palaces were rented out to shopkeepers and artisans; rich bankers and industrialists lived on streets inhabited by shoemakers, stone masons, indigent cloth workers and prostitutes [p. 23]." In these descriptions of the social geography of Florence, moreover, Brucker does not draw chronological distinctions.

For other examples of the opening of urban space in the center and inner ring of the city and the consequent displacement of workers and artisans in these areas during the course of the fifteenth century, see Isabella Hyman, *Fifteenth Century Florentine Studies: The Palazzo Medici and a Ledger for the Church of San Lorenzo* (New York, 1977); concerning the Medici palace: "The expansion in size and the decorative elaboration of private residences during the fourteenth and fifteenth centuries were important variations on the traditional formulae for Florentine houses of the well-to-do, but they caused relatively little alteration in the appearance of the city. While they bespoke the increasing prosperity, supremacy and power that gave early Quattrocento Florence its particular atmosphere of *benessere,* even they did not suggest that by the middle of that century it would be possible for a private citizen like Cosimo de'Medici to demolish twenty-two old houses in order to build one new one [p. 42]." And concerning the piazza and church of S. Lorenzo: "Space for the new piazza was to be provided by the destruction of buildings that the governing body of Florence wished to eliminate anyway for they were inhabited by prostitutes and other 'low types' who they believed should not have been living near the church [p. 115]." For other constructions which demolished workers' and artisans' homes during the second half of the fifteenth century, see Giuseppina C. Romby, *Descrizioni e rappresentazioni della città di Firenze nel XV secolo* (Florence, 1976); and R. A. Goldthwaite and W. R. Rearick, *Michelozzo and the Ospedale di San Paolo in Florence, Mitteilungen des Kunsthistorischen Institutes in Florenz.* Vol. 21, pt. 3 (1977), pp. 221–306; Luca Landucci, *Diario fiorentino dal 1450 al 1416,* edited by Iodaco del Badia (Florence, 1883), 102ff. For an expression of patrician consciousness of "good and honorable" neighborhoods during the fifteenth century, see L. B. Alberti, *The Family in the Renaissance,* pp. 184–185.

Table 5.4
Marriage Endogamies of the Popolo Minuto by Ecological Ring

	Endogamies				Exogamies			
	Parish (a)	Gonfalone (b)	Quarter (c)	Cluster (d)	Cross-quarter (e)	Cross-cluster (f)	Contado (g)	Total
Fourteenth century								
Periphery	62 33.07%	7 3.80%	21 11.41%	27 14.67%	62 33.70%	63 34.24%	32 17.39%	184
Inner ring	54 33.13%	11 6.75%	30 18.40%	35 21.47%	52 31.90%	58 35.58%	16 9.82%	163
Central city	12 17.91%	4 5.97%	24 35.82%	10 14.93%	17 25.37%	35 22.39%	10 14.93%	67
Fifteenth century								
Periphery	244 52.47%	47 10.11%	32 6.88%	65 13.98%	92 19.78%	106 22.80%	50 10.75%	465
Inner ring	14 20.29%	5 7.25%	8 11.59%	10 14.49%	17 24.64%	28 40.58%	12 17.39%	69
Central city	16 36.36%	—	6 13.64%	—	20 45.45%	26 59.09%	2 4.05%	44

Table 5.5
Endogamy within Ecological Rings

	Fourteenth century	Fifteenth century	Fifteenth century (weighted)	Fifteenth century endogamies (weighted)
Periphery	184	465	256.86	134.77
	44.44%	80.45%		52.47%
Inner ring	163	69	227.52	46.16
	39.37%	11.94%		20.29%
Inter city	67	44	93.55	34.01
	16.18%	76.1%		36.36%
Total				214.94
				37.19%

structure on the networks of social association among the *popolo minuto* by weighting the parish endogamy ratios for each of the three ecological rings in order that the fifteenth-century distribution of the *popolo minuto* would coincide with that of the fourteenth century. Thus, instead of 465 individuals considered from the outer ring, their numbers would be reduced by nearly 45%; the inner ring would be nearly quadrupled and the population of the Roman city doubled. Once the population of the *popolo minuto* has been redistributed according to the dimensions of the late Trecento population of laborers and craftsmen, the parish endogamies of the fifteenth century do indeed decline, from 47% to 37% and to 36% after adjustments for mobility (see Table 5.5). Nonetheless, even after these adjustments, the importance of parish during the late Quattrocento still exceeds that of the late Trecento, by 7 percentile points or by 23%, and by 13 percentile points or by 34% when the adjusted endogamy figures are considered, as a focus of neighborhood interaction.[4]

But should the effect of residential structure on the patterns of social association uncovered by the marriage statistics be selected out of our analysis? Are these urban structures truly independent variables or can they be considered, just as well, the results of certain changes in class definition, consciousness, and class struggle—another dimension of the "inward turning," fragmentation, and isolation that the popular classes experienced after the fall of the Ciompi and the rise of the Medicean state?

Thus far, art historians have studied only one side of the architectural

---

4. Even the unadjusted difference is significant; standard error of a proportion test: $p = 37.19$; $\pi = 34.06$; $N = 987.93$; $z = 2.08$.

expansion and urban renewal of Quattrocento Florence. Not only did
the *palazzi* of Via Larga and Via Maggio or the hospitals of S. Paolo
or S. Maria Nuova have a certain ideological effect, these massive monu-
ments to a family, a class, or a regime consumed considerable chunks of
urban space. By the period of Lorenzo, the claustrophobic image of
closely-bunched buildings reflected in the first view of Florence (the
Fresco of the Madonna della Misericordia in the Loggia del Bigallo, ca.
1342) was largely transformed. The parishes within the inner ring in
particular lost their dense populations. A disproportionate number of
these inhabitants were members of the *popolo minuto*. Mixed communities with extensive working class populations such as S. Pancrazio, S.
Paolo, S. Felice in Piazza, and S. Piero Scheraggio became during the
late Quattrocento much smaller communities with only a very thin
layer from the popular classes. Within the Roman street patterns,
palazzi such as the Strozzi Palace on Via Tournabuoni swallowed
parish communities almost whole.[5] In the century following the fall of
the Ciompi, Florence developed a much more clearly defined class
geography. The reverse side of the Renaissance palace construction on
Via Maggio and Via Larga, the new hospitals, churches, and monu-
ments to private families, was displacement and demographic redistribution. Concentrations of artisans and *sottoposti* within the 11 parishes
of Florence's periphery, the ghettos around *piazze* such as Camaldoli,
were the consequences of a more open, formal, and pleasing sense of
space in the city's center.

   The social distance between rich and poor which can be seen in the
changes in Florentine geography and changes in the social composition
of its parishes was reinforced, moreover, by a vertical dimension, by
relative changes in the concentration of urban wealth. Again, to
measure these changes we turn to information in the marriage records:
the amount of dowry payment. It might be argued that the tax surveys
would provide a more precise measure of changes in the concentration
of urban wealth. However, the tax structure between the late fourteenth
and the late fifteenth centuries, between the *Estimo* and the *Catasto*
(both in terms of the efficacy of tax assessment as well as the principles
on which the assessments were estimated) changed so dramatically[6]
that the dowry payment arguably provides a better standard for assess-
ing changes in the gradations of economic and social status between the
two centuries.

---

5. The parish community was S. Maria degli Ughi.
6. Herlihy and Klapisch, *Les Toscans et leurs familles: Une étude du castado florentin de
1427* (Paris, 1978), p. 44

When these dowries are arranged according to a curve of concentration or Lorenz curve,[7] we find in the distribution of dowry payments a greater concentration during the late fifteenth century. In the fourteenth century, the lowest 10% of the population exchanged dowries which were over three times the value (in relation to all dowries exchanged) of the dowries exchanged by the same percentage during the late Quattrocento; while in our fifteenth-century sample, the upper 10% of the population exchanged almost half the dotal treasures in comparison to 41% exchanged by the same population in the Trecento. The "line of equidistance" of the fourteenth-century Lorenz curve equals .613; while in the fifteenth century it increases to .672. (see Table 5.6 and Figure 5.1) More than a change in the distribution of wealth, the polarization of dowry payments in the fifteenth century might reflect the influence of the *Monte delle doti*. Even if this were the case, the social consequences would be the same—a growing bifurcation in the marital and, therefore, social interaction between the rich and poor.[8]

In conclusion, we have found that the social structure and networks of social interaction among the *popolo minuto*—that ambiguous group

Table 5.6
Lorenz Curves of Dowry Payments

Fourteenth century			Fifteenth century		
Percentage of population	Amount	Percentage of all dowries	Percentage of population	Amount	Percentage of all dowries
10	669.35	.00617	10	426.99	.001975
20	1720.77	.01587	20	1592.61	.00737
30	3403.98	.03140	30	4023.28	.01861
40	5631.22	.05194	40	7568.35	.0350
50	9115.71	.08409	50	12596.58	.0583
60	14379.36	.1326	60	20696.25	.0957
70	22444.67	.2070	70	34090.14	.1577
80	37396.79	.3447	80	58082.14	.2687
90	64413.85	.59418	90	112836.14	.5219
100	108408.85	1.00	100	216183.14	1.00

7. A description of the uses of Lorenz curves can be found in Giuseppe De Meo, *Saggi di statistica, economia e demografica sull'Italia meridionale nei secoli XVII e XVIII* (Rome, 1962), pp. 1–47.

8. See note 5, this chapter, and Herlihy, "The Distribution of Wealth in a Renaissance Community: Florence 1427," in *Towns in Societies*, edited by Abrams and Wrigley (Cambridge, 1978), p. 139, "Perhaps the most surprising result of our inquiry is the scant importance, by measure of numbers or possessions, of the middle levels of urban society . . . we do have indications that the highly skewed distribution of wealth in fifteenth century cities was a comparatively new development. . . ."

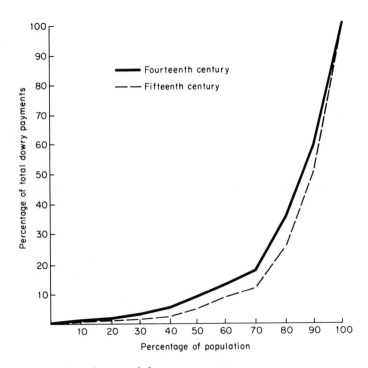

Figure 5.1. *Distribution of dowry payments.*

of laborers and artisans—were not static phenomena during the course of late medieval and Renaissance Florentine history. During the broadly defined period of the Ciompi, the structures of popular communities were similar to those of communities of upper guildsmen and patricians. Their residential patterns did not differ substantially; equal proportions of the populations resided in the various ecological rings of the city; both patricians and the poor attended the same parish churches. And the networks of association uncovered by our sample of marriage contracts carved out very similar geographies.

By the late fifteenth century, this picture had changed radically. The networks of association of the popular classes differed dramatically from those of their social betters. Both had changed significantly from the Trecento. While the patriciate had emerged from a neighborhood identification of themselves (at least in so far as the structuring of their consanguinal ties), the communities of the *popolo minuto* had become much more tightly focused around the large parish churches on the city's periphery. On the one hand, these networks of association isolated artisan and laboring populations from the residual population; on the other hand, these large and well-defined parochial communities fragmented the *popolo minuto* as a whole.

This fragmentation and isolation was accentuated by changes in the residential structure of Florence. No longer do our statistics reveal the ideal—typical medieval town—an integrated *Gemeinschaft* of rich and poor. From the fall of the Ciompi to the rule of Lorenzo, a class geography became more and more distinctive across the Florentine landscape. The other side of the "rational" formalistic city planning of the Quattrocento, the opening of space in the center city and the splendid palaces which branch out along strip developments such as Via Maggio and Via Ghibelline through the city's inner ring, was the development of working class ghettos in S. Lorenzo, S. Maria in Verzaia, and S. Frediano.

These ghettos were structured by more than considerations of class. From the late Trecento to the late Quattrocento, the supply of labor from beyond the city walls had changed, not so much in magnitude as in its character. Instead of the flow of Tuscan immigrants from the surrounding villages and towns, who quickly became integrated into the social structure of Florentine society (to the chagrin of the standard-bearers of Florentine culture), the bulk of late Quattrocento immigrants came from places further afield, foreign places. Many probably entered the city speaking foreign languages or other Italian dialects which would have been incomprehensible to the native Florentines and *popolo minuto*. Among these immigrants, the Germans were numeri-

cally most important. We find these *Gastarbeiter* occupying positions
at the bottom of the Florentine occupational structure. For the most
part they were *sottoposti* of the wool and silk industries. They most
certainly did not integrate themselves thoroughly within the Florentine
population. They settled into two neighborhoods and intermarried
tightly within the confines of these neighborhoods. Their geographic
endogamy was more constricted than any other subgroup of the Florentine population.

Beyond the dimensions of residential patterns and national/racial dif-
ferentiations, the Florentine urban population was further differentiated
by a growing gap in the distribution of wealth and in their capacity
to exchange prestigious dowry sums. Overlying these changes in urban
structure we still find significant changes in behavior patterns—the
networks of association—among the *popolo minuto* and among the
patriciate between the two centuries. In fact, most of the variables for
which we have tried to control in the previous two chapters—immigration, urban mobility, discrepancies in geographical representation—
have shown that our conclusions about the striking changes in the networks of association of the laboring classes—that sense of community
structured by the aggregation of conscious choices—should not be modified. Instead the dramatic differences discovered in Chapter 3 need to be
adjusted in the opposite direction: the changes in the character and
structure of the communities of the *popolo minuto* were even larger
than the raw statistics initially revealed. What then were the social and
political consequences of these changes in social structure? What do
these structures tell us about Renaissance Florence?

Chapter 6

Class Struggle I

I N the previous chapters we have examined two separate societies
contained within the Renaissance history of a single place: Florence,
1343–1383, and Florence, 1450–1530. We have found fundamental
differences between these two societies in the organization and structuring of their communities. While the patriciate of Florence was emerging from the vestiges of tower family formations, the structure of the
communities of workers and artisans was following an opposite trajectory. From communities and social associations which were similar to
those of the society as a whole and to the patriciate in particular, the
social networks of the laboring classes of Quattrocento Florence turned
inward. The parish church of fifteenth-century Florence dominated
the lives and communities of workers and artisans (quite unlike the
insurrectionary period of the Ciompi), while other nodes and places of
casual association—the street corner, the neighborhood tavern, the
work-place—lost their predominance in shaping popular culture.

Certain structural changes between the Trecento and Quattrocento
accentuated the fragmentation and isolation of the laboring classes both
from themselves and from other classes. Social distance between the
popolo minuto and the patriciate increased as the polarity of dowries
and wealth widened. Immigration shifted from a preponderance of
Tuscan migrants in replenishing the city's work force towards the reliance on long-distance immigrants, foreigners, speaking foreign tongues,
from other parts of Italy and beyond the Alps. These immigrants were
much slower and less likely than their Tuscan predecessors of the previous century to become integrated into the native Florentine laboring
classes. During the fifteenth century virtual ghettos, defined in terms
of residential concentrations and social interaction, appeared on the
urban horizon. Finally during the latter part of the Quattrocento, the
transformation of the old medieval city of the Trecento into the Renais-

sance city, characterized by a class geography, further accentuated the social distances separating classes. The other side of the palace building and architectural achievements which have imprinted the reputation of Renaissance Florence indelibly into the story of Western civilization was the uprooting of workers and artisans from the mixed neighborhoods which had existed within the Roman walls and inner ring of the city. These laborers became concentrated and isolated within the large parishes of the city's periphery. We must address the question: What were the political consequences of these broad structural developments?

In this chapter we begin to fill in some of the detail beneath the structures of our statistical analysis. In the words of the political historian, Gene Brucker, we have attempted to uncover "the transformation of the forms of association that underlie politics." [1] Now we must consider the relationship of the changes in the contours of communities—the ecology of the city, the changing character of social distances—to the political role of the *popolo minuto,* its subjective conditions and expressions of class during the fourteenth and fifteenth centuries.

Following Brucker's assiduous research, historians have turned away from a Marxist interpretation of the Revolt of the Ciompi, which (like Marx's own reading of Gino Capponi's description) saw this wool workers' revolution and temporary control of the Florentine Commune as a remarkable incident in Western civilization.[2] Historians now argue that the petitions of the Ciompi during the fall of 1378 and the short-lived measures enacted by their Balìa of 32 were hardly revolutionary. Instead they reflect, on the one hand, the cooptation of the masses by opportunists within the patriciate and, on the other hand, the traditional attitudes of a sluggish, sub-political population. According to Brucker:

> The most striking characteristic of these rebels was their innate conservatism, their respect for tradition, their adherence to the old forms and rituals. . . Perhaps it would be more accurate to say that, like every other group in Florentine society, the *popolo minuto* accepted the economic system. They had been nurtured in a milieu in which buying and lending, working for wages, were as familiar as the physical landmarks of the Arno city.[3]

This interpretation is further developed by economic historian Raymond de Roover:

---

1. Gene Brucker, *The Civic World of Early Renaissance Florence* (Princeton, 1977), p. 11.
2. Victor Rutenburg, *Popolo e movimenti popolari nell'Italia del '300 e '400,* translated by G. Borghini (Bologna, 1971; Moscow, 1958), p. 15.
3. Brucker, "The Ciompi Revolution," in *Florentine Studies: Politics and Society in Renaissance Florence,* edited by Nicolai Rubinstein (London, 1968), p. 352.

The demands of the Ciompi were by no means as radical or as revolutionary as one might suppose. The masses sought to improve their lot, but they certainly did not seek a complete change of the existing economic system. . . They did not even question the existing hierarchy; the best proof is that, in the excitement of their victory, they created several knights, among whom was Vieri di Cambio de'Medici (1323–95), probably the richest banker in Florence at the time. Even the symbolism—banners and coats of arms—adopted by the new guilds shows the prevailing influence of medieval customs and ideas.[4]

Relying in large part on the research of American historians since World War II, the French historians, Philippe Wolff and Michel Mollat, have derived similar conclusions:

The absence of an innovative spirit is striking enough. We have already noted how difficult it was for even the most ardent Ciompi to conceive a program which lay outside of the traditional mental categories. This explains the conservatism of most of the decisions of August, 1378. The Ciompi entered into the same institutional niches and ethical categories of those whom they had defeated.[5]

Finally, the connections between the government and the Ciompi, their entry into a coalition government, the retention of certain Communal institutions, and the innate conservatism of the *popolo minuto* are expressed most forcefully by Professor Brucker:

Neither in the petitions nor, presumably, among the Ciompi themselves was there an articulated demand for the destruction of the regime and the establishment of a new egalitarian order . . . Illustrative of lower-class conservatism was the Ciompi's acceptance of the constitutional structure under which it had been suppressed and exploited for a century.[6]

Before turning to the evidence concerning the Revolt of the Ciompi and the popular movements which preceded its outbreak, we need to question just what would be "revolutionary" in the views of those recent historians who have, since the early 1950s, revised or rejected completely the earlier interpretations of the Ciompi composed in large part by Niccolò Rodolico and Alfred Doren. From their criteria, one

---

4. Raymond de Roover, "Labour Conditions in Florence around 1400: Theory, Policy and Reality," in *ibid.*, Rubinstein, p. 309.

5. M. Mollat and P. Wolff, *Ongles Bleus, Jacques et Ciompi: Les révolutions populaires en Europe aux XIVᵉ et XVᵉ siècles* (Paris, 1970), p. 161.

6. Brucker, *Florentine Politics and Society, 1343–1378* (Princeton, 1962), p. 384.

wonders whether they would agree that the French Revolution or even the Russian Revolution were truly revolutionary. Brucker maintains:

> Of all the explanations advanced to account for the regime's collapse, the least plausible, in terms of evidence, is that which emphasizes the revolutionary role of the proletariat. The disorders of 1378 were not initiated by the Ciompi; they were instigated and directed by a faction within the regime. The first manifestations of violence involved guildsmen, not the disenfranchised cloth workers.[7]

Similarly, the French and Russian Revolutions were not initially directed by artisans or the proletariat, nor did the first manifestations of violence involve these groups. In the French Revolution, conflict began between the monarchy and the aristocracy; in the Russian Revolution, between the aristocracy and industrial interests. But because of these facts would we then deny the revolutionary role of the *sans-culottes* or the industrial soviets? In neither revolution, moreover, do we find a complete inversion of the *ancien régime,* a world "turned upside down." In both, certain institutions and technical expertise which were very much a part of the *ancien régime* had to be incorporated into the revolutionary state in order for the revolution to remain a part of "this world" and not of the next. From the standards applied to the Revolt of the Ciompi, it seems that only millennarianism—excesses which pertain more to the next world than to the present one—could possibly qualify as "revolutionary" in the current historiography of the Ciompi.

The other side of the Ciompi's "acceptance of the constitutional structure" was their participation in it, which radically changed that structure from representing less than 20% of the population to almost all of the adult male population. The creation of the three revolutionary guilds, moreover, which gave wage earners in the wool industry the right to buy and sell freely raw materials and finished goods, and which gave them the opportunity to participate in the decisions of production, fundamentally altered the relations of production in the dominant industry of Trecento Florence. Indeed, during the brief tenure of the Signoria under the direction of the Balìa of 32, the government made decisions which very certainly cut into the ancient prerogatives of the *lanaioli* and the merchant–banking class. First, the interest rates on forced loans—the principal means of taxation which in effect redistributed the incomes from direct taxation (the *gabelles*) back to the

---

7. *Ibid.,* Brucker, p. 388.

rich—were cut from 15% to 5%. Second, fluctuations in the ratio between gold and silver (before and after the Revolt of the Ciompi, a means of lowering the real wages of artisans and workers) was stabilized at 3.5 lire per florin. Third, the wool workers imposed production quotas on the wool manufacturers in order to reduce unemployment and under-employment. Fourth, by abolishing the *forestiere* and by placing members from the three new guilds in the courts of the *Arte della Lana,* the wool merchants could no longer exercise complete and arbitrary freedom of action over the personal and economic behavior of their workers.[8]

To understand the Ciompi, to put them in historical perspective, we must depart from an analysis which would evaluate their programs and actions according to the activities that we *might* expect from a late nineteenth- or twentieth-century work force. It is not necessary to consider the Ciompi a fully developed socialist movement; they clearly did not have an ideology or a plan of action that can be compared to late nineteenth-century working class movements. But the absence of such expressions and actions does not signify the opposite—a sub-political population, and the Revolt of the Ciompi a "traditional imbroglio." [9] What is necessary at this point is to move from abstract judgment to comparative analysis.

At the present state of historical research, perhaps the richest literature concerning typologies of popular protest exists in French historiography and turns in large part around the French Revolution. In the last 22 years, George Rudé and Charles Tilly have been its principal contributors. From this literature, one can generally identify two sets of tendencies in the forms, types, and composition of popular protest, from the Ancien Régime through the latter part of the nineteenth century. Tilly distinguishes between *communal* and *associational* forms of protest:

---

8. Nicolò Rodolico, *La democrazia fiorentina nel suo tramonto (1378–1382),* (Bologna, 1905), 136ff.; and Carlo Falletti-Fossati, *Il Tumulto dei Ciompi* (Florence, 1873), 55ff.

9. Brucker, "The Ciompi Revolution," p. 356. In his latest contribution to the history of Florentine society, *The Civic World of Renaissance Florence* (Princeton, 1977), Professor Brucker has somewhat altered his earlier interpretations of the Ciompi Revolution. Now, Professor Brucker emphasizes the revolt as the culmination of the "corporative" ideal in Florentine politics. But, the argument has not been changed essentially. Brucker does not see the *popolo minuto,* the Revolt of the Ciompi, or class struggle as forces in the transition from "corporative" to "elitist" politics—the theme of his latest narrative. Rather, the Revolt of the Ciompi is merely evidence which *reflects* the transition of these oligarchic types. To understand this process of transformation in Florentine society, Brucker focuses one-dimensionally on dynamics only within the oligarchy itself: "I agree with those scholars who have argued that the corporate foundations of the commune grew weaker in the fourteenth century; the historical significance of the Ciompi revolution was its revelation of that erosion [p. 11]." See also pp. 16, 40 and 325.

Communal: To the extent that contenders are communal, their collective actions—and hence the collective violence in which they engage—will tend to be localized, uncoordinated, dependent on normal rhythms of congregation like those of marketing, church-going, or harvesting, hard for the participants themselves to keep within bounds. To the extent that contenders are associational, their collective actions will tend to be disciplined, large in scale, deliberately scheduled, and organized in advance. . . Contenders vary in organization from simple, small, local groups recruiting largely through inheritance to complex, large, wide-ranging specialized groups recruiting through voluntary adherence and/or personal qualifications. . . In the European experience, lineages, religious congregations, villages, and members of local markets have been typical communal contenders, while political parties, secret societies, industrial firms, and trade unions have been typical associational contenders.[10]

---

10. Charles Tilly, "How Protest Modernized in France, 1845–1855," in *The Dimensions of Quantitative Research*, edited by Aydelotte, Bogue and Fogel (Princeton, 1972), p. 199.

In more recent articles and unpublished papers Tilly has drawn a tripartite periodization in the history of the forms and "repertoires" of popular collective protest from the period of absolutism to electorial politics. In "Collective Violence in European Perspective," H. D. Graham and T. R. Gurr, eds., *Violence in America: Historical and Comparative Perspectives* (Beverly Hills, 1979) Tilly breaks down the history of collective protest into three broad categories—primitive, reactionary, and modern. These correspond to different phases in the development of the modern state.

Primitive varieties of collective violence include the feud, the brawl among members of rival gilds or communes, and the mutual attacks of hostile religious groups . . . and share several features: small scale, local scope, participation by members of communal groups, as such, inexplicit and unpolitical objectives.

Reactionary disturbances are also usually small in scale, but they pit other communal groups or loosely-organized members of the general population against representatives of those who hold power, and tend to include a critique of the way power is being wielded. The forcible occupation of fields and forests by the landless, the revolt against the tax collector, the anti-conscription rebellion, the food riot, and the attack on machines were western Europe's most frequent forms of reactionary collective violence. The risky term "reactionary" applies to these forms of collective violence because their participants were commonly reacting to some change which they regarded as depriving them of rights they had once enjoyed; they were backward-looking. They were not, however, simple flights from reality. On the contrary, they had a close connection with routine, peaceful political life.

The *modern* varieties of political disturbance (to use another tendentious term) involve specialized associations with relatively well-defined objectives, organized for political or economic action. Such disturbances can easily reach a large scale. Even more clearly than in the case of reactionary collective violence, they have a tendency to develop from collective actions which offer a show of force but are not intrinsically violent. The demonstration and the violent strike are the two clearest examples, but the coup and most forms of guerilla also qualify. These forms deserve to be called "modern" not only because of their organizational complexity but also because the participants commonly regard themselves as striking for rights due them, but not yet enjoyed. They are, that is, forward-looking.

In "Hauptformen kollektiver Aktion in Westeuropa, 1500–1975" in *Geschichte und Gessellschaft* (1977), Heft 2, *Sozialer Protest*, ed. Richard Tilly, (Göttingen, 1977), 154–163, Charles

Tilly sees the fundamental shift in French history occurring in the 1850s: "Almost all these changes involved a shift away from casual congregation, communal organization, and uncoordinated protest toward the deliberate collective action typified by the demonstration or the strike." [11] How does the Ciompi fit into Tilly's typology? Certainly, we do not find all the forms of the associational model: industrial firms and trade unions, for example. On the other hand, there is evidence of the existence of strikes and secret societies. Moreover, the revolt of the Ciompi was not a village riot defined by lineages, religious congregation, or local markets. Rutenburg has even shown the regional interrelationships among Ciompi in Perugia, Siena, and Florence. The Ciompi uprising had a remarkable city-wide organization and participation that is particularly striking in comparison to the more localized participation revealed by the Bastille list of 1789, or more importantly, to the forms of protest found in fifteenth-century Florence. But to understand the Ciompi further, we need to break down these large ideal types into more detailed categories.

In his studies on the French Revolution, George Rudé offers six characteristics of the *pre-industrial crowd*: (*a*) the prevalence of the rural food riot; (*b*) the resort to direct action, and violence to property; (*c*) its spontaneity; (*d*) its leadership by those outside the crowd; (*e*) its mixed composition, with the emphasis on small shopkeepers and craftsmen in the towns, and weavers, miners, and laborers in the villages; and (*f*) its concern for the restoration of "lost" rights. [12] From other

---

Tilly analyzes the demands made by rebels and again breaks down the history of modern European social conflict into three categories. This time he calls them: competitive actions (conflicts within popular groups, such as the *charivaris*), reactive action (the forceful occupation of lands by the landless and the tax revolt), and proactive actions (strikes for higher wages).

The earlier distinction quoted in the text, however, *communal* versus *associational* forms of protest serves our purposes best: (*a*) because it is not altogether clear that the primitive forms or the competitive actions between rival groups within laboring communities are forms of class conflict, and (*b*) because we will consider in the next chapter not only collective forms of protest but also individual, isolated, and atomized acts of resistance to the state and to members of the merchant class. These acts do not fit into Tilly's tripartite divisions but are in fact a logical extension of the *communal* form of protest, which predominate as the form of social protest when the opportunity for *associational* forms becomes for various reasons more remote.

11. *Ibid.*, Tilly (1972), pp. 215–216.

12. George Rudé, *Paris and London in the Eighteenth Century: Studies in Popular Protest* (London, 1974), p. 23. In a recent article, William M. Reddy, "The Textile Trades and the Language of the Crowd at Rouen, 1752–1871," *Past & Present*, no. 74 (1977), pp. 62–89, criticizes the Tilly-Rudé distinction between pre-modern and modern forms of social protest by arguing that (*a*) the food riot was in fact in its socioeconomic context a form of strike, and that (*b*) the early strikes of the nineteenth century were not really strikes (conscious withholding of labor power) in the twentieth-century sense. I do not find Mr. Reddy's arguments convincing.

articles by Rudé, one could add to this list the critical relationship between the price of bread and the frequency of rioting. During the
French Revolution, Rudé distinguishes several periods or "motions" of
popular insurrection, 1789–1794. Briefly, the Champs de Mars, July,
1791, was a watershed. Before, there was a high percentage of foot riots
that bore a close relationship to the price of bread; afterwards, bread
riots declined, and protest in general was less sensitive to fluctuations
in bread or food prices. Strikes became more important, and the composition of the crowds included fewer women, shopkeepers, and artisans,
and a higher proportion of wage laborers of the manufactures.[13]

Let us now turn to the uprising of the Ciompi and those riots and
insurrections that survive in the criminal archives—the Podestà, the
Capitano, and the Esecutore—from the beginning of the records in
1343 through the restoration of the oligarchy and the trials of the
Ciompi insurrectionists, which continued through 1385. There are several problems in observing the trends in popular protest through these
documents. First, not all expressions of political conflict and consciousness on the part of the *popolo minuto* would have been adjudicated by
these courts. Political expressions, in fact, often the most advanced
expressions—strikes, for example—were not always violent, involving
the destruction of property or the injury of persons, and thus coming
under the jurisdiction of the criminal courts. Rodolico, for instance,
through the deliberations of the Arte della Lana, has uncovered evidence of a series of strikes in 1369 which show no trace in the records
of the criminal tribunals.[14] Second, even at the time of the compilation
of the inventories in the nineteenth century, there were *lacunae* in
individual *filze* and in records of various magistrates, as well as larger
gaps within the series of certain courts. The most serious of these is the
disappearance of all the records of the Capitano del Popolo between
March 14, 1352 and August 4, 1367. Third, the flood of November 4,
1966, seriously ravaged the earlier criminal archives.

In the period 1343–1385, 43 riots and insurrections which must have
involved thousands of men and women have been found, within the
confines of the city alone. From these we can observe over 350 persons
who were fined or sentenced to death. These riots ranged from small
attacks on individuals *berrovarii* (police officers of the courts) or on
officials of the Commune—from *numptii* to the *gonfalonieri*—to the
larger insurrections of the Otto di S. Maria Novella, and the mass

---

13. *Ibid.*, Rudé, pp. 131ff.
14. Rodolico, *Il Popolo Minuto: Note di storia fiorentina, 1343–1378,* 2nd. edition (Florence, 1968), pp. 73–76.

counter-revolutionary conspiracies which were adjudicated throughout the rule of *Arti Minori.*

Given the accepted models of insurrectionary activity in a pre-industrial period, the most striking characteristic of these Ciompi insurrections is the insignificance of the grain and food riot. The criminal archives shed light on only one grain riot. On August 19, 1368, five men, two from the rural suburbs and three then living in the city, were sentenced for congregating in front of a certain *loggia* where wheat and flour were sold.[15] These five men, along with the crowd which the officials of the Podestà estimated at more than 500,[16] then took "a certain quantity of grain beyond 20 starii" and marched to the palazzo de'Signoria, where they slammed the grain to the ground, yelled, *"viva il popolo"* and began storming the officials of the Podestà with stones. It is curious that, from the little one can detect about causes and political expressions, even this riot was no explicit protest against prices and hunger, but rather, a more general political protest against the Signoria itself and the government of Florence.

Second, within the rank and file of Trecento Florentine insurrectionists we do not find any women mentioned in the records. Unlike the riots from the *Ancien Régime* to the march on Versailles, where women played a predominant role, the composition of the crowds on the eve of the Ciompi (at least, of those apprehended by the courts) was almost completely masculine. Certainly, they must have been part of the larger crowds of insurrectionists, the crowd of 500 in 1368 and among those thousands outside the Palazzo Vecchio who brought a change in the Communal government on July 23, 1378. But they do not appear to have been the ringleaders, or at least among those sought out by the *berrovarii* of the Capitano, the Podestà, and the Esecutore. From these facts—the almost complete absence of grain riots and food riots, and the absence of women—it seems that the motivation for collective political unrest did not spring from dire material conditions and problems of immediate necessity to the hearth.

Moreover, when the most recent research on price trends and wages during the period of the Ciompi is studied, the data do not exactly support the strong correlation drawn by Professor Brucker between

---

15. The flood of November, 1966, damaged the criminal inquisitions and sentences in both the Capitano del Popolo and the Podestà which pertain to this case; only Rodolico's published transcription of the sentence found in the Acts of the Podestà is now accessible; *ibid.,* Document no. 11, pp. 97–99.

16. *ibid.,* p. 98, ". . . *ipsorum una cum pluribus aliis ultra numerum quingentorum quorum nomina in dicta inquisitione tacebantur ad presens pro meliori, . . .*" See Rodolico, *La democrazia fiorentina,* p. 124.

rising grain prices, immiseration, and incidence of political unrest. Charles de la Roncière charts a sharp rise in the price of general necessities around 1335 which continued until several years after the Black Death, to around 1352. In the middle 1350s through the 1360s prices fell; then, during the first half of the 1370s (a period of quiescence, according to Brucker) prices rose again, slightly surpassing the levels of the period of the Black Death. In the years immediately preceding the Revolt of the Ciompi, however, prices fell.[17] From information compiled by Richard Goldthwaite on grain prices, 1375 and not 1378 should have been the critical year of the Ciompi Uprising, had dire necessity been its principal underpinning.[18] Instead, 1375, according to Brucker's periodization of social unrest, falls within the trough separating the turbulent years at the beginning of the decade from the Ciompi uprising itself.[19]

Through the 1340–1378 period (which was characterized by only a slight overall rise in prices), wages (especially for the more menial forms of labor) increased sharply and the purchasing power of workers rose.[20] Charles de la Roncière has traced the wages of gardeners and construction workers; he finds that from the 1320s to 1381 wages for gardeners increased steadily, from 3.3 soldi per day in the 1326–1332 period, to 7.1 soldi from 1350–1356, to 8.2 soldi in 1371–1375, to 8.8 soldi from 1378–1381.[21] Similarly, the wages of the *manovali* or day laborers in the construction industry increased from 2.7 soldi in the 1340–1348 period, to 9.2 in 1350–1356, to 9.9 in 1378–1380.[22]

Although the Black Death certainly represents the watershed of these wages, real wages, nonetheless, continued to increase through the years immediately preceding the revolt of the Ciompi and through the years of the government of the Arti Minori. It might, however, be argued that these figures do not adequately reflect the well-being of the major portion of the Florentine urban work force—wage earners of the Arte della Lana. There is evidence that this industry was experiencing a

---

17. Charles de la Roncière, *Florence: Centre économique régional au XIVe siècle* (Aix-en-provence, 1977), pp. 118, 260–262.

18. Richard A. Goldthwaite, "I prezzi del grano a Firenze del XIV al XVI secolo, *Quaderni Storici*, Vol. 28 (1975), 33, Table B, Medie annuali, 1359–1477.

19. Brucker, *Florentine Politics and Society*, p. 378.

20. la Roncière, *Florence: Centre économique régional, p. 1302.*

21. la Roncière, "Pauvres et Pauvreté à Florence au XIVe siècle," in *Études sur l'histoire de la pauvreté*, edited by Michel Mollat, Vol. 2 (Paris, 1974), 672, and *Florence: Centre économique régional*, p. 344, table 58.

22. la Roncière, "Pauvres et Pauvreté," p. 681 and *Florence: Centre économique régional*, p. 371, table 62.

recession in the years 1366–1378, and that workers were being laid off.[23] Nonetheless, the point remains. The problems of the hearth, hunger and high bread prices (from which wool workers and the poor in general may have been suffering on the eve of the Ciompi), were not the triggers of this insurrection which led to their temporary control of the Florentine Commune. Rather, the causes are to be located in the principal industry of Florence, wool production, which drew its workers from the city at large. Its setting was associational—the firm; and the problems arising from the firm and the emerging capitalist structure of the Florentine economy were confronted squarely by the demands of the Ciompi in the petitions of July and the decrees of the Balìa of 32: the arbitrary jurisdiction of the guild court, the abolition of the *forestiere,* production quotas, and the right of working men to organize themselves into self-governing bodies which had a voice in guild and Communal affairs.

Besides the revolt of the Ciompi, moreover, we find in the criminal archives other examples of insurrections organized among workers *(discipuli et operarii)* in the wool industry. On October 9, 1343, Aldobrando di Ciecharino from Siena, called Trolquelio, who resided in the parish of San Lorenzo in the city of Florence, led an armed insurrection *("armati armis offensionibus et defensibus")* of wool workers who worked in the shops of Salvi di Messer Lotto and Matteo di Parigio de'Albizzi.[24] Less than two years later, the *scardassiere* ('skinner') Ciuto Brandini of San Pier Maggiore was captured and then hanged for organizing carders and skinners into *quedam fraternitas* with *consules* ('officials') and *capitudines* ('ordinances') in many places throughout the city. These organizations collected dues and held regular meetings.[25] Following the night of Ciuto's capture, the wool skinners and carders went on strike to demand his release.[26] The appearance of these workers,

23. Brucker, *Florentine Politics and Society,* 15; and Richard Trexler, *Economic, Political and Religious Effects of the Papal Interdict on Florence* (Frankfurt-am-Main, 1964), pp. 100–102; nonetheless, according to la Roncière, *Florence: Centre économique régional,* p. 387, table no. 64 and 1302, the wages of weavers rose through the period of the War of the Eight Saints and their general conditions were certainly improving during the two years preceding the Revolt of the Ciompi.

24. AP n. 23, fol. 87r–v.

25. The criminal documents pertaining to this case are again inaccessible because of the flood of 1966; Rodolico, *Il Popolo Minuto,* doc. no. 14, pp. 102–103, ". . . *et in dictis adunantiis et conventiculis inter alia dictus Ciutus proposuit arengavit deliberavit et ordinavit quod in dicta cohadunatione, congregatione et conventicula fieret postura seu collectio inter ipsos certam quantitatem pecunie colligende seu exigende a quolibet predictorum de dictis adunantiis . . .";* see also, Rodolico, *La democrazia fiorentina,* pp. 119–120.

26. *Ibid.,* p. 39.

Aldobrandino di Ciecharino da Siena and Ciuto Brandini, as leaders of industrial insurrection leads us to the question of leadership in the popular insurrections during the period of the Ciompi. In the models of Tilly and Rudé, insurrections of the *Ancien Régime,* or even the entire pre-modern, pre-industrial period (for Tilly, before 1850), had to rely on leadership from the outside, from the bourgeoisie or the aristocracy.[27] No matter how large a Luca da Panzano or Salviato dei Medici, or the knighting of Vieri dei Medici may loom in the accounts and interpretations of the Ciompi revolt of 1378, when the mass of insurrections— 1342 through 1378—is considered, one finds not just the presence of leaders emerging from the working and artisan population, as in the cases above, but in fact it is rare to find in these documents the presence of leaders coming from above.

There were of course exceptions. On November 3, 1343, Andrea degli Strozzi was condemned to death for arousing a crowd to charge and stone the Palazzo Vecchio and to throw stones against the Podestà and the Priores of the city.[28] Unfortunately there is no indication from the condemnation of the social status of those being led by Andrea.[29] In March of 1343, however, an inquisition was drawn up by the Capitano del Popolo against Pagnotto degli Strozzi, the brother of Andrea, who led an insurrection against the city to protest the condemnation of his brother.[30] In this inquisition, the notary of the Capitano transcribed the words allegedly spoken by Pagnotto to arouse sedition: "You wretched fools, who starve to death, who scrape for what should cost ten soldi a staio; even I could make a handful from this wretched bunch." [31] Thus, in this document it seems clear that Pagnotto was able to manipulate the crowd of impoverished urban dwellers for his own purposes—the overthrow of the Commune in a time of high grain prices.

But in the 15 other insurrections preceding 1378 which come down to us in the criminal archives, we do not find a single participant bear-

---

27. The Tilly-Rudé model might well be criticized here. The interrelationships between bourgeoise, gentry, artisans and laborers, often defined by overlapping ideologies and reciprocal social claims in preindustrial societies, might not have always resulted in simple one-directional relationships in times of social unrest: gentry leadership and popular following.

28. Rodolico, *Il Popolo Minuto,* doc. no. 8, 92–93; again, the original document is now inaccessible.

29. According to the chronicler, Marchionne di Coppo Stefani, *Cronica fiorentina,* edited by N. Rodolico Rerum Italicarum Scriptores, new ed., Vol. XXX, pt. 1 (città di Castello, 1903–55), 212, about 4,000 among wool skinners, *gente minuta* and the poor followed Andrea in this insurrection.

30. *Ibid.,* doc. no. 9, 93–94.

31. *Ibid.,* 94, *"canallia, canallia, canallia, che morete di fame, che avete cacciato quello che v'avrebbe dato ad dece soldi lo staio, ma anch'io ne farò una manecata di questa canallia."*

ing a prominent Florentine family name.[32] Although the relationship between those indicted by the court and the leadership of individual riots cannot be determined, it seems unlikely that the officials of the Podestà, Capitano, and Esecutore would have consistently arrested participants from the periphery and would often have refrained from entering the thick of the crowd to isolate its leadership. We know, however, from the phraseology of many of these condemnations—*"cum pluribus aliis quorum nomina in dicta inquisitione tacebantur ad presens pro meliori"*—that the police officials knew of others among the insurrectionists whom they chose not to reveal at the time of the condemnation of their comrades. But of these unmentioned insurgents, should we assume that they were necessarily the ringleaders or opportunist members of the patriciate?

With the condemnation in September, 1378, of the Otto di S. Maria Novella—the radical wing of the Ciompi which in August of 1378 elected officials and organized to push the revolution further—we begin to find again, for the first time since the early 1340s, members of the patriciate among the indicted *popolo minuto*. Among the *cardatori*, *pettinatori*, *scardassieri*, and *revitori*, we find a notary, Ser Agnolo Latini, Messer Luca di Totto da Panzano (who was the doctor of the Communal prison, the Stinche), a certain Maestro Andrea, Anibaldo di Bernardo degli Strozzi, and Luca del Melino da Montespertoli condemned to death by the government of Michele di Lando.[33] Yet, the chroniclers do not suggest that the workers and artisan insurgents were manipulated from above.[34] Indeed, *discepoli* comprised almost entirely the first Ciompi *consoli* in the new government of 1378: "li discepoli fussono li signori." [35] The lines of manipulation in fact ran from time to time in the opposite direction. The elected leaders from the ranks of

---

32. A(tti del) C(apitano del) P(opolo), n. 3, fol. 29r; n. 11, fol. 23r, 42r; n. 19, fol. 5v, 13v, 25r–v; n. 42, fol. 11r; n. 63, fol. 11r–12r; A(tti dell') E(secutore degli) O(rdinamenti di) G(iustizia) n. 17, fol. 17r–v; AP n. 23, fol. 87r–v; n. 116, fol. 3v; n. 127, fol. 336v; Rodolico, *Il Popolo Minuto*, doc. n. 11 and n. 15. Outside the city, on the other hand, we find numerous examples in the criminal sentences of *magnates et potentes* arousing villagers to join their riots and pillaging. Usually, these offenses were directed against other *magnati* or villagers, but rarely against the institutions of the Commune or its officers.

33. There are no surviving criminal records of these condemnations; instead, the lists come from two independent sources: *Cronica fiorentina*, pp. 336–337; and *Diario d'anomino fiorentino dall'anno 1358 al 1389*, edited by A. Gherardi (Florence, 1876), pp. 384–385.

34. From the chroniclers of the Revolt of the Ciompi, P. P. Fridolin and M. A. Gukovskij have composed lists of the Ciompi ringleaders. None of these organizers bears a prominent Florentine family name. According to Gukovskij, the "real heads" of the Ciompi insurrection of August, 1378, were two *sottoposti*, Meo del Grasso and Luca Melani. These studies have been summarized in Rutenburg, *Popolo e movimenti popolari*, pp. 307–308.

35. Stefani, *Cronica fiorentina*, 333.

the Ciompi cajoled a notary and a grammar teacher to write their petitions and grievances for the radical program of the Otto di S. Maria Novella in a presentable fashion.[36]

In the early 1380s, however, after the fall of the Balìa and the establishment of the broadly based coalition government of the *Arti Minori,* we find the city besieged (in the criminal documents) by a series of insurrections of a very different character from those which peppered the criminal archives of 1343–1378. These insurrections clearly originated from the "outside," both geographically and in terms of social class. In sharp contrast to the insurrections leading up to the Ciompi uprising, the tumults during the last two years of the regime of the *Arti Minori* possessed all the characteristics which an Edmund Burke, Hippolyte Taine, or a Pierre Gaxotte [37] would have wished of a popular insurrection. In the criminal archives, for the first time, there were substantial numbers of the patriciate intermingled with Ciompi. In a list of conspirators condemned by the Esecutore degli Ordinamenti di Giustizia, we find Messer Alberto di Pepo degl'Albizzi, Bernardo di Lippo di Cione Canni, Bindo di Gentile de'Bondelmonte, Bartolommeo di Gherardo di Messer Gheri da Prato, Iacopo di Bartolommeo de'Medici and his son Cristofano, Iacopo di Messer Rinieri Canicioli, Messer Lapo da Castiglionchio, Niccolò di Rineri Peruzzi, Pigello di Messer Luigi degli Adimari, Tommaso di Rinieri Cavalcanti, and Advardo di Bartolommeo Pulci. Of the 29 condemned to death, only one was identified as a *sottoposto,* a certain Niccolò di Berto di Bando *tiratore* (a 'stretcher'). This group of conspirators allegedly ran through the *contado* and district of Florence capturing persons, carrying off movable goods and animals, murdering persons, burning fields and buildings and homes, and kidnapping virgins, women, and men.[38]

On January 2, 1380, Lanfranco di Messer Luca da Panzano, Cione di Antonio da Panzano, Ugolino di Naldo Gherardini, Iacopo di Boccaccio Brunileschi, Totto di Antonio Gherardini, Bese di Guido Magalotti, Gherardino di Piero Velluti, the notary, Ser Piero di Ser Gasi, formerly from Prato (then living in the parish of S. Firenze) and his three sons,

---

36. Rodolico, *La democrazia fiorentina,* 193; and Stefani, *Cronica fiorentina,* 329.

37. Cf. Chapter I, p. 1; and see G. Rudé, *Paris and London in the Eighteenth Century,* 125–126.

38. AEOG n. 870, 37r–38v, "... *henormia crimina commictenda . . . debellandos et capiendos infinitos homines et personas dicte civitati et comitatui et districti ac eorum bestias animalia res et bona capienda et exportanda, homicidia, incendia et edificiorum domorum et cappannorum, raptum quorum virginium et mulierum et bominium in comitatui et districti Florentie commictendum et perpetiandum . . .*"

Ser Piero, Ser Nofri, and Ser Bruno were condemned as rebels for congregating outside the city walls of Siena and conspiring to besiege the Commune's fortress at Figline. Among the 18 *rebelles*, only two bore Ciompi occupations, the *pettinatori* ('combers') Giovanni di Putro del Schreggia and Sandro di Feduti called El Ghianda.[39] The Capitano del Popolo condemned to death on January 1, 1380, 19 members of the Florentine patriciate from among the 51 *rebelles* who were arrested. They had allegedly conspired in the city of Bologna during the month of November, 1379, and had besieged Florence at six o'clock at night sometime in December. Among the 51, only five were clearly of Ciompi status: two weavers, two combers, and a skinner. The conspirators entered the city of Florence raising the cry of *"Viva el populo et Parte Guelfa"*; they bore the insignia and banners of the Parte Guelfa.[40]

The motivation, moreover, for insurrection expressed in some of these sentences again seems to fit the Taine–Burke model. A utopian image of power, vainglory, and even cash impelled some of the desperate *popolo minuto,* then in exile or out of favor with the government of the *Arti Minori,* to ally and conspire with members of the patriciate. In a conspiracy condemned by the Esecutore in October, 1381, a certain Ricco cajoled Tommaso Buzaffi of the parish of S. Lorenzo to join the armed insurrection against the present regime of *Arti Minori* with the following words: "If you are not one of the *Priores,* here, within six months, you'll never be; because there will be another new scrutiny, you will be made rich and you will never have to have any more to do with poor men." [41] In addition, on September 16, 1380, the forces of the Capitano apprehended three men from Laterina, one man from Monte Longo and another conspirator from the Florentine parish of S. Felicità for an attempted seizure of the castle of Laterina. In the inquisition it is made clear that these men were paid 200 florins each by the nobleman, Nannino di Messer Canagni da Arezzo, to subvert

---

39. ACP n. 1198, 47v–49v.

40. ACP n. 1198, 54v–59r; the patricians indicted were: Messer Lapo di fu Lapo da Castiglionchio, Messer Giovanni di Pocciamo di Bettolo de'Coppoli da Perugia, Benedetto di Somone de'Peruzzi, Adovardo di Bartolommeo de'Pulci, Bernardo di Lippo di Cione de'Canni, Giovanni di Bartolo di Cenne de'Biliotti, Messer Alberto di Pepe di Antonio degli Albizzi, Giovanni di Guereno di Tribaldo de'Rossi, Pigello di fu Messer Luigi degli Adimari and his brother, Talano, Maricino di Lando di Antonio degli Albizzi, Tommaso di fu Ranieri de'Cavalcanti, Cenno di fu Naddo de'Rotellani, Niccolò di Iacopo de'Bordoni, Bernardo di Iacopo de'Beccanugi, Iacopo di Bartolommeo de'Medici and his wife, Niccolosa, Niccolò di Sandro de'Bardi, Messer Guido di Silvestro di Bandene, and Bingenio di Piero de'Rotellani.

41. Rodolico, *La democrazia fiorentina,* doc. n. VII (AEOG of 1381), 477, *"Se tu non sarai de'priori de qui a sei mesi, tu non sarai mai perchè si fara un altro scrutinio nuovo, tu si fatto ricco, et non vuoli più usare coi poveri uomini."*

and rebel against the castle. And if successful, Nannino promised his *"amici"* a part of the new regime.[42]

But not all of the insurrections following the defeat of the Otto di S. Maria Novella in September, 1378, had the same composition or motivation. By 1382, after the fall of the coalition government of the *Arti Minori* and the restoration of the oligarchy, we find a new period of Florentine insurrections; these counter-revolutionary movements, organized outside the city of Florence and staffed, in large part, by members of the patriciate, disappear from the criminal archives. On March 13, 1382, the Podestà condemned three men to death and condemned their property to be destroyed because of rioting and the destruction of property along the streets running into the piazza of S. Michele Berteldi.[43] In the *"coventicula conspiratio"* ('conspiracy'), the influence of the patriciate is no longer apparent. Less than two weeks later, the Podestà condemned 12 men to be beheaded for congregating and inciting to riot *(fecerunt conventicula)*. Of the 12, only one bore a family name—a certain Pietro di Giovanni del Zuta de'Covoni—and, unlike most other lists of the condemned, nine were identified by profession. We find a *merciator* ('peddler'), four *cardiouli* ('carders'), two *tintores* ('dyers'), a *lavator* ('washer of woolen cloth'), and a *cimator* ('shearer'). Thus, of those identified by profession, eight were clearly members of the Ciompi, and all nine could be considered members of the *popolo minuto*. Instead of the cry of *"Viva la parte guelfa e il popolo"*—the slogan of the *popolani grassi*—these insurrectionists raised the cry of the Ciompi, *"Vivano vinti e quattro arti."*[44] A month before these sentences, the oligarchy had been restored to power and had completely obliterated the remaining accomplishments of the revolt of the Ciompi, 1378—the revolutionary guilds of wool workers (the *Arti dei Farsettai* and *dei Tintori*) had been abolished.

In 1383, the oligarchy began its efforts in earnest to round up and purge from the Commune those remaining parties which might threaten the stability of the restored regime. On September 11 and 12, 1383, the Esecutore condemned 82 men to death. Of this crowd, only four possessed family names: Francesco di Messer Giorgio degli Scali, and his brother Ghino, Messer Tomasso di Marco degli Strozzi, and Alessandro di Benedetto Gacci. Of the remaining 78, 17 were identified by

---

42. ACP n. 1313, fol. 26r-27r, *"Et tunc dictus Nannes pro implendendo . . . dando . . . videlicet Nicolao, Tribaldo, Mactheo et Iohanni ducentos auri pro quolibet se predictam rebellionem, subversionem dicti castri Latarine facuerint et executioni mandaverint."*

43. AP n. 3053, fol. 102v-103v, *". . . inter vias publicas in plateam Sancti Michaelis Birteldi . . . fecerunt elevandum rumorem . . . plures dannos bonorum . . ."*

44. AP n. 3053.

profession. There was perhaps only one major guildsman, a druggist; six minor guildsmen—a belt-maker, two cobblers, a grocer, a maker of armor, and a tavern keeper; and another 13 who were outside the Florentine guild structure—five skinners, a comber, a doublet-maker, a tailor, a carder, a dyer, a tanner, a cook and an official of weights and measures.[45] The slogans and actions of this crowd, despite the participation of at least three persons of notable family backgrounds, again distinguishes this insurrection from those conspiracies against the regime of the *Arti Minori*. Instead of hailing the arch-patrician club—the *Parte Guelfa*—these rebels marched through various parts of the city, carrying the three banners corresponding to the three revolutionary guilds of *sottoposti* and raising the insignia of the lamb against the field of the city, the sign of two of the new guilds. According to two sets of sentences in the Esecutore, the rebels chanted, "Long live the 24 guilds and death to the traitors who make us starve."[46]

In conclusion, the insurrections following this suppression of the Otto di S. Maria Novella on August 31, 1378, fall into two categories, separated by a single chronology. In the period from 1378 to January 2, 1382, the broadly based government of the *Arti Minori*, which retained a representation of a large portion of the laboring population, was under seige from conspiracies organized outside the city and comprised in large part by exiled members of notable families: the Alberti, da Castiglionchio, the Albizzi, the Medici, etc. In marked contrast to those lists of condemned insurrectionists in the period preceding the Ciompi, 1343–1378, where we find only two participants with notable family names, one-third of the conspirators in these riots and conspiracies, 1379–1381, bore prominent family names. Moreover, those identified by the professions of the Ciompi are rare; they do not dominate the insurrectory crowds as they did in the 30 years preceding the Ciompi. Of 81 persons condemned to death in the years 1379–1381, only 8 were *sottoposti*—a spinner, four combers, two weavers, and a skinner—while 45 bore prominent Florentine family names. Second, the ideology or motivation for action, of which the notaries' inquisitions give us only a glimpse, was clearly different from the riots of the preceding period. Personal vainglory, money, and opportunism dominated the designs of the leadership and were the means for manipulating their following. The chants raised by these groups were in support of the *ancien régime* symbolized by the *Parte Guelfa*.

---

45. AEOC, n. 950, fol. 25r–27v and 29r–30v.
46. *Ibid.*, 27v and 29v, "*Vivano le vinti quarto arti et muorano i traditori che fanno morire de fame.*"

In the period 1382–1383, the insurrections described in the criminal sentences reflect a different crowd. With the restoration of the oligarchy, the target of insurrection had changed; the counter-revolutionary groups of exiled noblemen disappear, and in their place we find, once again, crowds dominated by the rank-and-file of the Ciompi. They banded together to protest the cancellation of their advances of 1378: political recognition and the right to bind together in workingmen's guilds. Their slogans, moreover, did not represent the designs of the patriciate—*"Viva la Parte Guelfa"*—but instead, the interest of working men and women—*"Vivano li vinti et quarto arti."*

Let us now go beyond the question of leadership and manipulation to investigate more closely the composition of the crowd. From the analysis of the patrician influence, it should be clear that the riots during the period 1343–1383 should be divided into three phases: (*a*) those before the fall of the Otto di S. Maria Novella; (*b*) the counter-revolutionary conspiracies, 1378–1381; and (*c*) the last attempts of the Ciompi to defeat the restoration of oligarchic rule, 1382–1383.

We do not pretend to have collected all the information on those riots which might still survive in the criminal archives of Florence for each of these periods. For the most part, we have simply relied on those insurrections uncovered by Gene Brucker and Niccolò Rodolico. In addition to these insurrections, we added several others found in the sentences of the Capitano del Popolo and the Podestà. The notions used here for political violence, riots, or popular protest, therefore, conform closely with those of Professor Brucker. We have considered, then, incidents involving collective attacks against any officers of the courts, the Podestà, the Capitano, and Esecutore, or officials of the Commune, as well as attacks against merchants and their property or those arising in wool or silk shops. Neighboring brawls, however, have not been considered a form of political protest. From the laconic descriptions contained in the criminal sentences, it is not always possible to distinguish the neighborhood brawl from a political insurrection. In both cases, the notary copied the formulaic language: *"Animo et intentione ac proposito turbandi et pervertendi statum pacificum civitatis Florentie . . ."* If the contenders, however, in these mass altercations attacked their opponents shouting political slogans such as *"Vivano il vinti quarto arti,"* the gathering was considered an insurrection. Between 1343 and September, 1378, we can identify 18 separate political insurrections in which 120 persons were tried.[47] During the regime of the

---

47. In *Florentine Politics and Society*, Professor Brucker was able to note several other riots in this period. The flood of November, 1966, and other current problems with archival storage have made these documents for the time being inaccessible.

Arti Minori, there were at least three insurrections in which 101 persons were tried. After the restoration of the oligarchy, 14 cases of insurrection were tried and 151 persons condemned.

Unfortunately, as we have noted in our study of the marriage relationships, the notaries of the late fourteenth century were not wont to identify individuals by profession. The Trecento notaries of the courts were no different. In the 18 insurrections which preceded the condemnations of the Otto di S. Maria Novella, only 24 individuals, or 28% of those condemned, were designated by a profession; in the period of counter-revolutionary conspiracies, 1380–1381, ten or slightly less than 10% of the participants were identified by an occupation; and in the 14 insurrections following the restoration of the oligarchy, the notaries identified 32 persons, or 21%, by a profession.

For the period preceding the revolt of the Otto di S. Maria Novella, we find that an extraordinary percentage of those who were identified by a profession, a title, or family name, were *sottoposti* of the wool and silk industries (81%). There were spinners, three dyers, a doublet-maker, and a tailor. Of the others identified by a profession, there were two furriers, a tanner, and a *balestriere* ('cross-bowman'), a craft which was outside the Florentine guild structure, and, therefore, should be considered as part of the *popolo minuto*. In the period of counter-revolutionary conspiracies, all 10 of those individuals identified by a profession practiced crafts which were outside the guild structure, and eight were Ciompi. When we consider all those whose status is clear from the documents, however, we find (because of the large numbers of notables bearing titles or family names) that these eight Ciompi comprised only 15% of the identifiable members of the crowd. Finally, in those insurrections following the restoration of the oligarchy, the importance of the Ciompi and the *popolo minuto* again is striking; 47% were *sottoposti* of the wool industry, and 57% were outside the Florentine guild system. If we then combine the two periods of revolution against the oligarchic regimes, we find that 38 persons, or 60% of those identified by profession, title, or family name were wage earners in the wool or silk industries. The composition of these crowds bears an interesting relationship to the composition of crowds during the French Revolution. In the list of *vaingueurs de la Bastille,* only 16% of those identified by profession were wage earners or workers in the manufactures of Paris.[48] Rudé argues that as the Parisian crowds became more politicized through the period 1791–1794, a greater proportion of wage earners comprised the revolutionary crowds, but at no point did wage earners dominate the leadership or composition of these

---

48. Rudé, *Paris and London in the Eighteenth Century,* 109.

crowds as they did in those insurrections of the Ciompi, 1343–1378 and 1382–1383.[49]

At this point, it might be argued that the meager percentages of those identified by occupation cannot adequately portray the composition of the Florentine crowds, that there may have been a bias in the identification of Ciompi occupations. For the period of the Ciompi, there does not exist a Bastille list as such. After the petitions of July, and the ousting of the oligarchies, no one was arrested. The revolt of the Ciompi was a success. With the fall of the radical wing of the Ciompi, the Otto di S. Maria Novella on August 31, 1378, however, there were arrests. For this incident, moreover, we possess two lists which do not rely on the notarial conventions of identification practiced in the courts. One comes from the chronicler Marchionne di Coppo Stefani, the other from the *Diario d'anonimo Fiorentina*, now believed to have been the writing of a member of the Machiavelli family.[50] In combining the two lists, we find 35 different individuals, of whom two bear family names, and 14 designated by occupation. We can thus determine the status of nearly half of the condemned—which more than doubles the percentage of those whose status we could observe in the lists of condemned found in the criminal sentences. Of those from the Otto di S. Maria Novella, there were a baker, a tavern keeper, a grave digger—lower status occupations within the *Arti Minori*. The remaining 11 identified by occupation were *sottoposti* in the wool industry: four skinners, three carders, a comber, a wool finisher, and a dyer. Thus, in this list of condemned insurrectionists, in which there exists a fair sampling of occupational identification, we again find a high proportion of the crowd as wage earners in the wool industry (69%).

Now that we have considered the leadership and the composition of the crowds during the period of the Ciompi (broadly conceived, 1343–1383), let us consider the question of ideology or motivation in more detail. As we have seen, the slogans which are sprinkled through some of the inquisitions of these insurrections leave us few and feeble traces for reconstruction. Much of the confusion in the interpretation of the Ciompi has resulted from the failure of historians to distinguish between the three historical phases of insurrections which we have outlined above. Some historians, minimizing the revolutionary role of the Ciompi, have thus concentrated on the two-year period, 1380–1381, the period of counter-revolution, and have pillaged these insurrections for materials

---

49. *Ibid.,* Rudé, 129 and 141.
50. *Cronaca fiorentina di Coppo Stefani,* rub. 807 and *Diario d'anomino fiorentino,* 384–85.

supporting a conservative interpretation of the Revolt of the Ciompi and the political role of the *popolo minuto*. The French historians, Philippe Wolff and Michel Mollat, for instance, have concluded:

> Such are the circumstances which explain the last and violent upheaval of the revolution at the end of August 1378. A mere incident or pretext was enough to catalyse the disappointment and the aspirations of the *minuti*. The judicial records of the repression which followed the new disorders throw a pitiful light on the credulity of the crowd in face of the mirage of apocalyptic prophecies; and on the naivete of its revolutionary dreams, devoid of any political sense. Thus Antonio di Ronco, one of the Ciompi, said: "The time will come when I shall no more wander about like a beggar, because I expect to be rich for the rest of my life; and if you will join me, you will become rich and we shall enjoy a brilliant situation in Florence." [51]

Unfortunately, Mollat and Wolff do not cite the source of this document. But, for the period preceding the fall of the Otto di S. Maria Novella, we do not find another like it; rather, it resembles closely the aspirations of those Ciompi who were manipulated during the early 1380s to join the counter-revolution against the government of the *Arti Minori*. But to understand the Ciompi, we must finally turn back to the Revolt of the Ciompi itself and consider its leadership and petitions. Just how much did it appear to have been dominated by demagoguery or millennarian ideals? How much was it the product of the personal clientelage of the Medici, Scala, and Strozzi? Was it really "devoid of any political sense"? Here the questions of ideology, motivation, and leadership or manipulation become intertwined.

As we have said, the Revolt of the Ciompi, the overthrow of the oligarchy on July 20–22, 1378, was successful. Afterward there were no arrests; nor did the Ciompi government or the government of the *Arti Minori* later grant titles, similar to the *vainqueurs de la Bastille*, to the insurgents of July, 1378. Thus, we are not left with a Bastille list to aid in analyzing its leadership and motivation in detail. [52] From the chronicle of Alamanno Acciaioli, a member of the overthrown Signoria of 1378, we learn that on the night of July 19, a certain Simincino, called Bugigatto, was captured, tortured, and interrogated. Far from being spontaneous or spasmodic, it becomes evident from Simincino's

51. Mollat and Wolff, *Ongles bleus*, p. 155.

52. See Jacques Godechot, *The Taking of the Bastille, July 14th, 1789*, translated by Jean Stewart (London, 1970), pp. 221–26; and Rudé, *Paris and London in the Eighteenth Century*, pp. 256–288.

testimony that the Ciompi uprising of July 20 relied on an organized
leadership and secret meetings held in various parts of the city:

> Yesterday, during that day, I (Simincino) and Pagolo del Bodda, Lioncino
> di Biagino, Lorenzo Ricomanni, Nardo di Camaldoli, Luca di Melano, Meo
> del Grasso, Zoccolo, and Guido Bandiera, Salvestrino from San Giorgia, il
> Guanda di Gualfonda and Galasso, we were twelve in all, went into the
> Hospital of the Priests in San Gallo street; and when we were there, others
> came from a place called de 'Belletrani and others of San Gallo; and there
> it was decided to begin the insurrection at three o'clock; and thus the order
> was given by certain officers, which we made at the Ronco outside and
> beyond the gate of San Piero Gattolino.[53]

Despite the connections of these 12 men with certain *ammoniti* and
the patrician Salvestro de'Medici, the organization and manipulation
of the masses was quite different from Andrea or Pagnotto Strozzi's
leadership of the hungry in 1342, or the later conspiracies against the
government of the *Arti Minori,* organized, led, and staffed in large part
by citizens of Florence bearing notable family names. Of the 12 revealed by Simincino, those who organized the secret meetings and
planned the strategies for insurrections—the leadership in the streets—
we do not find any patricians, but rather men who clearly appear to
have been common artisans, petty shopkeepers, and *sottoposti.*

After the ousting of the old oligarchy, the *popolo minuto* elected
their own Balia of 32, which effectively ran the government of the
Commune until the insurrection of the Otto di S. Maria Novella. Because of discontent with the justice rendered by the Podestà and the
Capitano, moreover, the government of the Ciompi on July 25 and
29 nominated their own judges and officials of the courts. Of the 12
elected (3 from each quarter), we again do not find the presence of
notable men; they were men without family names.[54] Among them
there were a certain Magister Christofanus Gensi (perhaps a grammar

---

53. *Cronache e memorie sul tumulto dei Ciompi,* edited by Scaramella, *Rerum Italicarum
Scriptores,* new edition, Vol. XVIII, Pt. 3 (Bologna, 1917), pp. 20–21.

"Ieri, in quello dì, io (Simoncino) e Pagolo del Bodda, Lioncino di Biagino, Lorenzo
Ricomanni, Nardo di Camaldoli, Luca di Melana, Meo del Grasso, Zoccolo, e Guido
Bandiera, Salvestrino da San Giorgio, il Guanda di Gualfonda e Galasso, e fummo in tutto
dodici, n'andammo nello spedale de Preti di via San Gallo; e quando fummo quivi,
vennono a nostra chiamata de'belletrani e altri di San Gallo; e quivi si determinò di
levare il rumore in sull'ora della terza; e così era data l'ordine per certi sindachi, che noi
facemmo nel Ronco fuora della Porta a Sanpiero Gattolini più di sono.

54. Falletti-Fossati, *Il tumulto dei Ciompi,* Doc. X, 119.

school teacher or a stone worker), a notary, and a son of a notary. In addition, we find a *riveditore* ('cloth finisher'), and a baker. Finally, despite his later cooptation (which has been carefully documented by Niccolò Rodolico) the Gonfaloniere of Justice, Michele di Lando, came from humble origins. And notwithstanding his later social success, during the summer of 1378, he was found among the ranks of the *Popolo di Dio*.[55]

The petitions of July 21 and 22, the changes in the officials of the Podestà and Capitano on July 25 and 27, and the changes instituted during the brief tenure in office of the Balìa of 32, moreover, do not reflect the heavy hand of a faction within the patriciate operating surreptitiously behind the scenes. The revolt of the Ciompi was indeed an amalgam of struggles; its success depended on their alliance with the *arti minori, ammoniti,* and even individuals such as Salvestro de'Medici, well ensconced in the oligarchy of Florence. From this amalgam should we be so cynical as to always expect the force and direction to have come from above, and conversely assume the passivity of the laboring classes? We find similar alliances and divisions of conflict in the French, Russian, and Chinese Revolutions.[56] On a more local level, the success or failure of labor movements in American cities during the early part of the twentieth century depended in large part on just how well welded the links were between workers and the community at large.[57]

Gene Brucker, Mollat, Wolff, and de Roover, on the other hand, have argued that the demands of July 21–22 were modest, and even reflected a deep-seated conservatism. Brucker has argued that the creation of the three revolutionary guilds was a throwback to former times— the restoration of the guild world of Dino Compagni. But the three guilds of 1378, which interlocked the whole of the *popolo minuto,* had only the name *arte* in common with the 72 or more guilds that structured the medieval economy of Dino Compagni.[58] Instead of a plethora

55. Rodolico, *La democrazia fiorentina,* pp. 200–06.

56. See, for instance, Albert Mathiez, *La Révolution Française* (Paris, 1922–1927); Georges Lefebvre, *The Coming of the French Revolution,* translated by R. R. Palmer (Princeton, 1947); Albert Soboul, *The French Revolution, 1787–1799,* translated by Forest and Jones (New York, 1974); E. H. Carr, *A History of Soviet Russia,* Vol. 1: *The Bolshevik Revolution, 1917–1923* (London, 1950); Charles Bettleheim, *Class Struggles in the U.S.S.R.: First Period, 1917–1923* (New York, 1977); and Mao Tse-Tung, "The Role of the Merchants in the National Revolution," and "Analysis of All the Classes in Chinese Society," in *The Political Thought of Mao Tse-Tung,* edited by Stuart R. Schram (New York, 1969), pp. 206–209 and 210–214.

57. See Herbert Gutman, *Work, Culture and Society in Industrializing America* (New York, 1977); and James Green, "The Brotherhood of Timber Workers, 1910–1913," *Past & Present,* no. 60 (1973), 161–200.

58. *La Cronica,* edited by I. Del Lungo in Rerum Italicarum Scriptores, 9, pt. 2 (Città di Castello, 1913), pp. 95–96.

of brotherhoods isolated and organized around various steps of production and crafts and outside the political world of the Commune, the three guilds of 1378 unified the wage earners of Florence in such a way that they could for the first time make demands which would alter the political and economic policy of the Commune. We have already reviewed their demands: those that concerned debts and debtors, the juridical authority of the Arte della Lana, production quotas, and the fiscal and monetary policy of the Commune. But it was, perhaps, their zeal to become incorporated within the political system of the Florentine Commune that lies at the crux of our argument. Brucker and others have seen this demand as obvious evidence of the Ciompi's nonrevolutionary character, of their desire to bolster rather than destroy "the system." We argue that these demands reflected instead a remarkable political consciousness for working men in an emerging capitalist society, especially a fourteenth-century one. Charles Tilly, in studying the transformation of protest in nineteenth-century France (which occurred roughly before and after 1850) has found the following distinction between old and modern forms of protest in regard to their position towards the state:

> The reactionary forms [of protest] (which include the invasion of fields, the tax revolt, food riot, the anticonscription rebellion, and perhaps machine breaking) all expressed the resistance of communal members of small polities to the claims of the national governments and national economies. The modern forms (the violent versions of strikes, demonstrations, revolutionary movements, and the like) typically involve associational contenders for power, *accepting rather than resisting* the priority of the national government over its rivals.[59]

In Florence, the centralized authority was the city–state, the government of the Commune of Florence.

It would be folly, however, to associate the revolt of the Ciompi, 1378, with strikes, working-class associations and protests in industrialized Europe of the second half of the nineteenth century. We do not find anticipations of an indigenous working-class ideology or (despite Ciuto Brandini's efforts) lasting working-class institutions. On the other hand, given the criteria for the "modernity" of protest outlined by Charles Tilly and George Rudé, the revolt of the Ciompi appears incredibly modern; we see more evidence of *associational* contenders than *communal* ones. The presence of women was uncommon; food riots were rare; the frequency of riots (1343–1383), occurred

---

59. Tilly, "How Protest Modernized," p. 201.

over a period of generally falling bread prices and rising wages. Although the Ciompi allied themselves with certain members of the patriciate, their leadership generally came from among their own ranks, and they organized their own secret meetings for planning strategy. And when they came to power (although they may have knighted Vieri de'Medici) they elected, in large part, members of the *popolo minuto*—a class which had previously been barred from office-holding—to administer justice and the affairs of the city. We find those forms of protest typical of *communal* contenders only during the brief period, 1379–1381, a period of counter-revolution against the broadly based coalition government of the *Arti Minori*. The leadership of these conspiracies was clearly the exiled aristocracy who successfully manipulated, paid off, or influenced by promises of vainglory and utopian rule certain destitute members of the *popolo minuto*.

But the "modernity" of the forms of protest during the period (broadly conceived) of the Ciompi must be put in context.[60] As argued

---

60. Tony Judt's suggestion in "A Clown in Regal Purple: Social History and the Historians," *History Workshop,* no. 7 (1979), pp. 66–94 that the work of Charles Tilly "ignores, and is ignorant of, politics" is altogether risible (to use Judt's oft-used adjective). In "Getting It Together in Burgundy, 1675–1975, *Theory and Society,* 4 (1977), 478–504, "Hauptformen kollektiver Aktion in Westeuropa, 1500–1975," and "Collective Violence in European Perspective," Tilly traces the transformations in the forms and repertoires of popular resistance in relation to the development of capitalism and, more importantly, in relation to the development of the state from absolutism to the modern nation state:

A food riot is nothing at all without a baker, merchant or city official to attack, a strike nonexistent unless a boss is somewhere on the scene. If that point seems obvious, its implications are not so self-evident. For it means that no explanation based entirely on the experiences of the rioters or strikers can be adequate. . . . Over the historical experience discussed in this paper, two large processes made the greatest difference to the interests of the ordinary people. One was the expansion of capitalist property relations, the other the rise of the national state. . . . We have seen statemaking at work concretely in the tax rebellion and the anticonscription riot, but also in the demand for female suffrage. The expansion of capitalism and the rise of the national state together created the world we live in. They set the frame for the changing forms of collective action, and therefore of collective violence. . . . As a result, the history of collective violence reflects the history of human collective experience as a whole ["Collective Violence in European Perspective," pp. 56–57].

The broad parallelism between the state and forms of popular protest which Tilly constructs over the *longue durée* of modern European history, however, is of little help in understanding the transformations in the "repertoires of resistance" over our nearly 200 years of the Renaissance in Florence. History does not always present neat parallelisms within "stages of history"; often the disjunctions and disequilibria in economic, social, and political developments are crucial for understanding change and historical processes. In Florence with the development of the Renaissance state, instead of a corresponding advance in the forms of popular protest, "the resources" available to the laboring classes were very much limited by the very development of this early modern state. As a consequence we will find the working in the earlier part of this book, the *popolo minuto* cannot be understood in isolation, in and of themselves; rather, they must be understood in relation to other classes in society and, in particular, in relation to the ruling elite. One wonders what forms the protests of the Ciompi would have assumed had the Commune of Florence resembled in structure the monarchy of Absolutist France, or even the oligarchy of Venice. In Trecento Florence there was a curious disequilibrium between the structures and organization of production, the organization of labor, and the development of the state. The burgeoning capitalist economy of fourteenth-century Florence was contained within a state apparatus that was essentially medieval. After the defeat of the Ciompi and the development of statecraft through the Quattrocento rule of the Medici, this balance was to shift. Before beginning an examination of this shift in polity, and its consequences for the *popolo minuto*, let us now attempt to describe the nature of protest during the second period of our analysis, the mid-Quattrocento.

---

classes of the late Quattrocento regressing into more defensive and primitive forms of resistance. For another study which stresses the importance of disequalibria in historical development over the long term, see the magisterial work of Robert Fossier, *La terre et les hommes en Picardie*, 2 vols. (Paris, 1968); for one which considers the short term, see Leon Trotsky, *The Russian Revolution: The Overthrow of Tzarism and the Triumph of the Soviets*, ed. F. W. Dupree (New York, 1932).

Chapter 7

Class Struggle II

$\mathcal{T}$HE fact that the *popolo minuto* was not a static force during the *longue durée* of the Renaissance can be seen in the transformation of the forms and frequencies of popular protests between the late fourteenth and late fifteenth centuries. In contrast to the middle and late fourteenth century, the most salient characteristic of the *popolo minuto* in late fifteenth-century Florentine society, was their silence. But how does one argue from silence? Might the change, instead of reflecting a change in political activity or political consciousness, reflect changes in the documentation and changes in those institutions which so directly touched the lives of the popular classes—the criminal tribunals?

Indeed, during the Quattrocento, with the rise of humanist historiography, the chronicle tradition of Florentine history (one of the major sources for our knowledge of the Ciompi) declines.[1] We do not find another substantial chronicle of Florentine history with an ear to the ground, interested in the opinions and problems of the *popolo minuto,* until the last decade of the fifteenth century. Second, the court system of Florence and its apparatus of surveillance experienced a fundamental transformation from the late Trecento through the early modern period which does affect the documentary basis of popular insurrection. With the defeat of the Otto di S. Maria Novella, the Commune of Florence created the Otto di Guardia on September 2, 1378. By the middle of the Quattrocento, this court and its apparatus for surveillance had become the dominant criminal tribunal in Florence.[2] It was a summary

---

1. Marvin Becker, "Florentine Politics and the Diffusion of Heresy in the Trecento: A Socioeconomic Inquiry," *Speculum,* XXXIV (1959), 74–75.

2. Giovanni Antonelli, "La magistratura degli Otto di Guardia a Firenze," *Archivio Storico Italiano,* CXII (1954), 3–40.

court, not presided over by a foreign notable as in the medieval Italian tradition of jurisprudence; rather, its powers rested directly under the control of the Signoria.

Eight citizens, almost always from notable Florentine families, tried the indicted by vote; fundamental procedures of fairness—a written inquisition of the alleged crime, the testimony of the defense, and the testimony of the prosecution—were eliminated. As a result, the records of the Otto di Guardia, unlike the pages of information which often filled the records of even a single case in the Capitano del Popolo, the Podestà, or the Esecutore, are bare indeed. In the cases of the Otto, we usually find only the name of the defendant and his sentence. Often there is not even a clue about the crime allegedly committed, much less the precise information contained in the records of the late medieval courts—the name(s) of the victim(s), the place of the crime, an exact description of the injuries inflicted. Moreover, the records of the Otto before 1468 have been lost almost completely. There is a *filza* covering the semester, 1408–1409, and two *filze* covering 8 months of business in 1460.

From Giovanni Antonelli's study of the Otto di Guardia, we can follow through the *provvisioni* the evolution of this court's importance in criminal jurisprudence from its foundation until 1502, when the remaining medieval criminal courts, the Podestà and the Capitano, were abolished.[3] Through the Quattrocento, furthermore, the Otto's "opinions" impinged more and more on the court proceedings of the Capitano and the Podestà. Indeed, for the suppression of political violence, or the threat of such violence, the Otto generally collaborated with the forces of the Podestà and the Capitano—their *famuli* and, to a point, their courts, notaries, and judges. Thus, the possibility of observing insurrections, conspiracies, and political violence in general may not be as faint for the mid-Quattrocento as a glance through the inventories of the Otto and the nature of their deliberations might at first appear.

Despite the decline of the chronicle tradition and the problems imposed by changes in the courts and their documentation, we have the testimony of silence from Niccolò Machiavelli. In the preface to his *Istorie fiorentine*, Machiavelli justified the writing of another history of Florence by criticizing his humanist predecessors, Leonardo Bruni and Poggio Bracciolini.[4] Although these narratives, according to Machiavelli, were excellent when they concerned conflict between the Floren-

---

3. The Esecutore degli Ordinamenti di Giustizia was abolished in 1434 with the coming to power of the Medici.

4. Niccolò Machiavelli, *Istorie fiorentine*, in *Opere*, Vol. VII, edited by Franco Gaeta (Milan, 1962), p. 65.

tines and other foreign powers, he found them deficient in their analysis of internal, civil discord. By civil discord, it becomes clear that Machiavelli means something more than those intrigues staged by one ruling family against another: *"Ma di Firenze in prima si divisono intra loro i nobili, di poi i nobili e il popolo, e in ultimo il popolo e la plebe."* [5]

The first half of the *Istorie* brings the history of Florence to the return of the Medici in 1434. A central event of this half of Florentine history from its foundations was the Ciompi uprising; it was the turning point, as important to the course of Florentine history as the return of the Medici. In the second half of the *Istorie*, Machiavelli could fall victim to the same criticism he leveled against his humanist predecessors. The narrative is almost completely entangled with affairs which we might call diplomatic history, the intrigues and struggles between the Florentine state and its foreign neighbors. Below this level of conflict, only those struggles *"intra loro i nobili"* find place. The importance and impact of the *popolo minuto* on the affairs of state or on Florentine society more generally almost completely disappear following the collapse of the Arti Minori in 1382. Now, the reader might well question why this is so. After all, the circumstances of its commission made the *Istorie* skirt gingerly certain topics relating to the Medici's coming to power.

In a letter written by Donato Gianotti, a close friend of Machiavelli, the conflict of interests presented by Machiavelli's patronage and his solution to the dilemma are clarified. According to Donato, Machiavelli had commented on the sincerity of his *Istorie fiorentine*:

> I cannot write this history from the time when Cosimo came to power to the death of Lorenzo as I would write it if I were in all respects free; the actions will be true and I shall omit nothing only I shall leave in the background the discussions of the general causes of things; for example, I shall describe the events and the happenings that followed Cosimo's taking the state, but I shall leave in the background the discussion of how and by what means and cleverness a single individual came to such a height. Let him who would like really to understand me note well what I make his opponents say; what I would be unwilling to say as coming from myself I shall put into the mouths of the opponents. [6]

But the source of conflict in interest and ideology between Machiavelli and the Medici was on the level of those conflicts *intra loro i nobili*,

---

5. *Ibid.*, N. Machiavelli, p. 69.
6. Myron Gilmore, Introduction to *Machiavelli: The History of Florence and Other Selections,* edited by Gilmore (New York, 1970), xxvii.

and here Machiavelli does not refrain from presenting these conflicts either surreptiously or explicitly. The other levels of conflict, and especially those *fra il popolo e la plebe* would have presented no serious conflict of interest. Machiavelli was no republican in a nineteenth-century sense, and certainly no proto-socialist. His interpretation of the tumult of the Ciompi leaves little doubt about his class identity and sympathies. Machiavelli's silence, instead, must reflect something about the social and political realities of Quattrocento Florence, which are corroborated by the silences in the criminal records of the Capitano and the Podestà—the almost complete disappearance of those long lists of condemned *popoli minuti* accused of *"starent . . . in turbationem seditionem et tumultum presentis status pacifici et tranquilli civitatis Florentie. . . ."*

To probe into the nature of a class conflict, to cut beneath those political intrigues, principally among the patriciate, with which the Quattrocento historians concerned themselves, we have scrutiniezd 11 years of the surviving criminal records from the Podestà, the Capi-tano, and the Otto di Guardia. This period extends from the first semester of court proceedings in 1454 through 1466. This decade was chosen for several reasons. First, from the perspective of constitutional order and unrest between the Medici and various factions within the oligarchy, the decade 1454–1466 was certainly the most critical of Cosimo's rule, and perhaps even the most important time of struggle for power until 1494, the Pazzi Conspiracy of 1476, notwithstanding. In 1454, the patriciate were able to institute reforms which refur-bished the constitutional, electoral, and administrative structures of the oligarchic rule which preceded the Medici Balìa of 1434.[7] In 1457, there was an abortive anti-Medici conspiracy, followed by a sharp reaction from the Medici. The leader of the patrician faction, Girolamo Machia-velli, was exiled in August, and, shortly afterwards, the Commune exiled another 150 citizens.[8] These purges, 5 days later, led to the "Parlamento of 1458":

> On 9 August, Astorre, Lord of Faenza, was expected with 300 cavalry and 50 infantry. On the tenth, the Signoria ordered all citizens over 14 to come the next morning unarmed to the Piazza. When they arrived, they found the Piazza and the streets leading to it heavily guarded by mercenary troups and armed citizens. Then, the Signoria appeared on the rostrum in front of the palace, and a notary read out the text of a law

---

7. Nicolai Rubinstein, *The Government of Florence Under the Medici, 1434–1494* (Oxford, 1966), p. 88.
8. A(tti del) C(apitano del) P(opolo) n. 3866, fol. 34r–35v.

creating a new Balìa. . . Its main purpose was twofold, to resuscitate the system of control which had been ended in 1454–1455, and to put it on a permanent basis by making it a part of the constitution.[9]

Following the Parlamento, cautious of any alliance between organized opposition within the city, the Balìa extended the sentences of exile in 1434, and banished as well the sons and descendents of the exiled.[10] Finally, the secession of Piero in 1464 led to another temporary breakdown in the Medici hegemony. Factionalism, perhaps in part structured along recurrent lines of *novi homines* and the established families of Florence, flared again.[11] Luca Pitti, Niccolò Soderini, and others within the patriciate tried once more to wrench control from its locus on the Via Larga and to reinstate either a pre-Medicean oligarchy or to restructure Florentine government along the lines of the Venetian "mixed government." [12]

Second, the first signs of a deterioration in labor relations in the silk industry (perhaps as important an employer by the middle of the century as the wool industry) are revealed in the reforms of the statutes of Por S. Maria instituted in 1458. The consuls were empowered "to impose corporal punishment, send delinquents to the pillory or even subject suspects to torture, because so many offenders, it is explained, were poor people unable to pay fines." [13]

Third, Professor Molho has discovered in the *ricordanze* of Francesco di Tommaso Giovanni, an officer of the Otto di Guardia, the only popular insurrection of any proportion known from the protests of the *Arti Minori* in 1414 to the time of Savonarola.[14] Although this incident, which involved the wresting of a thief from the hangman's noose by a group of neighbors, cannot compare with the massive insurrections of the middle and late Trecento, Francesco Giovanni's description of the surrounding crowd and the ensuing rock-throwing let loose by the incident reveals the seething bitterness of the *popolo minuto* and the tensions beneath the generally harmonious constitutional structure of Cosimo's rule.

---

9. Rubinstein, *The Government of Florence*, 103–104.

10. ACP n. 3867, 17v, 18r–v, 19r.

11. Guido Pampaloni, "Fermenti di riforme democratiche nella Firenze Medicea del quattrocento," *Archivio Storico Italiano*, XCIX (1961), 37–38.

12. *Ibid.*, Guido Pampaloni, p. 37.

13. Raymond de Roover, "Labour Conditions in Florence Around 1400: Theory, Policy and Reality," in *Florentine Studies: Politics and Society in Renaissance Florence*, edited by Rubinstein (London, 1968), p. 293.

14. Anthony Molho, "Cosimo de'Medici: Pater Patriae or Padrino," *Stanford Italian Review* (1979), pp. 13–15; and Carte Strozziane, Serie II^a, 16 bis, 24v.

Finally, these political crises occurred against a backdrop of economic recession, with recovery commencing by the latter part of 1458. In 1457, there was a major epidemic, and in 1458 the Commune issued fiscal reforms and administered the first *catasto* survey since 1433. These events and conditions would suggest that if we are to attempt to find the *popolo minuto* politically active or generally riotous, the decade 1454–1466 would be as profitable to probe as any decade during the fifteenth century, at least before 1494.[15] We shall be able to view the *popolo minuto* both in a period of hardship and in one of economic recovery.

As has been mentioned, the Otto di Guardia frequently intervened in the business of the Podestà and the Capitano. At these junctures, the characteristic formula of the courts headed by the foreign magistrates yielded to that of the Otto. These sentences are introduced by the Capitano or Podestà and then are followed by the statement: "And with the force of this particular pronouncement of the magnificent eight lords in the custody and authority of the said city of Florence . . ."[16] According to Giovanni Antonelli, the Otto intervened or collaborated with the agencies of the Podestà or Capitano to suppress and try political crimes, insurrections, offenses, and threats to the state.[17] But what does this mean? In the period under observation, these cases ranged from homicide[18] to theft[19] to embezzlement[20] to blasphemy[21] to conspiracies against the government and perhaps mass insurrection.[22] For the most part, however, it is impossible to discern the exact nature of the violation contained in these cases. Of 68 interventions of the Otto into the affairs of the Podestà and Capitano during our period, 38 cases do not provide any description whatsoever of the offense. There appears only the formulaic introduction, the name or names of the accused, and the sentence.

Nonetheless, the mere appearance of the Otto in the criminal pro-

---

15. The criminal records, 1455–1466, are not a continuous series. Of the records of the Podestà and the Capitano, the sentences from nine semesters are missing. These cluster in the period roughly between 1461 and 1464.

16. A(tti del) P(odestà) n 5065, fol. 31r; "*Et hoc vigore ciuisdam buletini Magnificorum dominorum otto custodie et bailie dicte civitate Florentie. . .*"

17. Antonelli, "La magistratura degli Otto," p. 7.

18. ACP n. 3866, fol. 37v and 47v.

19. ACP n. 3867, 6r.

20. ACP n. 3950, fol. 2r.

21. ACP n. 3950, fol. 126 and no pagination, 26 March, 1464.

22. ACP n. 3842, fol. 6r; n. 3852, 16r–19v; n. 3866, 35r, 30r, 30v, 34r; n. 3867, fol. 3r; n. 3868, fol. 7v–9r; n. 3981, fol. 30r; AP n. 5108, fol. 53r–v.

cedures of the other courts suggests, on the one hand, unusual concern on the part of the Signoria, and, on the other hand, social tensions and potential threats to the Signoria's domination. During our period, these interventions increased dramatically in 1459 and 1460. By 1461, they begin again to taper off. Even though there is a paucity of data for the years 1462–1463, by 1464, when the documentation again approaches completeness, these interventions are only a small proportion of what they had been at the turn of the decade.

From those cases that do contain the barest descriptions, these interventions of the Otto suggest a markedly different sort of criminality from those cases that otherwise predominated in the protocols of the Podestà and Capitano: simple debts, theft, card games, rural poaching, trespass, *mezzadri* refusing to work the land, and contempt of court. Of the 33 cases whose nature can be in some part discerned, 14 concerned alleged conspiracies or armed insurrections. Of these, more than half pertained to those exiled by the Parlamento of 1458, the strengthening of control by the Medici faction immediately following the Parlamento, and the renewal of the sentences of exile of 1434 and an extension of these sentences to the male heirs.

Beyond these threats to Medici domination from factions within the Florentine oligarchy, four other insurrections appear in the criminal archives, three of which provoked the intervention of the Otto. Of these, three occurred in the subject towns—S. Miniato al Tedesco, Castiglion Fiorentino, and Cortona. Three clearly were directed by members of the patriciate and, as far as the records reveal, were composed entirely of patricians. In the single conspiracy within the city of Florence, the Capitano del Popolo indicted Carlo di Benedetto de'Bardi on November 19, 1457, for conspiring with Piero de Giovanni de'Ricci, Alammano di Giovannello di Arnario, and Giovanni di Niccolò in the house of Dioneo di Matteo di Arnario on the corner of del Gilglo in Via della Scala, near Prato Ognissanti.[23] The notary of the Capitano del Popolo recorded a conversation allegedly between the conspirators. Piero's first questions:

> Why do we not have 100,000 florins apiece? If we had it, we would know well how to spend it and would now be having a good time.[24]

The others replied:

---

23. ACP n. 3842, 6r.
24. ACP n. 3842, 6r, *Perchè non abbiamo cento milia fiorini per uno? Perchè al mancho ce farramo bon tempo et sapere modi despendere?"*

Do you believe that 50 gentlemen like ourselves with the same spirit and will could incite the people? [25]

Carlo answered:

Why yes, and even with a smaller number.[26]

The others confirmed his confidence:

Yes, and even with less than the mentioned 50 men . . . considering that the *popolo minuto* is starving to death.[27]

Carlo then revealed his ambitions:

I would like to be a grand master who could squeeze the many who have sucked this land in the time of war. There would be few who are sent back to their offices or returned to the Monte office and few would be spared.[28]

Piero added:

Cosimo, if I would like to spare him . . .? [29]

But Carlo contested:

That one would be the first to go.[30]

Alammano, at this point, intervened:

O let us talk about something else.[31]

But Carlo insisted, ironically:

There are a hundred things to talk about, but to talk thus would only postpone the fun.[32]

---

25. *Loc. cit.*, "Credete voy che cinquanta homini da bene come noy di uno medesemo animo et volunta levassero quisto popolo?"

26. *Loc. cit.*, "Che si et anchi menor numero."

27. *Loc. cit.*, "Sic et menor numeras dictorum quinquaginta hominium . . . consideratum quod populus minutus moratur fame."

28. "Io vorrei essere uno grande maestro che potese demagrar parichi che fanno pop(p)ata questa terra nel tempo de la guerra. Che serreno pochi che non facese reporre su et remandarli al Monte et pochi ne preservarci."

29. *Ibid.*, 6v, "Cos(i)mo, se vorrei preservare. . .?"

30. *Loc. cit.*, "Quello serebbe el primo."

31. *Loc. cit.*, "O però ragioniamo d'altro."

32. *Loc. cit.*, "Ce sonno cento ragionamenti, ragioniamo d'altro adtendiamo ad godere."

This interchange reveals several things. First, it confirms that there existed severe economic conditions for the Florentine *popolo minuto* during 1457. Second, the patriciate regarded these conditions with an eye for furthering their individual ambitions. Third, there was very little ideological basis for the popular insurrection. Beyond his own ambition to be master and to enjoy the fruits of the land, Carlo de'Bardi expressed little more than discontent with the war faction in the Medici regime and bitterness toward Cosimo himself. But their plans failed. Their discontent did not precipitate an aristocratic conspiracy, much less an armed insurrection with popular support. Were their plans entirely stifled by the Medici power of surveillance and repression? Would the starving *popolo minuto* have been willing and ready to support an ambitious faction within the patriciate against the Medici government?

The other three conspiracies were confined to incidents occurring in the subject towns, Cortona, S. Miniato al Tedesco, and Castiglion Fiorentino. Unfortunately, the inquisitions of the Capitano and Podestà are not nearly so rich as they would have been in the Trecento. The inquisitions provide only certain formulaic phrases: *"turbulenta insulta," "fecerunt congregationem cum armis,"* and the names of the condemned and their sentences. In August, 1457, five men, three of whom were brothers, and four of whom were distinguished as "Ser," "led many men" and seized the castle of S. Miniato, which housed the local officials of the Otto.[33] They demanded that the *cavaleri* of the Otto free their brother (whose name is not mentioned in the document). On August 6, 1461, the Otto prosecuted eight men of uncertain status, none of whom possessed a family name. The majority of the condemned originated from small places in the *contado* or the surrounding territory of Cortona—Mesigliuolo, Montalla, S. Marco, Terontola, Bacciolle, and Foligiachi de Perugia.[34] These men, for reasons not revealed in the brief inquisition, stole several books from the archives of Cortona which were necessary for governing the city *(gubernantie causam)*, and thereby violated the *dignitatem rei publice Florentine.* The eight men were sentenced to 10 years of exile in the Commune of Pisa.

Finally, the most important insurrection during our period broke out in Castiglion Florentino. Three separate cases concerned this insurrection which the Otto di Guardia tried through the auspices of the Podestà and Capitano on June 7, June 16, and June 25, 1466.[35] A Ser Michele di Ser Martino di Iacopo, Paolo di Marco *fabbro*, a Ser Martino,

---

33. ACP n. 3866, 34r.
34. ACP n. 3901, 7r.
35. AP n. 5108, 53r–v; ACP n. 3981, fol. 30r, 34r.

and a certain Santo di Domenico del Mencho, all *Priores* of the city of Castiglion Florentino, organized a congregation of "many armed men" at the palace of the Priores for the purposes of rousing unrest throughout the Commune of Castiglion Florentino.[36] These Priores were exiled from the *"terra"* of Castiglione for a year. The insurrection, clearly organized from the top by the Priores of the city, but perhaps encompassing lower-class participants, was clearly the protest of a subject town against the centralizing domination of Florence.

None of these conspiracies, obliquely revealed through the records of the Podestà and Capitano, suggests popular insurrection, although the muscle of the *popolo minuto* may have buttressed the patriciate's designs and discontents. How can we then talk about class struggle in the middle of the fifteenth century? Do the criminal records leave any clues, show any overt manifestations? First, the threat of patrician conspiracy was not the only threat which deserved the Otto's scrutiny; but certainly, the members of patrician families were its major focus. In those cases in which the defendants can be identified either by profession or a family name, sixteen involved persons with family names, five involved minor guildsmen, and six, *sottoposti*. However, if we count the individuals instead of the number of cases, over 85 persons appear with family names; whereas, the number of minor guildsmen and *sottoposti* were equivalent to the number of cases pertaining to them, thus, five and six respectively. Moreover, from these condemnations of prominent members of the patriciate, the number of individuals involved remains uncertain. The condemnations were often directed not against particular individuals, but against families and, in particular, the male line of these families *(omnes et singuli filii descendentes per lineam masculinam)*. On November 6, 1458, the Otto renewed sentences of exile against prominent families who were condemned by the Parlamento of 1434; De Castellanis, De Bardis, De Ardingellis, De Belfradelli, De Strozzis, De Peruzzis, De Guasconivus, De Rondinellis, De Branchaciis, De Guadagnis, De Baltovinettis.[37] In this condemnation, no individual is named, only these families and *omnes et singuli filii et descendentes quicumque et qualiter cuiusque per lineam masculinam infrascriptarum familiarum*. In addition, the Otto di Guardia found it judicious to intervene in the business of the Podestà and Capitano to prosecute *sottoposti* in the wool and silk industries as well as members

---

36. ACP n. 3981, 30r, ". . . *essent de prioribus dicte terre Castiglione . . . noctis tempore fecerunt congregrationem pluribus et pluribus hominibus cum armis offendibilibus et defendibilibus in dicto palatio priorum pro commictendo scandelam in dicte terre."*

37. ACP n. 3868, 7v–9r.

of the *Arti Minori*. Some of these condemnations, in which only the sentence—usually a severe one such as long exile in the region of Pisa or death—was reported, might suggest, nonetheless, the possibility of popular protests or organization and preparation for insurrectionary activity.

For instance, on August 21, 1461, a certain spinner, Fioravante di Meo di Mancino of the parish of S. Lorenzo, was exiled for life to remain beyond the borders of the city, *contado*, and the district of Florence.[38] On November 21, 1459, a certain Salvestro di Francesco di Lorenzo, a *reveditore* ('wool finisher'), was condemned *ad penum rebelionis*.[39] The Otto refrained from reporting the nature of the crime in order to apprehend *alios rebelles* who were associated with the wool finisher Salvestro.

Beyond these incidents, which may have in fact been insurrections of considerable dimensions or may have included only several wool or silk workers involved in petty misdemeanors, there are other incidents reported in the Capitano and Podestà which certainly did not bring large numbers of workers together with any internal planning or organization. These incidents, highly individualistic, which pertained perhaps only to a single grievance against a single land owner or patrician, suggest best the character of class conflict in the middle of the fifteenth century. On August 23, 1459, the Otto intervening in the business of the Podestà sentenced a certain Nardo di Meo di Nardo alias Nardello of the parish of S. Maria a Carraia in the *contado* of Florence to ten years of hard labor. He attacked, "armed with certain weapons," Buoncorso di Luca di Messer Giovanni Rucellai of the parish of San Pancrazio. Nardo's blows drew blood and, according to the inquisition, *"fecit scandelam tam in civitate quam in Comune."*[40] The actual conditions and motivations for Nardo's attack, of course, are not explained.

In March, 1460, a Eugenio di Pier del Lepre from S. Lorenzo, *homo superbus rissosus et scandalosus* stabbed Antonio di Angelo de'Pepi, a citizen of Florence. Through their *bulletini*, the Otto exiled Eugenio from the city, *contado*, and district of Florence.[41] On July 23, 1464, the Podestà sentenced several *contadini (lavoratori di terra)* from the suburban parish of S. Maria a Settignano for calling the patrician lady, Margherita di Dolfo di Canto di Dolfo *lanaiolo*, the wife of Antonio di Gamberello de'Gamberelli of Florence, a "putana, troia et ribalda."[42]

---

38. AP n. 5035, fol. 33r.
39. ACP n. 2866, 30r.
40. *Ibid.*, 25r.
41. *Ibid.*, 43r.
42. AP n. 5098, 48v.

Finally, on March 26, 1464, a certain Piero, son of a former Giovanni di Piero Bruscianese called Caviglia from the village of S. Maria al Mole, set fire to and destroyed a tile-covered barn and 12 stariora of land located at Monte Calvoli belonging to Bartolommeo, the emancipated son of Messer Carlo di Agnolo di Filippo de'Pandolfini, citizen of Florence.[43]

It is curious to note that Benedetto, who suffered these acts of primitive rebellion against his rural properties from the hand of at least one of his *contadini*, was the grandson of Agnolo Pandolfini. Until the middle of the nineteenth century it was believed that Agnolo Pandolfini was the author of Leon Battista Alberti's third book of *Della Famiglia, Economicus*. Sometime during the late Renaissance a member of the Pandolfini family had changed the names in Alberti's manuscript and had attributed the text's authorship to the ancestor of their *stirpe*.[44] In the *Civilization of the Renaissance in Italy* Jacob Burckhardt singles out this work to exemplify the Renaissance's ideal of the life on the rural estate: its pastoral bliss and security.[45]

The criminal archives of the middle of the fifteenth century, moreover, reveal a type of social conflict that did not appear in our samples for the late fourteenth century: the household revolt, domestic slaves and servants poisoning or attempting by other means to murder or injure their masters. The Capitano, on June 16, 1460, condemned Lucia Tarta, the domestic slave of Zanobi, son of the former Bernardo di' Gerolini of the parish of S. Romolo.[46] According to the inquisition of the Capitano, Lucia, in order that she could live with her patron and "satisfy her immoderate appetites" *(immoderatos eos appetitios satisfacere)*, entered a shop in S. Piero Maggiore and bought a potion of poison which she planned to mix in the lunch prepared for her patron's wife. For the attempted crime, Lucia was to be flagellated while being led from place to place in the city until she reached the place of justice. There, "before her eyes" her nose was to be amputated and then she was to be burnt at the stake.

On October 14, 1460, the Capitano accused the Tartan Chiara, a former slave of donna Agata, the daughter of former Domenico di Iacopo de'Benini of Florence, the wife of Lorenzo di Zanobi de'Brogietti of the parish of S. Paolo and presently the servant of Marco di Bernardo, an armor manufacturer, of assaulting her former patron in the face and

---

43. *Ibid.*, 163r.

44. Girolamo Mancini, *Vita di Leon Battista Alberti*, 2nd edition (Florence, 1911), pp. 233–240.

45. Jacob Burckhardt, *The Civilization of the Renaissance in Italy*, translated by C. S. Middlemore (New York, 1954), pp. 297–299.

46. ACP n. 3867, 52r–v.

thereby drawing blood. The incident allegedly occurred in the Via Benedicta in the parish of S. Paolo. Chiara was absolved.[47]

From these laconic descriptions in the criminal inquisitions, it is difficult to say very much about assaults by the lower orders of Florentine society against the patriciate. The burning of the Pandolfini's barn, after all, could have been caused by simple negligence. Lucia's scheme to murder her *patrona* perhaps may have derived simply (as the inquisition states) from her immoderate sexual appetite and desire for her patron. Yet these incidents, along with other charges of slander and physical abuse directed against patricians which can be found in the criminal archives, reflect resentment, highly individualistic to be sure, and hardly politically efficacious, that nonetheless from time to time crystallized into an act of violence and protest. These individual acts might be labeled acts of atomized rebellion.[48] This category, quite unlike the networks for collective protest of the late fourteenth century, brackets the dimensions and possibilities of fifteenth century popular protest.

Nonetheless, popular protest did persist, and these acts taken in the aggregate determined (at least in part) the limits of just what bosses, landlords, and magistrates felt they could get away with. The impact of these individual acts of protest and the lack of deference that regularly surface in the criminal records is impossible to measure and, given the terseness of the Quattrocento records, even difficult to describe. From other studies, however, of slaves in antebellum North America,[49] workers in Nazi Germany,[50] forced labor in twentieth-century Southern Rhodesia,[51] bandits in various civilizations,[52] and yeomen in eighteenth-century England,[53] we would be foolish to assume that these atomized acts were in fact as isolated or independent from the social fabric and political relations as their cases appear in the criminal records. On the

---

47. ACP n. 3891, 21v.

48. For a similar description, see E. P. Thompson, "Crimes of Anonymity," in *Albion's Fatal Tree*, edited by D. Hay, P. Linebaugh, J. Rule, Thompson and C. Winslow (New York, 1975), pp. 255–308.

49. Eugene Genovese, *Roll, Jordan Roll: The World the Slaves Made* (New York, 1972)

50. Timothy W. Mason, *Sozial politik im Dritten Reich: Arbeiterklasse und Volksgemeinschaft* (Opladen, 1977); and Molly Nolan, "Social Policy, Economic Mobilization and the Working Class in the Third Reich: A Review of the Literature," *Radical History Review*, IV, 2–3 (1977).

51. Charles van Onselen, "Worker Consciousness in Black Miners in Southern Rhodesia, 1900–1920," *Journal of African History*, 14 (1973), 237–255; and *Chibaro: African Mine Labor in Southern Rhodesia, 1900–1933* (London, 1976).

52. Eric Hobsbawn, *Bandits* (London, 1969)

53. E. P. Thompson, *Whigs and Hunters: The Origin of the Black Act* (London, 1975); and "Crimes of Anonymity."

one hand they required the cooperation of others not indicted or at least the silent collusion of fellow laborers and parishioners. On the other hand, news of these "individual outbursts" must have traveled, albeit with weak undulations, both among the land-owning, mercantile, and ruling classes and throughout the communities of laborers and peasants. The repercussions of these acts which defined the outer limits of the hegemony of Renaissance culture would require another study—a study, given the documentation, that might be impossible for fifteenth-century Florence. But from the evidence presented in this chapter it is at least safe to assume that the descriptions by Lionardo Alberti, Giovanni Rucellai, and Angelo Poliziano [54] of the subordinate classes' supposed passivity and deference cannot be taken on face value. Rude acts of resistance and protest intermittently punctuated the ideology of pastoral bliss and late Quattrocento paternalism.

The collective manifestations of fifteenth-century popular protest are the exceptions which prove the rule; they are limited indeed. Thus far, we have found only two examples, both occurring within a year of each other during the period of severe recession in Florence, 1457–1458. Six men, four identified professionally as silk weaver, vegetable vendor, carpenter, and cobbler, one night in August, 1457, armed with long iron lances and knives *("armati lancis longis feratis et cultelesis")* stabbed Cambio di Giovanni di Cambio, an officer *(familiarius)* of the Otto di Guardia, then residing in the parish of S. Lucia Ognissanti. The six stabbed Cambio near his home. The description of this insurrection against the Otto is found only in the inquisition of the Podestà; there is no trace of the crime in the records of sentences.[55] Presumably, the case was then subjected directly to the jurisprudence of the Otto di Guardia, whose deliberations for the year 1457 are missing. Once again, the motivations which brought these six men together to attack Cambio and thereby to offend, more generally, the strong arm of the state, the Otto di Guardia, are not stated in the criminal documents. The configuration of residences of these contenders, nonetheless, suggests something about the character of their protest. Five of the six lived roughly in the same neighborhood as the injured, Cambio, in parishes adjacent to S. Lucia Ognissanti. Only one participant, Bernardo di Iacopo, a silk weaver, came from another quarter and ecological cluster in the city, the parish church of S. Michele Visdomini, in the quarter of S. Giovanni; whereas, four of the six were neighbors of the same parish

---

54. Molho, "Cosimo de'Medici," pp. 16–17.
55. AP n. 5008, 2r–8v.

church, S. Paolo, which by the middle of the fifteenth century was not a particularly large parish in population or in territory.

The description of the second incident of collective violence initiated by members of the *popolo minuto* is more vivid; it derives not from the terse, clinical descriptions contained in the judicial sentences, but from the *ricordanze* ('personal memoirs') of a member of the Otto di Guardia, Francesco di Tommaso Giovanni. Recently, Anthony Molho has analyzed this incident in detail. Below is an abridged version of Francesco's description:

On the seventh of July, while the *Capitano* of the *Otto* was sending Antonio di Piero Boccino di Vercaia, a thief, to be executed, the condemned man's mother, seeing her son led away, began wailing in the Piazza della Signoria. No sooner had she started than a tumult (*romore*) began, the armed escort was assaulted by the onlookers, the thief freed, led to the church of San Firenze and then taken to Santa Croce where he was hidden in the church's roof. . . The Otto were immediately mobilized, especially because "the people had risen in a tumult" (*levandosi il popolo a romore*). Clearing the crowd from the Piazza de'Signoria, they made their way toward Santa Croce, amid a hostile crowd which pelted the passing officials with rocks. Finally, gaining access to the church with the aid of four *maestri* sent over by the priores, they found the thief hiding behind a beam in the room, brought him down, and dragged him back to the Piazza de'Signoria which was *piena di popolo*. Summarily condemned for his new crime, he was decapitated in front of the *Porta del Capitano* before "a huge crowd" (*infinito popolo*). "And in this way," Francesco concludes . . . "we disabused the people of their bad habits" (*isgannano il popolo perchè non s'avezzi*). But the story does not end here, for a few days later the Otto discovered that what had seemed only a spontaneous and accidental series of events was nothing of the sort. Indeed, on the day preceding the incident, a conspiracy had been spawned by the thief's *vicini ed amici* who had gathered by the church of the Camaldoli, carefully planned the operation and preordained that the mother's wailing was to be the sign to charge the Capitano and free the prisoner. Eighteen men were arrested as promoters of the conspiracy, and "because they were poor people" it was decided to punish them not by the imposition of a fine, but by exiling them from Florence.[56]

The 18 men were certainly not linked together by occupation. Of the 11 identified by occupation, all were probably within the ranks of the *popolo minuto*. There were a carpenter, a house painter, two weavers,

---

56. Molho, "Cosimo de'Medici," pp. 13–14.

a wine seller, a messenger, a cook, one who lived or worked in the Communal brothel, a goldsmith's assistant, a cobbler, and a baker. According to Francesco's *ricordanze*, six were identified by popolo, and all six lived in those two parishes, S. Frediano and S. Maria in Verzaia, that straddled the Piazza of their meeting place, Camaldoli.[57]

Although from the spontaneous rock-throwing we may deduce the general resentment of the *popolo minuto* against the strong arm of the Medici state (the Otto di Guardia and its officials), the motivation for the incident which sparked their resentment originated in a communal setting. The neighbors of the working-class quarter of Camaldoli sacrificed their necks to assist a friend and a neighbor who had been condemned by the Otto not for a political crime or for attempting to organize wool or silk shops, but, instead, because of theft.

Both the character of insurrection and the configuration of social networks illustrated by these two examples of collective violence and popular protest from the middle of the fifteenth century contrast sharply with the character of late fourteenth-century protest.[58] As with the casual networks reflected by our marriage statistics for the fifteenth century *popolo minuto*, the networks of trust and association—the rudiments of popular organization in the face of adversity—present in these two tumults were truly parochial; they lacked city-wide or even significant cross-neighborhood participation. We have already examined in detail the political content of these Trecento insurrections. Now let

---

57. The inquisition for this incident found in the records of the Podesta n. 5008, 9r–10r, are somewhat at variance with Francesco di Tommaso Giovanni's report. First, the condemned Piero is not identified as from Verzaia, but rather from the adjacent suburban parish of S. Piero Monticelli. Furthermore, six others are identified in the inquisition by parish. Two were from the parish of S. Frediano, and another was from the adjacent parish of S. Maria in Verzaia. But, the other three came from across the Arno, from the parishes of S. Lorenzo and S. Piero Maggiore in the quarter of S. Giovanni and from S. Stefano of the quarter of S. Croce. Giovanni di Deracherato della Schetella of S. Stefano, however, does not appear in Francesco's list of conspirators. Rather, Giovanni, who lived in a parish adjacent to the Piazza de'Signoria may not have been one of the original conspirators nor one of those later rounded up by the Otto in the neighborhood of Camaldoli; very likely, Giovanni was one of those onlookers, who after the incident had been launched, began to unleash his anxieties against the authorities and was subsequently apprehended by the *famulus* of the Podestà. We learn, moreover, from the inquisition that rock throwing and rioting spread rapidly and spasmodically through the working-class districts of the northern part of the city—the parishes of S. Lorenzo and S. Piero Maggiore.

58. For a third example of this parallelism between the character of insurrection and the geographic configurations outlined by the residences of the insurrectionists, we might look outside our period to the abortive food riot of 1411. According to Professor Brucker, *The Civic World*, 327, "The alleviation of hunger was a primary goal of the leaders, who intended to sack the communal granary . . . Of the fourteen identified conspirators, the majority were residents of the working class (and adjacent) parishes of San Frediano and Santa Maria in Verzaia in the Quarter of Santo Spirito."

us turn back to the middle and late Trecento insurrections to examine their *associational* character in more detail, to investigate the networks of association which the lists of condemned insurrectionists might uncover.

Again, the lists of insurrectionists found in the criminal sentences present the problem: The courts apprehended and prosecuted only a small proportion of the participants within the insurrectionary crowds. On the other hand, unlike the sketchy information regarding profession in the criminal records of the late fourteenth century, the condemned were consistently identified by place or parish of residence. For the revolutionary periods, 1343–1378 and 1382–1383, we find seven insurrections in which five or more of the participants were identified by place or parish of residence. The most parochial constituency found in the seven incidents was, in fact, the least explicitly political.

On April 14, 1348, 11 men from the parish of S. Paolo, accompanied by four men from the adjacent parish of S. Lucia Ognissanti, a man from the neighboring parish of S. Trinità, and another man from across town, then residing in the parish of S. Maria del Fiore, attacked two brothers of the degli Infangati family.[59] The courts as usual do not state the reasons for the alliance of these members of the *popolo minuto* and their particular grievances against the degli Infangati brothers.

On December 14, 1344, ten men, all bearing only a patronymic or a nickname, nine of whom were identified by parish, attacked with stones various messengers and police of the Podestà.[60] The majority came from around the Piazza di S. Spirito: three were from the parish of S. Felice in Piazza, north of the Santo Spirito; another came from a few blocks south of the Piazza, a small parish on the Arno, S. Iacopo sopr'Arno; and three from the parish of Santa Spirito itself. They were joined, however, by two men from across the Arno, from the parish of S. Simone of the eastern quarter of the city, S. Croce.

An incident of July 9, 1345, shows another remarkable geographic array of friendships and networks of mutual assistance. The Podestà condemned nine men for besieging a creditor's agents and two policemen of the Palazzo Vecchio in order to rescue from their hands the delinquent debtor, Niccolai, a miller of the parish of S. Michele Visdomini.[61] Of Niccolai's nine *amici*, not a single one was from his immediate neighborhood, the parish of S. Michele; instead, they came to his assistance from all four quarters of the city: two were from the

---

59. ACP n. 63, 11r–12r.
60. AP n. 116, 3v.
61. AP n. 127, 336v.

northeastern parish of S. Piero Maggiore; two were from further east, the parish of S. Ambrogio. Another two came from the parish of S. Iacopo tra le Fosse in the quarter of S. Croce; and the other three came from S. Firenze (S. Croce), S. Michele Berteldi (on the border of the quarter of S. Giovanni and S. Maria Novella), and S. Felice in Piazza, across the Arno and in the quarter of S. Spirito.

In the grain riot of 1368, of the five identified by parish, two were from S. Piero Maggiore (S. Giovanni), and the other city dweller came from south of this parish and across the quarter and the ecological boundaries, from the parish of S. Piero Scheraggio (S. Croce), located within the old Roman walls. The two other ringleaders came from the *contado* parishes, just beyond the city walls, the parishes of S. Piero Monticelli and S. Quirico a Legnaia.[62]

In the condemnations of the insurrectionists of the Otto di S. Maria Novella who attempted to push the revolution further than the designs of Michele di Lando, the chronicler Stefani lists the parishes of 23 of those 35 condemned.[63] Again, all quarters of the city are represented. There were city-wide linkages; yet there seem to have been several nodes for drawing together the revolutionaries: six were from the parish of S. Frediano, and another two from its neighborhood cluster, S. Felicità and S. Pier Gattolino; another six came from the cluster of S. Lucia Ognissanti, four from the parish itself, one from S. Paolo, the other from S. Maria Novella; five were from the northern part of the city— spreading from west to east, two came from S. Lorenzo, one from S. Piero Maggiore, and one from S. Ambrogio; three resided within the central city, from the parishes of S. Remigio, S. Maria del Fiore and S. Firenze; and finally, one of the Otto di S. Maria Novella came from the suburban, rural village of S. Donnino.[64]

In the second period of revolution, moreover, following the fall of the government of the *Arti Minori* (1382), the provenances of the condemned show similar patterns of participation and networks of association among the *popolo minuto*. Of the condemnations involving over 100 men executed by the executor of the ordinances of justice during

---

62. Niccolò Rodolico, *Il Popolo Minuto: Note di storia fiorentina, 1343–1378*, 2nd. edition (Florence, 1968), Doc. n. 11, 97–99.

63. *Cronaca fiorentina di Marchionne di Coppo Stefani*, edited by Rodolico, Rerum Italicarum Scriptores, new ed., Vol. XXX, Pt. 1 (Città di Castello, 1903–1955), rub. 807.

64. For a description of the geographic dimensions of the revolt of the Otto di S. Maria Novella, see *ibid.*, p. 333, *"Pure levatisigli dinanzi, furono presi, e messi sotto la scala, e la novella ando a S. Maria Novella. Di che la abrigata, che sapea bene non dovere avere quello che volea, comincio a sonare a S. Paolo; e S. Friano rispondere, e S. Giorgio e S. Niccolo e Belletri e S. Ambrogio, e ultimalente si raccolsero a S. Friano."* (These parishes and places encircled most of the urban geography of Renaissance Florence, see Figure 1.1.)

the fall of 1383, the contenders came from all zones and quarters of the city with highest representations from the working-class neighborhoods of S. Lorenzo, S. Frediano, and S. Piero Maggiore.[65] On December 9, 1383, the Capitano del Popolo condemned two Ciompi from the parish of S. Paolo for attempting to revive the three suppressed revolutionary guilds.[66] On closer scrutiny, we find that they had organized secret meetings throughout the city in the principal working-class districts, Beletri, Palazolo, S. Ambrogio, S. Piero Gattolini, and Camaldoli.[67, 68]

When we turn back, finally, to the outbreak of the Revolt of the Ciompi itself, we learn from Simoncini's testimony that the Ciompi (quite in contrast to the outbreak of the French Revolution, July 14, 1789, which comprised *sans culottes* principally from only two adjacent working-class neighborhoods of Paris) drew their support and planned their revolt throughout the entire city of Florence (see Figure 7.1). The insurrectionists, on the eve of the Tumult of the Ciompi, met first in the Ospedale dei Preti in via S. Gallo, near what is presently the Piazza della Libertà, and later in the place called El Ronco, just beyond the Porta S. Piero Gattolino (today, Porta Romana), the southern-most point of the city. They planned four separate uprisings: one from the church of S. Spirito (comprising 1000 men); the second from the church of S. Stefano, in which 400 men from the quarter of S. Croce would join; the third and fourth, linking together the northern districts of the city, were to originate from the churches of S. Lorenzo in

---

65. A(tti degli) E(secutore di) O(rdinamenti di) G(iustizia), n. 950, 17r–18v, 25r–27v, 29r–30v, 35v–36v; AP n. 3053, 102r–103r; n. 3147, 47r–48r.

66. Rodolico, *La democrazia fiorentina*, Doc. n. VIII, 479–484.

67. *Ibid.*, 479, ". . . *quod predicti et quilibet ipsorum debebant coadunare et congregare penitus ordinaverunt multos et multos homines et personas infrascriptarum contratarum civitatis Florentie videlicet: Beletri, Palazolo, populi S. Ambroxii et S. Petri gattolini ac etiam Camaldole. . . .*"

68. When we consider, moreover, those incidents of insurrection for which the notaries of the criminal tribunals have not left us the names and places of at least five participants, the same patterns of social networks among the contenders, cutting across parish and neighborhood boundaries, are confirmed. For instance, on September 3, 1344, the court of the Capitano condemned two *popoli minuti* for plotting to overthrow the government. One of the rebels was from S. Remigio in the quarter of Santa Croce; the other was a soldier *(balistiere)*, who lived across town in the parish of San Paolo in the quarter of S. Maria Novella (ACP n. 11, 23r). Of the two stone masons condemned for writing an inflammatory letter against the regime in power in 1364 and in praise of the rule of the Duke of Athens, one came from the parish of S. Trinità (S. Maria Novella); while the other lived in the parish of S. Piero Gattolini, located across the Arno in the southernmost corner of the city (Brucker and Becker, "Una lettera in difesa della dittatura nella Firenze del Trecento," *ASI*, CXIII, 257–258). Finally, of two convicted for assisting two heretics (a man and his son) to resist the police of the Inquisition and of the Podestà, one was from the same parish as the heretics; the other lived across the Arno in the working-class district of S. Frediano (AP n. 3178, 136r–v, 153v–154v).

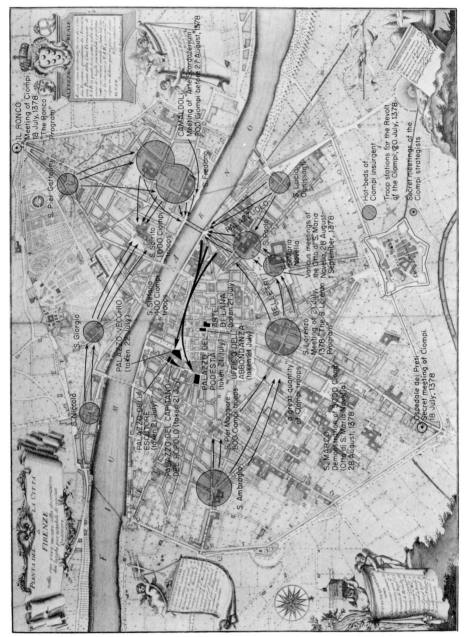

Figure 7.1. *The general sweep of Ciompi insurrections, 1343–1383.*

the western half, and S. Piero Maggiore to the east.[69] In several descriptions of the mass movements of the Ciompi, moreover, we find the Ponte Carraia which linked together the sweep of working-class neighborhoods running from S. Ambrogio to S. Piero Maggiore to S. Lorenzo to S. Lucia Ognissanti and then across the Arno to the "hotbed" of insurrection, the working-class districts of S. Frediano, S. Maria in Verzaia, and Camaldoli mentioned as a crucial geographical point in the military strategies of the Ciompi.[70]

Thus, the networks of association traced by the arrested participants in the mass insurrections of the period of the Ciompi contrast sharply with those gathered from the few examples of collective political activity on the part of artisans and workers during the Quattrocento. While the Ciompi of the mid- and late Trecento cut patterns of friendship and trust which stretched across wide geographic districts, the geographic configurations of contenders in the mid-Quattrocento show relationships based on narrow neighborhood, truly parochial, solidarities. Similar to differences in the marriage patterns of workers and artisans between the two periods, the patterns of political participation and rioting in the fifteenth century, in contrast to those of the late fourteenth century, show the artisan and laboring classes on the defensive, turned inwardly within their parish communities, and probably no longer capable of organizing mass insurrections of city-wide dimensions.

In conclusion, the insurrections of fifteenth century Florence appear to have had a very different character from those of the late fourteenth century which led to the outbreak of the Ciompi. First, they were predominantly staffed and inspired by patricians in protest against the Medici state or a faction within it. Second, they originated for the most part in the subject towns and appear to have challenged the centralizing policy of the capital—Florence. In the Tilly model these revolts were clearly *communal* and "reactionary" forms of social protest. When we turn to the *popolo minuto*, their actions appear in the shadows. We do

---

69. *Cronache e memorie sul tumulto dei Ciompi*, edited by G. Scaramella *Rerum Italicarum Scriptores*, new ed., Vol. XVIII, Pt. 3 (Bologna, 1917), pp. 20–23.

70. See Brucker, *Florentine Politics and Society, 1343–1378* (Princeton, 1962), p. 379; Rodolico, *La democrazia fiorentina*, pp. 424, 427 and doc. IX, 482; and Stefani, *Cronica fiorentina*, 214, describes the movement of an insurrection in 1343: ". . . *la brigata ruppero il serraglio del ponte alla Carraia . . . E di via Maggio trasse tutto il popolo, e da S. Spirito e S. Piero Gattolino. . . .*" See also pp. 423 and 426. It is interesting to note, moreover, that in commemoration of the Revolt of the Ciompi, 30 or 40 ciompi met on the night preceding July 21, 1383, at the Ponte alla Carraia. From this point, strategic to the Ciompi insurrection, the leader of this small band of ciompi remnants, a certain Cecco, raised the banner of the Popolo di Dio (now condemned by the restored oligarchy) and led his group through the principal streets of Florence that circulated through the traditional foci of the ciompi militants of 1378 (Rutenburg, *Popolo e movimenti popolari*, 353.)

not find the banners, slogans, and mass movements of the late fourteenth century. Instead, their actions appear fragmented, individuated, and might be classed under the rubric of atomized rebellion: the burning of the Pandolfini's barn, a domestic slave poisoning her *patrona,* and the stabbing of an important member of Florentine politics and society. Third, we have thus far uncovered only two incidents of collective violence initiated by the *popolo minuto* against officials of the state. The context and character of protest in these two incidents are decisively more parochial, more *communal* than the *associational* ties which bound together the more highly politicized insurrections of the late fourteenth century.

This narrative evidence mixed with a statistical evaluation of the participants in insurrectionary crowds shows clearly that the *popolo minuto* was not a static force over the *longue durée* of the Renaissance in Florence. Not only did their political expressions change; the very "forms of association that underlie politics" [71] changed—from the quotidian setting of conscious marriage choices to the networks of trust and friendship cast by the condemnation lists of political protest. Our conclusions are not impaired by the fact that the fifteenth-century materials do not provide enough information for an adequate comparison with the richer materials of the period of the Ciompi. But the silence of the documents—despite obvious evidentiary problems—is, in fact, the point. What Machiavelli could not write about—not because of his censors, but rather because of sociopolitical realities—ultimately tells us more about the nature of the *popolo minuto* and the Quattrocento than the frank and vivid narrative of Francesco di Tommaso Giovanni, or the clinical descriptions of the Podestà's inquistions, could possibly convey. The fact is: The *popolo minuto* of the middle fifteenth century had become a very different animal from what it had been 75 years before— not only in its political activism, but, more profoundly, in its sociological character, in the networks of association, both casual and political, which underlay their forms of political expression.

The final chapter will examine some of the causes of this radical change in Florentine society. To understand the fifteenth-century trough in popular culture and class struggle the locus of inquiry must shift from its usual place in the study of working-class history. We must do more than simply observe the *popolo minuto* and their political activity—not only because of the paucity of materials regarding their activity during the Quattrocento, but because of the very change in the nature of class struggle. We must be open to class struggle initiated

---

71. Brucker, *The Civic World of Early Renaissance Florence* (Princeton, 1977), p. 11.

from above and not only in the short term—the brutal suppresion by the state of an insurrection or of a temporary victory of the working classes.

We must diverge slightly from the course that our argument has so far plotted. We will continue our examination of the criminal archives, but this time it will not be to seek out the dramatic incidents of conflict; instead, the analysis will be more systematic. "Criminal behavior," however, will not be the only subject of this inquiry. From the day-to-day records we hope to understand the very interstices between classes. This will mean that the popolo minuto themselves will not be the subject, but instead *their relationship* to the dominant classes will be the focus of our inquiry. We will attempt to interpret that other side of the criminal statistic so seldom considered by historians of criminality—strategies of prosecution and social repression, and in so doing we seek to gain new insight into that problem which Jacob Burckhardt over a hundred years ago proposed as crucial for understanding the civilization of the Renaissance—"the state as a work of art."

Chapter 8

Criminality and the State
in Renaissance Florence

E finally come to the question: What happened to the Ciompi during the Quattrocento? The period of Cosimo de'Medici, a time of cultural and aesthetic effervescence and presumably of social peace, might not appear at first glance to be a likely place to observe the struggles and structure of the Florentine *popolo minuto*. First, there are certain problems of evidence—the changing complexities of the criminal tribunals and their jurisdictions and the growth of the summary judiciary, the Otto di Guardia, whose records, where they exist, contain only bare lists of names and the penalties to be exacted. For the period of investigation, only a single filza from the Otto's deliberations, containing four months of business, survives. But, more importantly, there is the problem posed by the social and political realities themselves—the almost complete disappearance (as we discovered in the previous chapter) of those most visible manifestations of struggle: attacks against officials of the Commune, mass insurrections, and strikes. Given the focus of research on mass movements and working-class history more generally—the tendency to concentrate on (or even to romanticize) the "great events" of working-class history—the silence of the mid-Quattrocento becomes interesting.[1] A comparison of the structure of the *popolo minuto* and the nature of class struggle between the fourteenth and fifteenth centuries, moreover, will provide a perspective for better understanding one of those "great events" of European working-class history (heretofore studied almost solely in and of itself)—the Revolt of the Ciompi and its epoch.

It is possible to move toward an explanation of the apparent social peace of Quattrocento Florence. The inquiry could proceed from a

---

1. See E. J. Hobsbawn, "Labor History and Ideology," *Journal of Social History* (1974), 371–381.

number of documentary funds found in the treasures of the *Archivio di Stato:* we have chosen to collect and to analyze statistically various samples from the criminal archives. These sources, more than any others that come to mind, are at the very interface of class confrontation. On the one hand, there are the accused—from the atomistic rebels who burned the barn and fields of the Pandolfini, to the long lists of insurrectionists who staged the last efforts to preserve the rights of working-class men and women to associate in guilds and to participate in the government of Florence; on the other hand, there is the prosecution— the actions of the state, its courts and systems of law enforcement and surveillance, and the private actions of individuals from the merchant class, their vigor in the prosecution of debtors, rural poachers, and *mezzadri* who allegedly broke their work contracts.

To be sure, the zeal for justice or retribution did not always bring together litigants of opposing classes. We seek, nonetheless, through a statistical analysis of criminality, to explore beneath the most obvious level of class conflict presented by the criminal archives. In the previous two chapters, we studied class struggle by focusing on the *popolo minuto* itself, their collective and individual assaults on the state and against the merchant class. In this chapter we will not hunt through the criminal archives for what was in fact the exception, whether it was an act of primitive rebellion or a mass insurrection. Rather, we will compare criminality as a whole in two periods of Florentine history—not in order to write a history of crime as such, but to consider changes in the interaction of two forces which underlie every statistic on criminality: actual criminal behavior and the nature of prosecution.[2] Through untangling this interaction we seek to reveal changes in the relationship between the majority of the defendants (who were in fact the *popolo minuto*) and the apparatus of the state—its courts, the organization of social control, and its strategies of prosecution. To understand the changes in class equilibrium after the Ciompi the historian must look not only at what was happening in the streets: analysis must push into the realm of the patriciate and the state, it must be open to the possibility of the offensive coming from above. We will argue that the criminal statistics of late fourteenth and mid-fifteenth centuries chronicle fundamental changes in the class equilibrium of Renaissance

---

2. All the historical analyses of criminality which I have read have treated criminal statistics one-dimensionally. They have, in other words, used these statistics only for estimating actual criminal behavior. They consider the other side of these statistics—their reflection on changes in regimes, strategies of prosecution, the development of certain apparatuses of the state—only as qualitative problems in the estimation of criminal behavior; the state and the forces of repression, in these studies, are never the subjects of inquiry.

Florence; moreover, these transformations (lodged within the political sphere) radically altered the structures of popular life from the period of the Ciompi through the end of the period of Cosimo de'Medici.

A consideration of shifts in criminality from the mid-Trecento through the mid-Quattrocento presents several immediate problems. First, when considering criminal behavior over a long period of time, there emerges the problem of the possibility of changes in the definition of what exactly constituted a crime, in terms both of the law and of morality. Given the sources at our disposal, it is almost impossible to assess, independently of the criminal statistics themselves, such changes of morality. Changes in the statutory definitions of crime, however, might be examined through the various compilations of the statutes of Florence.

From the late twelfth century, the bodies of Florentine law were divided among various institutions over which foreign notables presided. The Commune created the institution of the Podestà as early as 1193,[3] then the Capitano del Popolo (1250),[4] and finally the Esecutore degli Ordinamenti di Giustizia (1307).[5] There was no clear division of tasks nor of jurisdictions between these courts. Why a certain case of assault and battery, for instance, would be tried in one court and not another is still an open question.[6] These institutions, moreover, were more than tribunals; each possessed its own organization of law enforcement, its own body of *berrovarii* (police). Only the Esecutore degli Ordinamenti di Giustizia, at least in theory, seems to have had some autonomy of legal jurisdiction. This court, created after the Commune had defeated the *Magnati*, had exclusive jurisdiction over crimes committed by noblemen. By the mid-Trecento (when the earliest surviving records appear), however, we find the Podestà and the Capitano apprehending and trying criminals identified as *Magnates et Potentes*. On the other hand, the Esecutore was the principal court to prosecute and try those Ciompi who made a last stand to preserve the revolutionary guilds of wool workers immediately following the restoration of the oligarchy in 1382. By the middle of the Trecento, the day-to-day business of the Esecutore shows that it no longer played a major role in Florentine

---

3. Lorenzo Cantini "Dell' Ufizio del Podestà di Firenze" in *Saggi istorici d'antichità toscane,* edited by Cantini (Florence, 1796).

4. A. Gherardi, "Il Podestà e il Capitano del Popolo," in *Miscellanea fiorentina di erudizione e storia,* edited by I. del Badia, Vol. III, pp. 43–45.

5. Gaetano Salvemini, *Magnati e popolani in Firenze dal 1280 al 1295* (Florence, 1899).

6. The court in which a particular crime was tried depended generally on which law enforcing agency apprehended the criminal or reported the crime. For cases brought to trial by private parties, the choice of tribunal is more difficult to discern.

criminal justice. Its chief function seems to have been the scrutiny of the law officials—from the judges to the police—of the other two tribunals. Although there were several changes in procedure in the reform of 1295, there was only one major compilation of the body of law under the aegis of this tribunal, the Ordinances of Justice, redacted in 1293. The institution was abolished in 1434 with the return of the Medici.

There were three major compilations of the criminal statutes for the other two tribunals (the Podestà and the Capitano) first in 1322, then in 1355, and 1415. Unfortunately, a study of changes in criminal law during the fifteenth century or between the late fourteenth and the late fifteenth centuries (the two points of our analysis) would be much more difficult than an inquiry simply for the fourteenth century. It would require a close scrutiny of the voluminous *fondo* of the *provvisioni* of the Signoria. Such an exhaustive study of the fifteenth-century documents, however, might bear little fruit, at least in uncovering significant changes in the contours of criminal law. Unlike the civil law, the criminal law appears to have been remarkably stable over the period of the Renaissance. It excited very little notice from the Florentine legists of the mid- and late Quattrocento (whose opinions have been categorized and summarized by the seventeenth-century lawyer, Antonio Strozzi). Only murder elicited any concern; otherwise, their attention was turned to matters of civil law—problems of business partnership, property, land tenure, inheritance, and the dowry.[7]

Second, the years (and the flood of 1966) have carved out serious gaps in the series of sentences of the medieval tribunals—the Esecutore degli Ordinamenti di Giustizia, the Capitano del Popolo, and the Podestà. Third, despite these gaps, these archives are still far too immense for a systematic analysis over the 160 years of their existence. For an examination of the changes from the period of the Ciompi (broadly defined as the years 1343–1383) through the regime of Cosimo de'Medici, we will consider Florence as two separate societies: Florence, 1343–1383 and Florence during the last 12 years of Cosimo's reign, 1455–1466. The materials for the earlier period, moreover, are much more vast than those which have survived for the mid-Quattrocento.[8]

---

7. I wish to thank Professor Fredrick Krantz of Concordia University for providing me with this information.

8. For both periods only the criminal sentences will be examined. For a semester tenure of any particular Podestà or Capitano, the notaries of the court kept information regarding criminal cases in several different books. If the court brought charges against a defender, the notary described the case in the *Liber inquisitionum,* which included the name(s) of the accused, the name(s) of the victims, the place and date of the crime, accomplices to the crime, whether the crime occurred at night, after the ringing of the second bells of the parish

We have thus compiled for the two periods different sorts of samples. In the latter period all the surviving sentences of the medieval tribunals will be considered. For this period, though unscathed by the flood of 1966, only half of the *filze* of criminal sentences now survive. For the earlier period, particularly before the Black Death, there are as many as 15 times the number of sentences per semester as one finds for the same period during the mid-Quattrocento. For comparison with the data compiled from the latter period, we have, therefore, drawn on all the sentences for only two years during the period of the Ciompi—one before the Black Death, 1344–1345; the other afterward and during the period that Gene Brucker has described as a time of relative social calm, 1374–1375.[9] Fourth, changes in juridical practice and jurisdiction present problems for comparison. As was mentioned above, in 1434 the Esecutore was abolished, but, more importantly, the Otto di Guardia, created after the fall of the radical wing of the Ciompi on September 2, 1378, assumed more and more power during the Quattrocento.[10]

churches (in which case, the penalties were doubled), and a description of the alleged injuries inflicted on the injured party. Usually, the notary in this book followed the history of the case (the various summonses of witnesses, the accused, and the plaintiff(s)) through its progress in the quarter court. If a private person instead of the court brought charges, the same notarial procedures were followed in the *Liber accusationum*. The testimonies of the accused and the plaintiff were kept in two books, the *Liber testium ad defensam* and the *Liber testium ad offensam*. Third, the *Liber prosecutionum* contained the miscellaneous deliberations, commissions, and business of the court between its notaries, judges, and *famulus* (or police force). Fourth, if the accused failed to appear in court (committed contumacy), the notary inscribed the defender in a book which listed those banned from the city, *contado*, and territory of Florence, the *Exbandimenta*. These books were redacted and organized by quarter for city and *contado*. Only the book of sentences, *Condempnationes et absolutiones*, covered the entire city, *contado*, and territory. These books, moreover, were more than simple lists of the accused and their sentences; they contained large portions from the *Liber inquisitionum* or *accusationum*, sometimes the entire description redacted by the notary of the previous quarter session. For more information on criminal procedure, see G. O. Corazzini, "Cenni sulla procedure penale in nel secolo XIV," in *Miscellanea Fiorentina*, II, pp. 17–23; J. Kohler and G. degli Azzi, *Das Florentiner Strafrecht des XIV Jahrhunderts* (Mannheim-Leipzig, 1909); and Umberto Dorini, *Il diritto penale e la delinquenza in Firenze nel secolo XIV* (Lucca, 1923). In addition, each court handled civil proceedings, which were divided into various offices, each with its own set of registers.

9. At present there is no compilation of the total number of condemnations for either the fourteenth or fifteenth centuries. Moreover, since a researcher can order no more than two *filze* from the criminal archives per work day, it would require more than two years just to order the *filze* in order to trace the number of criminal sentences per year from 1343 through 1502. The inventories of the criminal archives, however, usually indicate the number of *fogli* contained in each *filze* of condemnations, and changes in the number of pages roughly reflect changes in the number of condemnations. By this guide, the year 1344–1345 appears typical of the period 1343–1348, and the year 1374–1375 representative of the period 1349–1379.

10. Giovanni Antonelli, "La magistratura degli Otto di Guardia a Firenze," *Archivio Storico Italiano*, n. 402, Anno XCII (1954), 3. In addition to the Otto di Guardia, the Commune of Florence created two other summary tribunals during the early Quattrocento, the

Unlike the other late medieval tribunals, judgments by the Otto were not established through the procedures of inquisition, testimony of the prosecution, and testimony of the defense. The Otto was a summary court; the decisions, interspersed through the daily business of their deliberations, were extremely laconic. Often no more than the sentence and the name of the accused appear in these ledgers. From its inception, moreover, until 1468, only three *filze* survive: one for the period 1408–1409; the other two for eight months in 1460–1461.[11] Despite the absence of these records, we maintain that an investigation of the existing sentences (along with estimates drawn from the deliberations of 1460) can lend insight into changes in Florentine society from the late Trecento through Cosimo's rule.

For each of these points in time (1344–1345, 1374–1375, and 1455–1466), we have categorized those crimes which involved at least one resident from the city of Florence into 10 criminal groupings; otherwise, the crime was simply counted as from the *contado*.[12] Of these statistics, the most striking differences are the shifts in the total number of sentences over time. In the period before the Black Death there are 1682 indictments per annum for city and *contado;* for the year 1374–1375 the number falls precipitously to 440; and in the last decade of Cosimo's rule the figure handled by the Medieval tribunals (the Podestà and Capitano) dwindles still further to 106.2 per annum. To explain these changes, two considerations immediately come to mind: the growth of the criminal jurisdiction of the Otto di Guardia and changes in population. First, the importance of the Otto would affect only the total number of indictments for the third period. From a single *filza* of deliberations of the Otto (May–August, 1460) we find 153 condemnations. This suggests that the Otto may have condemned as

Onestà and the Ufficiali di Notte. The Onestà specialized in crimes concerning prostitutes and pimps and made arrests in connection with crimes which broke out in the public houses of prostitution. For the 83 year history of this tribunal, Professor Richard Trexler calculates that there were 1092 cases or 13.16 cases per annum. These cases, however, are distributed irregularly through the 83 years of court records. Periodically, the authorities found it necessary or politically astute "to crack down" on the affairs of prostitutes and pimps and those crimes associated with them. For our Quattrocento period, 1455–1466, one *filza* of sentences of the Uficiali di Notte survives: Ufficiali di Notte n. 9 (August 14, 1461–July 8, 1462). For this year there were 51 condemnations.

11. ASF, Otto di Guardia e Balia (La Repubblica), n. 10 and 11.

12. These categories are (*a*) assaults and batteries, (*b*) murder, (*c*) theft, (*d*) rural crimes—poaching and stealing farm animals, wood, and grain, arson, trespass, and *mezzadri* neglecting to work the land, (*e*) urban trespass and breaking and entering, (*f*) fraud and swindle, (*g*) violations against morality—sodomy, rape, prostitution, blasphemy, (*h*) indebtedness, (*i*) contumacy and false testimony, and (*j*) political crimes from individual attacks on officials of the Commune to mass insurrection.

many as 459 persons a year. Since a clear distinction was not always made in the ledgers of the Otto di Guardia between condemnations and deliberations on a case, this number might slightly overstate the actual number of sentences. It is clear, nonetheless, that the total number of indictments in the Quattrocento certainly did not dwindle from the period 1374–1375; instead, they increased perhaps 28%. When we then add those cases from the other summary courts established during the fifteenth century—the Onestà and the Ufficiali di Notte—the number of condemnations may have increased by as much as 52%.[13]

When we consider, furthermore, the shifts in population over this 120 year period, the arrangement of our aggregate figures assumes a different configuration.[14] After the data has been corrected for changes in jurisdiction and population, there do not appear to have been striking changes in *per capita* prosecution between the period before the Black Death and the mid-Quattrocento. Over the long term the rates decline by less than 10%.[15] It is, instead, the second term of our analysis, 1374–1375, that becomes the anomaly. From the period before the Black Death to the eve of the Ciompi, the number of indictments fell dramatically from 1682 to 440 cases, which yields a *per capita* decline of 56%. But what do these aggregate rates suggest? Either there was a critical change in the criminal behavior of Florentines during the 20 years following the Black Death, or on the eve of the Ciompi there was a serious breakdown in the traditional forms of law enforcement and surveillance. At this point, however, we will go beyond the possible implications of the aggregate statistics.

To go beyond the aggregate statistics, to construct a picture of what can be called the composition of criminality, we must rely on the only window open to relative changes in the various sorts of crime over the long duration: the medieval tribunals, the Podestà, the Capitano del Popolo, and the Esecutore. For this analysis the summary courts of the Quattrocento can only serve to test or control our conclusions and to suggest adjustments in the findings. We will argue that the relative

---

13. The number of condemnations per annum for the period 1455–1466 would then total 629 (106 from medieval tribunals, 459 from the Otto di Guardia, 51 from the Ufficiali di Notte and 13 from the Onestà). See note number 10, this chapter.

14. According to Rodolico, *La democrazia fiorentina*, 40, there were 13,372 households in urban Florence in 1379; he estimates the total population of Florence to have been 66,860. Herlihy and Klapisch, *Les Toscans et leurs familles: Une étude du catasto florentin de 1427* (Paris, 1978), Table n. 16, 183, estimates that the city had a population of 37,361 in 1458–1459. For the first point of our analysis, 1344–1345, we will assume Giovanni Villani's pre-Black Death population estimate of the city of 90,000.

15. For the period, 1344–1345, there were 1869 condemnations per 100,000 per annum; for the period, 1455–1466, 1686 per 100,000 per annum.

changes in the ratios of crimes prosecuted by the Commune of Florence within these medieval tribunals alone will reflect changes in the strategies of prosecution of the Florentine state and hence will reflect changes in the character of the state and society.

For the three periods of our analysis we will consider the number of crimes within a certain category of criminality, such as trespass, murder or crimes of immorality (blasphemy, gambling, and violations of sexual mores) as a ratio of the total number of sentences or of another particular category of criminality. When this composition of criminality is analyzed, the shifts in the ratios suggest a different periodization from the one suggested by the simple aggregate changes in the number of indictments. To characterize these changes in the composition of criminality over the three periods, we have drawn six relationships: first, the number of assaults and batteries as a ratio of the total number of crimes which involved at least one resident from the city; second, the ratio of murders to assaults and batteries; third, the number of rural crimes—poaching, chopping and stealing young trees, rural arson, trespass, and *mezzadri* neglecting to work the land—as a ratio of the total number of city crimes; fourth, the number of indictments for indebtedness to the total; fifth, offenses against morality—sexual crimes, gambling, and blasphemy—to the total; and finally, the ratio of those crimes in which both parties resided outside the city to the total number of sentences.

When these ratios are considered, we find a closer correspondence in each category of crime between the two earlier periods, 1344–1345 and 1374–1375, than either shows in comparison with the period of the mid-Quattrocento (see Table 8.1, 8.2, Figure 8.1 and Appendixes H.1–H.3). Crimes of morality and murder assumed the most gentle slopes over time. On the other hand, we find dramatic shifts between the periods of the Ciompi and the last decade of Cosimo's rule when those crimes which comprised the greatest bulk of the indictments are observed. Crimes involving parties from the countryside exclusively increased in the periods 1344–1345 to 1374–1375 from 39% of all indictments to over 47%, but in the mid-Quattrocento they declined by almost three-fourths of the 1374–1375 ratio to less than 16% of all indictments. Similarly, assaults and batteries, by far the most common indictments for both periods before the Ciompi, remained constant relative to other crimes after the Black Death but then in the fifteenth century fell rapidly from nearly 39% of all urban crimes to less than 18%. On the other hand, curiously enough, the relative number of indictments for murder increased slightly through the three periods, and, as a ratio to assault and batteries, it soared from the late Trecento to the

Table 8.1

Composition of Criminality: Summary

Crime	1344–1345	1374–1375	1455–1466
1. Assault and battery (1–9) :: total city crimes	402	91	79
	.3918	.3889	.1767
2. Murder (10–11) :: total city crimes	23	9	27
	.0224	.0346	.0604
3. Murder (10–11) :: Assault and battery (1–9)	.0572	.0989	.3418
4. Theft (12–13) :: total city crimes	40	8	24
	.0390	.0342	.0850
5. Rural crimes (14–21) :: total city crimes	101	27	88
	.0984	.1154	.1969
6. Crimes of morality (26–32) :: total city crimes	38	9	24
	.0370	.0346	.0537
7. Personal indebtedness (33) :: total city crimes	145	28	19
	.1413	.1197	.0430
8. Total indebtedness (33–36) :: total city crimes	146	38	92
	.1423	.1624	.2058
9. Crimes of the *contado* :: total crime	656 :: 1682	206 :: 440	84 :: 531
	.3876	.4682	.1582

mid-Quattrocento by 346%, from less than two to almost seven murders per every 20 indictments for assault.

How do we summarize these shifts? Do they not confirm our general knowledge about Renaissance Florence: after the Black Death, tensions among classes were mitigated; because of the relative prosperity, the

Table 8.2

Differences in the Intervals, 1344–1345 through 1374–1375 and 1374–1375 through 1455–1466

Categories of crime [a]	Interval no. 1 (1344–1345 through 1374–1375)	Interval no. 2 (1374–1375 through 1455–1466)
1	.29	21.22
2	1.22	2.58
3	4.17	24.29
4	.48	5.08
5	1.70	8.15
6	.24	1.91
7	2.16	7.67
8	2.01	4.34
9	8.06	31.00
Total of differences	20.33	106.24

[a] These numbers are the absolute differences between the periods indicated. For a description of the criminal ratios, numbers 1–9, see Table 8.1.

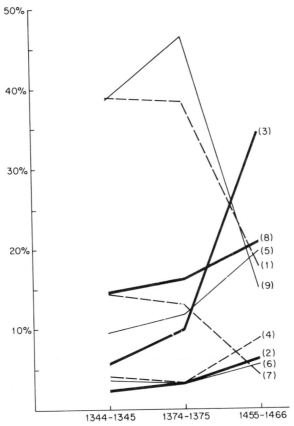

Figure 8.1. *The composition of criminality (the numbers in parentheses correspond to Table 8.1).*

popolo minuto entered a period of quiescence; and in general, disputes were settled more by civil arbitration than by street violence.[16] Only the incidences of murder and rape conflict with this portrayal. These crimes, however, were numerically a small component of total criminality for all three periods.

But let us for the moment entertain another interpretation. These transformations show not only a change in litigation from offenses against persons to those against property, they reflect, in addition,

16. See, for instance, Gene A. Brucker, "The Florentine *Popolo Minuto* and Its Political Role, 1340–1450" in *Violence and Civil Disorder in Italian Cities,* edited by Lauro Martines (Berkeley, 1972), pp. 182–183; and Marvin Becker, "Changing Patterns of Violence and Justice in Fourteenth and Fifteenth Century Florence," *Comparative Studies in Society and History,* 18 (1976), 296.

changes from a predominance of crimes which usually involved litigants of like social status—such as assaults and batteries—to crimes in which members of the merchant class normally prosecuted artisans, laborers, and peasants—cases of indebtedness, rural trespass, poaching, and neglecting to work the land. An examination of those who litigated in criminal offenses supports the impression that there was a fundamental shift in the nature of prosecution rather than in criminal behavior. First, for that numerically most important category of crime during the Trecento—assaults and batteries—84% of the disputes in the first period and 91% in the second involved litigants who from the documentation appear to have had similar social origins. Either both litigants were identified by only a patronymic, or a profession belonging to the minor guilds, or to one which identified *sottoposti*, workers in the wool and silk industries; or the litigants were both designated as magnates or major guildsmen or both bore a family name. Of these conflicts between equals, only 5% involve magnates or members of the Florentine patriciate. In those conflicts which involved combatants of unequal status, most often, for both sample periods of the Trecento, it was a lower-class contender who accused one from the upper-classes of assault. In 11% of the cases in the first period and 6% in the second, the plaintiff was a man or woman of undistinguished status and the defendant was either a magnate, a major guildsman or a person bearing a prominent Florentine family name. The most negligible percentages for both periods (5% and 4%, respectively) were disputes which involved the opposite relationship; one in which a commoner allegedly assaulted a man or woman of patriciate status.

These relations between assailants and the assaulted (or the prosecution) contrast sharply with those found in the sentences of the Podestà and the Capitano, in the period 1455–1466. First, only two-thirds of the cases of assault in the third period were disputes among equals. It might be suggested that these differences reflect merely the tendency to identify persons more thoroughly in the sentences of the Quattrocento than the notaries had done earlier. But the possibility of changes in notarial practice would not explain differences in class confrontation which existed in the residual 34% of cases of assault and battery. Whereas, in both periods of the Trecento, less than half of those cases of unequal class confrontation (29% in the first period and 43% in the second) involved a plaintiff who was a patrician, in the mid-Quattrocento the balance shifts: in three-fourths of the unequal encounters, a patrician prosecuted a *popolo minuto* or a *contadino*.

These changes may in part reflect changes in the nature of class conflict, which can be observed from the most dramatic events contained in the criminal archives. From the period of the Ciompi to that of the Medici, the large-scale insurrections that racked the city disappear. In their place we find desperate attacks of atomized and primitive rebels: neighbors assaulting an officer of the Otto di Guardia,[17] the burning of the Pandolfini barn and fields,[18] slaves and servants poisoning their masters.[19]

Since collective forms of resistance were frustrated, it might be argued that the change in the balance of power between classes led during the fifteenth century to an increase in the number of individual attacks by the poor against the prominent. More plausibly, the shift in the balance of power would have affected actual criminal behavior in the opposite direction; that is, we should have expected (had the reporting and prosecution of crime remained unchanged) a decline during the fifteenth century in the number of assaults and batteries inflicted against the rich and powerful by a *popolo minuto* less politicized and more intimidated than their Ciompi predecessors. It is the other side of the criminal statistic, not criminal behavior per se, but rather its bearing on the nature of prosecution, that these statistics more reasonably convey. They reflect, in other words, a change in the nature of class struggle that must be observed from the perspective of the state rather than the people: selective police surveillance and repression (Table 8.3)

The statistics on murder and their relation to indictments of assault and battery further suggest that our statistics reflect changes more in the apparatus of the state—the courts and the organization of social control, and levels of prosecution—than in actual changes in criminal

Table 8.3
The Class Nature of Assaults and Batteries

Period	Intra-class	Inter-class	Low status assaults high status	High status assaults low status
1344–1345	304	58	7	17
	83.98%	16.22%	29.17%	70.83%
1374–1375	71	7	3	4
	91.03%	8.97%	42.86%	57.14%
1455–1466	46	24	18	6
	65.71%	34.29%	75.00%	25.00%

17. A(tti del) P(odestà) n. 5008, 2r–8v.
18. AP n. 5098, 163r.
19. A(tti del) C(apitano del) P(opolo) n. 3867, 52r–v and n. 3891, 21v.

behavior. Unlike assault, murder rates fluctuated less sharply from the late Trecento to the mid-Quattrocento. Even when the data from the Otto are not considered, the absolute rate declined, insignificantly, from 15 to 13.5 murders per 100,000 persons. Historically, cases of murder have been the criminal statistic least susceptible to changes in morality or law enforcement.[20] Almost universally, they are investigated and prosecuted the most zealously and its end product—the body—is more difficult to conceal than the results of other crimes. Murders are generally not performed by professionals, but instead, arise from unpremeditated, but passionate and often spontaneous grievances among friends, neighbors, and members of the same family.[21] Most often, these grievances result in violent acts against acquaintances, that is assaults and batteries; occasionally, the victim dies.[22] Thus, if the levels of surveillance, police enforcement, and the practice of the courts remained constant, one would expect a relatively stable relationship between indictments for assault and indictments for murder. Instead, we have found that from the late Trecento to the mid-Quattrocento the ratios of murders to assault soared by 356%. If murders were being no more assiduously prosecuted than before, an enormous number of assault cases were not reaching the courts by the later period. Therefore, the nature of police surveillance and the selectivity in prosecution must have changed. Crimes once routinely handled were now regarded as of insufficient importance to handle.

Let us now turn to other areas of our criminal statistics. When we consider crimes of indebtedness, changes in the class relations of the litigants are not, on first observation, so striking. The relationships between litigants residing in the city and those residing on the countryside remain about the same. In the first period, 21%, in the second 24%, and in the third, 22% of the litigants were rural debtors to creditors who resided in the city. The number of those undistinguished by upper guild status or family name who were indebted to creditors of patri-

---

20. Cf. J. S. Cockburn, "The Nature and Incidence of Crime in England, 1559–1625: A Preliminary Survey," in *Crime in England, 1550–1800,* edited by Cockburn (Princeton, 1977), p. 57; and Henry P. Lundsgaarde, *Murder in Space City: A Cultural Analysis of Houston Homicide Patterns* (New York, 1977), p. 10.

21. Cf. Carl I. Hammer, Jr., "Patterns of Homicide in a Medieval University Town: Fourteenth Century Oxford," *Past & Present,* no. 78 (1978), 20; Barbara Hanawalt (Westman), "The Peasant Family and Crime in Fourteenth Century England," *Comparative Studies in Society and History,* 18 (1976), 297 and 320; R. F. Hunnisett, *The Medieval Coroner* (Cambridge, 1961), p. 31.

22. From evidence in contemporary American cities, Lundsgaarde, *Murder in Space City,* 156, concludes: "The violent behavior that ultimately leads to injury and death is therefore, quite similar although, in principle, the victim's condition—whether dead or alive—conveniently and legally serves to categorize the offense."

cian status did, however, rise steadily from the Trecento to the mid-Quattrocento, from 14% to 21%, and then 31%. More importantly, from the mid-Trecento to the last decade of Cosimo's rule, our statistics indicate qualitative changes in the procedure of these cases of indebtedness. In the period 1344–1345, personal indebtedness, that is, cases presented by private parties as opposed to corporate bodies, constituted almost all of the criminal procedures against debtors (99%). After the Black Death, the number of cases brought by the guilds and the merchants' court (the *mercanzia*) increased slightly to less than 16%.

The critical changes in these statistics, however, occurred again during the Quattrocento. By the end of Cosimo's rule, the number of prosecutions for personal indebtedness had dwindled to a little more than one-third of all the cases of debt (37%); while those cases which had originated in the guild courts and the *mercanzia* predominated. For these cases, the criminal courts were increasingly reserved for reinforcement of earlier decisions of the merchants' courts, to insure the collection of debts by creditors of the merchant class. These changes in the character of litigation once again reveal the accentuation of class cleavages within the medieval tribunals from the late Trecento to the mid-Quattrocento.

Finally, when we glance at those rural crimes which involved a party from urban Florence, changes in city–*contado* and class relations appear more vivid. For the period 1344–1345, residents of the city prosecuted persons from the *contado* in 61% of these cases. In 12%, both litigants resided in the city and in the remaining 27%, residents of the countryside prosecuted citizens of Florence who had violated their property rights. In the succeeding periods, prosecutions brought by *contadini* against citizens of Florence declined sharply to 4% in 1374–1375, and in the last period of our analysis they disappear completely. Correspondingly, prosecutions brought against *contadini* by citizens of Florence climbed from 61% to 83% to 89%.

When we consider, moreover, the class differences between the litigants in cases involving rural offenses, the first and second periods appear more similar. Of those cases prosecuted by residents of the city of Florence against *contadini* in the first period, 12% of the citizens were patricians; in the second period the figure rises to 32%; and in the third period, it jumps to 62%. The most important fact, however, regarding rural crimes cannot be gleaned from an analysis of the relations between citizens and *contadini* found in these cases. The aggregate statistics, here, tell us more. Those crimes in which both parties, the plaintiff and the defendant, were *contadini* increased slightly from the first to the second period, from 39% to 47% of all cases. But during the mid-Quattrocento, they diminished significantly to only 16% of all indictments.

Were these changes simply the result of changes in jurisdiction, possibly the creation of new rural tribunals which would, in the fifteenth century, have tried the bulk of those day-to-day problems among *contadini* which filled the sentences of the mid-Trecento? At this stage of research there is no evidence of the creation of new courts in the *contado*.[23] Indeed, the centralization of other agencies of the Florentine state during the Quattrocento, including the encroachment of the Florentine courts—the Podestà and the Capitano and especially the Otto di Guardia—on the affairs of the subject cities and their territories, suggest that a decentralization of the courts within the traditional *contado* of Florence would have been unlikely.[24] Should we then assume that those numerous conflicts between *contadini* and *contadini* during the Trecento—fist fights, stabbings, boundary disputes, petty theft, and trespass over seeded fields with flocks of sheep or beasts of burden—simply disappeared? More plausibly, these shifts once again give us more information about changes in the courts and, in particular, changes in the strategies of prosecution.

In summary, from an analysis of the composition of criminality and prosecution, the preponderance of certain types of crime changed fundamentally from the Trecento to the mid-Quattrocento. Fist fights, knifings, neighborhood brawls—those disputes which in most of the cases in all three periods of analysis brought together members of the *popolo minuto*—declined sharply from the Trecento to the mid-Quattrocento. In the later period, moreover, they reflect a curious class inequality. While serving less and less the urban artisan and wage earner in the

---

23. For the fourteenth and fifteenth centuries there are no surviving sentences kept by the rural courts within the traditional *contado* of Florence. (See Giulio Prunai, *Gli archivi storici dei comuni della Toscana. Quaderni della "Rassegna degli archivi di Stato,"* Volume 22 [Rome, 1963].) Presumably, as with the quarter courts within the city, these courts passed along their inquisitions, accusations, and testimonies to the court of the Podestà or the Capitano del Popolo, where the sentence was pronounced and where the cases were then combined into a unitary volume of sentences covering the four quarters of the Commune. According to Prunai, *Gli archivi,* p. 7, the Commune of Florence did not pass legislation which provided for the establishment of archives for the rural courts until the second half of the sixteenth century.

24. For an analysis of the encroachment of the city on the contado of Florence, see Marvin Becker, "The Florentine Territorial State and Civic Humanism in the Early Renaissance," in *Florentine Studies,* edited by N. Rubinstein (Florence, 1968), p. 132; Herlihy, *Medieval and Renaissance Pistoia* (New Haven, 1966), pp. 155–179; "The Distribution of Wealth in a Renaissance Community: Florence 1427," in *Towns in Societies,* edited by Abrams and Wrigley (Cambridge, 1978), pp. 131–157; and Herlihy and Klapisch, *Les Toscans et leurs familles,* pp. 291–300.

resolution of his or her own grievances, the courts and the organization of police by the mid-Quattrocento became instruments, at the disposal of the Florentine patriciate for solving problems and conflicts with his or her social inferiors. Similarly, in the countryside, the urban patriciate was able to use the courts more and more to settle problems on their rural estates, from acts of arson to the poaching of pigeons, while the courts appear systematically to have neglected grievances among rural parishioners. Finally, prosecution against debtors increased in relative importance but, more importantly, these prosecutions changed qualitatively. From cases of personal indebtedness between individuals, the courts of the Podestà and Capitano in the period 1455–1466 acted in the majority of these cases not only on behalf of a creditor litigating against a debtor, but as the strong arm of the guild and merchant's courts.

But can we be sure that these shifts in the composition of indictments do not simply reflect shifts in jurisdiction, most importantly the growth of the Otto di Guardia? First, we argue that changes in jurisdiction would not explain the internal variation in the indictments of the medieval tribunals described above, the changes in the ratios of cases of murders to cases of assault and battery or changes in the class status of the prosecution and the defense. Second, when we consider the surviving *filze* of the deliberations of the Otto during the mid-Quattrocento, those cases in which the nature of the crime can be discerned show that the Otto did not fill the gaps left by the shifts in the medieval tribunals from the Trecento to the Quattrocento. Instead, the condemnations of the Otto opened new areas of surveillance, prosecution, and criminality.[25]

First, its jurisdiction substantially widened the territory of the city's tribunals. In the deliberations of 1460, from May 3 to August 29, 35% of the accused resided beyond the city walls, but the majority of these condemnations did not settle or vindicate squabbles in the traditional *contado;* instead, three-fourths of these cases sentenced residents of the subject towns and their districts. Second, the Otto widened the area of criminal adjudication socially. It assumed sole responsibility over the affairs of Jews, who were again allowed to settle in the city of Florence after 1434, and at least 10% of their deliberations pertained to this new minority. Finally, within Florentine society as a whole—throughout the city, *contado,* and district—the Otto extended its jurisdiction, surveillance, and prosecution into new areas. These areas hinged on changes in criminal procedure which the summary character of the

---

25. Otto di Guardia (della Repubblica), n. 11 (May through August, 1460).

Otto's tribunals made possible.[26] No longer was it necessary for the notary to draw up an inquisition describing the crime and its circumstances; no longer was it necessary to consider the testimonies of the prosecution and the defense; no longer was it even necessary for the condemned to have actually committed a crime. He or she could be convicted simply *pro sospetto* or *pro suspicione*.[27]

These breaches of concepts of fundamental procedural fairness are most apparent and best known at the top of society. Because of the Medici's suspicion of certain factions within the patriciate, entire male lines past, present, and future of several important Florentine families— the Machiavelli, the Strozzi, the Castellani, and others—were exiled from the territory of Florence by a series of *bullettini* issued by the Otto following the Parlamento of 1458.[28]

A closer search through the deliberations of the Otto of 1460 reveals that similar procedures occurred throughout the social ladder of Florentine society. Besides cases of individuals from the *popolo minuto* exiled or fined *pro sospetto*, charges against game-playing—usually *zardi*— were prominent in the deliberations of the Otto. These games had been prohibited by statutory law since the early Trecento,[29] and in the sentences of the Trecento we occasionally find prosecutions against gamblers. In almost every case, however, the accused was indicted for another crime, usually an assault which had occurred during the course of the game. In the deliberations of the Otto, on the other hand, condemnations for playing *zardi* stand alone. One suspects that these games did not offend public morality any more in the Quattrocento than they had in the period of sumptuary legislation following the Black Death. Instead, their increase probably reflects the entrance of the Otto into new spheres of surveillance and repression. Since the beginning of the fourteenth century the Commune had always been cautious and concerned about the possible political ramifications of formal as well as informal groupings of the *popolo minuto*, whether these occasions were

---

26. Antonelli, "La magistratura," pp. 3–40.

27. See, for example, Otto di Guardia, n. 11, 7r, 52r, n. 14, 3v, 10r, 15r, 16v, 17v, and 22r. For earlier instances of the Otto apprehending suspected persons, see Brucker, *The Civil World of Early Renaissance Florence* (Princeton, 1977), p. 339.

28. See N. Rubinstein, *The Government of Florence Under the Medici (1434–1494)* (Oxford, 1965), pp. 103–104 and ACP n. 3866, 34r–35v; n. 3867, 17v, 18r–v, 19r.

29. *Statuti della Repubblica fiorentina*, Vol. 1, Statuto del Capitano del Popolo (1322–1325), edited by Romolo Caggese (Florence, 1910), p. 147, IV. "*De ludis vetitis et mutuantibus ad ludos et ludum retinentibus, et de contractibus factiis causa ludi.*" It is interesting to note that this prohibition is not organized among those statutes which condemned certain practices of immorality, such as sodomy and blasphemy. Rather, the statute condemning games of risk comes immediately after two statutes which condemned the formation of congregations and political insurrection.

religious or for the purposes of a friendly drink and the tempting of lady luck.[30]

Another summary court created during the early Quattrocento, the Ufficiali di Notte (the Officials of the Night) perhaps best of all illustrates the incursion of the State into areas of jurisprudence left free by the medieval tribunals.[31] Although sodomy was an offense during the fourteenth century, every case of homosexuality adjudicated in the medieval tribunals in our two samples, 1344–1345 and 1374–1375, was in fact a case of homosexual rape. These tribunals or the Otto di Guardia continued to adjudicate cases of rape through the fifteenth century. On the other hand, the cases which the Officials of the Night began to try during the fifteenth century clearly were not rape cases; instead they arrested and sentenced lovers. In many cases the documents make this plain; the notaries of the court indicate the duration of the relationship. They range from three months to over a year and a half preceding the time of arrest.[32]

Second, the manner by which the courts apprehended these "criminals" was clearly different from procedures practiced by the medieval tribunals. For the year 1461–1462, for instance, the same individual, a certain Francesco di Lapuccio, a silk weaver who resided in the parish of S. Ambrogio beyond the city walls, accused 9 of the first 12 offenders. Francesco had had affairs with all of these men.[33] Agnolino di Cristofano d'Agnolo, who was variously identified as a ragman and an apprentice to a cobbler *(sta al calzolaio)*, brought charges against at least eight of his lovers.[34] In one case, Domenico di Giovanni Lunghi from Modena, a candy vendor *("che vende sconfortini in Mercato Vecchio")* lured the little boy Agnolino into his apartment by tempting him with candy.[35] But in other cases the descriptions show no signs of deception or violations against the will of the plaintiff. The reappearance of the same plaintiffs in case after case suggests that the Officials of the Night rounded up a few known homosexuals and then forced these men or boys to implicate their lovers. Clearly, this court was cutting into private affairs, matters of morality which the medieval tribunals (at least in practice) left untouched.

But if we can be assured that the changes in criminality detected in the medieval tribunals between the fourteenth and fifteenth centuries

---

30. Brucker, "The Florentine *Popolo Minuto*," p. 170.
31. I would like to thank Sherrill Cohen for bringing my attention to these records.
32. Ufficiali di notte, n. 9, 12v, 20r–v, 21r, 25r–v, 28v.
33. *Ibid.*, 1r–9r.
34. *Ibid.*, 12r, 13r, 15v, 17r–v, 21v, 22v.
35. *Ibid.*, 17r.

were not the results of changes in the jurisdictions of the courts, can we still be absolutely certain that there were not changes in criminal behavior? Indeed, changes in the levels of criminal violence against persons might in part be explained by changing patterns of community and networks of association among the *popolo minuto*. We have found, after all, a fundamental change in the social structure of the *popolo minuto* from the late Trecento to the late Quattrocento. From a population which during the period of Ciompi insurrections was assuming a city-wide identification of itself in terms of its social networks of association, the *popolo minuto* of the late fifteenth century turned inward; its communities became fragmented and isolated, clustered tightly around the large parishes of the city's periphery. This regression of the artisan and laboring classes of Quattrocento Florence into a social formation more characteristic of a pre-capitalist society [36] reflects a class dominated more (than it had been during the revolutionary climate of the Ciompi period) by neighborhood, family, and customary or subliminal controls—controls which went beyond and beneath the bounds of articulated governmental policy and jurisdiction. In contrast the Trecento patterns of social association characterized a *popolo minuto* more political and more volatile than the laboring classes of Florence in the following century. These Trecento social patterns, moreover, must have affected other areas of social life. The emergence of the *popolo minuto* from the customary bonds of the parish community, which my statistics on marriage patterns underscore, must have had consequences that were less memorable than the grand events of Ciompi insurrection. In comparison to the latter half of the Quattrocento criminality persisted at staggering levels, and physical violence among members of the *popolo minuto* was rampant. In other words, the loosening of the old parochial social and religious bonds during the Trecento had consequences for both inter- and infra-class conflicts.

Beyond these changes in social relations, certain "social facts" of the latter half of the Quattrocento might explain in part the remarkable decline in assault and batteries. First, our statistics have shown that population densities must have declined during the fifteenth century: the population was slow to recover from the periodic returns of the Plague, while at the same time the population became more evenly

---

36. See Karl Marx, *Grundrisse: Foundations of the Critique of Political Economy,* translated by Martin Nicolaus (New York, 1973), p. 489; Anthony Giddens, *Capitalism and Modern Social Theory: An Analysis of the Writings of Marx, Durkheim and Max Weber* (Cambridge, 1971), p. 101; Max Weber, *The Theory of Social and Economic Organization,* translated by A. M. Henderson and Talcott Parsons (New York, 1947), 324–391; and C. Tilly, L. Tilly, and R. Tilly, *The Rebellious Century, 1830–1930* (Cambridge, Mass., 1975), pp. 4–13.

distributed across the urban territory of Florence because of "urban renewal" within the city's center.[37] Second, possible improvements in living standards may have created a less aggressive *popolo minuto*.[38] But are we really to believe that that mass of altercations, verbal as well as physical, among neighbors and relatives within the communities of the poor, that filled the ledgers of the Podestà during the Trecento, simply disappeared?

The other side of these criminal statistics, the changes in the levels and strategies of prosecution, speak more loudly. An interpretation of these changes is supported by structural changes in the institutions of law enforcement. In the first period of analysis, 46% of all cases of assault and murder were reported and brought to court *(ad relationem)* by the laic *cappellani* of the parish churches. Almost every church in the city—even those very small communities in the central city—had at least one and usually two of these officials who were elected twice a year by the entire *popolo* of the parish. For the most part, these chaplains were minor guildsmen, and we even find *sottoposti*, wage earners of the wool industry, holding these posts of responsibility for the parish's protection.[39] In the Communal statutes of the early fourteenth century, however, it does not appear that this office (at least from the perspective of the merchant class) was considered an honor or provided privilege: "Concerning the election of the chaplain . . . no one who is from one of the twelve major guilds can be forced against his will to be a chaplain."[40] Nonetheless, during the Trecento the basic unit of surveillance

---

37. For theories on the relationship between population density and criminal behavior, see Louis Chevalier, *Laboring Classes and Dangerous Classes in Paris during the Last Half of the Ninteenth Century*, translated by F. Jellinek (New York, 1973), p. 193.

38. Whether the standard of living in the second half of the fifteenth century was substantially higher than what it had been during the late Trecento is still a matter for debate. We now know from the mammoth research of Charles de la Roncière, *Florence: Centre économique régional au XIVe siècle* (Aix-en-Provence, 1977), 5 vols., that wages and the standard of living of the poor in general were rising during the third quarter of the Trecento. From our work, moreover, on the distribution of dowries, it appears that the poor (at least relative to the general population) were capable of amassing greater dowries during the period of the Ciompi than they were a century later. The "golden age" of the wage earner had probably ended by the second half of the fifteenth century. Population and grain prices were again beginning to rise. See Marco Lastri, *Ricerche sull'antica e moderna popolazione della città Firenze* (Florence, 1775); and Richard Goldthwaite, "I prezzi del grano a Firenze dal XIV al XVI secolo," *Quaderni Storici*, 28 (1975), pp. 5–36.

39. During the spring and summer semester of 1345, both of the cappellani of the parish of S. Michele Visdomini as well as a cappellanus of S. Pier Maggiore were wool combers *(pettinatori)*, ACP, n. 127, 172r, 287r and 325r.

40. *Statuti della Repubblica*, vol. 2, 49, Statuto del Podestà (1325), *"De electione cappellanorum . . . Et quod nullus qui sit ex aliqua duodecim maiorum artium invitus cogatur esse cappellanus."*

was the parish church. Particularly in the period 1374–1375, entire parish communities were frequently summoned to court and fined because of a violation, usually an unsolved murder or a brutal slaying, which had occurred within the parish's jurisdiction. The community had failed to ring the church bells, to raise the hue and cry or to apprehend the culprit.[41] Every individual of the parish was fined, and the schedule of penalties was progressive. Everyone who lived in and owned a shop (in which was practiced one of the trades of the 21 guilds) was fined a standard 40 soldi. All other residents were fined 20 soldi, and those who resided outside the parish but who held a shop (*"quemlibet apothecam habitantem et non habitantem in dicto popolo"*) within its borders were charged 10 soldi.

In the period 1455–1466, the laic *cappellani* disappeared completely from the records of inquisitions and sentences of the medieval tribunals. A centralized and secular structure of law enforcement had supplanted the medieval parochial organizations. In the city, police enforcement relied on the 100 *berrovarii* of the Podestà and Capitano and, more importantly, on the force of the Otto di Guardia, its 200 *balestieri*, its 200 *famigli*, and its network of spies.[42] In the countryside, the larger jurisdiction of the Commune and the *podesterie* supplanted the parochial structure.[43] Quite unlike the laic rectors who were residents of the parish and elected by their *popolo*, the officials of the larger secular units were appointees of the expanding Florentine bureaucracy. From the offices of *castellani* to *capitani*, almost universally, the patriciate of urban Florence—the Machiavelli, the Soderini, etc.—in many cases perhaps beginning their careers in the civil service, held these posts in the subject towns or in obscure zones of the *contado*.[44]

---

41. ACP n. 2768, 21r,

> Omnes et syngules homines populi, universitatis et comunitatis Sancti Petri Maioris in mense novembris studiose cessaverunt et neglexerunt curre, clamare (et) campanas, pulsare, capere et captum (esse) in fortiam dictis communis . . . civ. Flor. ponere et mictere Bartolommeum Johannis vocatur Dodecim qui deliberate, appensate, ex proposito et male modo contra fornam iuris . . . percussuit et vulneravit Loctum Andrencii de populo Sancti petri Maioris cum cultello ferreo . . .

See also 25r, 27r, 31v, 38r, 39r, 49r, 50r, 55v, 57r, 67r; AP n. 2770, 72r; ACP n. 803, 4r, 4v, 5r, 5v, 21r, 23r, 36r, 38r; and Dorini, *Il diritto penale*, 209–211.

42. "La magistratura," pp. 10–11, 21.

43. The *podesterie* and the communes were ancient jurisdictions whose origins push back into the thirteenth century, but their predominance over the ecclesiastical units of jurisdiction—the *popoli*—emerges only during the course of the fifteenth century.

44. Periodically through the sentences of the Podestà, 1455–1466, the officials of the courts, the Capitani, the Podestà, and the *castellani* of the provincial forts of the *contado* and the subject towns were absolved from any crimes which they may have committed during their

The parallels between the changes in the composition of criminality and changes in the structure of law enforcement and jurisdiction—the centralization of the courts and the police and the concomitant destruction of the local parochial units that relied on the cooperation and service of artisans, laborers, and peasants—suggest that the dramatic decline in those crimes that predominated in the criminal records of the Trecento—assaults and batteries among peasants, artisans, and laborers—was not the result of a critical change in criminal behavior nor a slackening of the repressive forces of the state. Quite the contrary, alongside the development of the Otto di Guardia and its more repressive measures for political and criminal surveillance, the medieval tribunals of the Podestà and the Capitano increasingly assumed a class character. One aspect of this development was the increase in the relative number of indictments against peasants who allegedly committed violations on the rural estates of the urban patriciate and an increase in the number of cases in which the guild and merchants' courts used the criminal apparatus of the Podestà and the Capitano to prosecute their debtors. The other side of this development was the systematic neglect of protection and of responsibility for serving as the means of arbitration for artisans, laborers, and peasants within their own rural or working-class parishes. No longer, by the middle of the fifteenth century, did cases involving fist fights or knifings among peasants, artisans, or workers clog up the courts; no longer was a team of notaries required to fill pages on end with the particulars of these crimes in the ledgers of the criminal inquisitions, accusations, testimonies, and sentences.

On first impression, this observation might seem paradoxical. We might imagine that centralization and improved efficiency of the law enforcement machinery would lead to increased concern and surveillance of all criminality through all strata of society. After all, random fist fights and disorder in the working-class parishes might spread into more disruptive violence that would threaten the stability of the Florentine community as a whole or even threaten the stability of the Florentine state. But, in certain American cities today we find the same inconsistency: an obsession with "law and order" and, at the same

---

six-month tenures in office; see, for instance, AP n. 5098, 13r, 15r, 53r, 59r, 63r, 71r, 77r, 84r, 87r, 91r, 92r, 101r, 105r, 110r, 115r, 123r, 129r, 137r, 143r, 157r, 159r, 167r, 173r, 178r, 184, 190r, 194r, 202r, 210r, 218r, 224r, 228r, 230r, 236r, 240r, 246r, 252r, 256r, and 257r. For a discussion of the development of the Florentine state and its bureaucracy, see Becker, "The Florentine Territorial State," pp. 109–140; A. Molho, "The Florentine Oligarchy and the Balìa of the late Trecento," *Speculum*, XLIII (1968), 23–51; and Gene Brucker, *The Civic World*, pp. 6–11.

time, a nonchalance towards criminality or even homicide in the ghettos or among minority groups.[45]

In conclusion, the structural changes in criminality, the strategies of prosecution and the organization of law enforcement outlined by the statistics on indictments for the fourteenth and fifteenth centuries in Florence may not have been so far removed from political conflicts supposedly on the surface of history. They seem, instead, to have been the consequence as well as the instrument of changes in the balance of class power between the *popolo minuto* and *reggimento* (or ruling class) which developed from the fall of the Ciompi through the Quattrocento. These changes undoubtedly rested on changes in the ecology of the city. From the period 1340–1383 to the second half of the fifteenth century, the city assumed a class geography. In the mid- and late Trecento, the populations of the poor appear from the notarial and tax records evenly dispersed across the landscape of urban Florence. By the later part of the Quattrocento, the social ecology of the city had changed. Over 80% of the poor resided in ghettos clustered on the city's periphery, within the large parishes of S. Ambrogio, S. Lorenzo, S. Frediano, and S. Maria in Verzaia.

Because of this class segregation it would have been much easier for the merchant class of fifteenth-century Florence to ignore everyday

---

45. In a recent study of murder in Houston, the anthropologist Lundsgaarde, *Murder in Space City*, pp. 10 and 190, observes:

> On the one hand, there are both public officials and private citizens who do not view homicide as cause for alarm. This lack of concern stems in part from the observation that most killings and fighting occur among racial minorities and others at the bottom of the social hierarchy. . . . The Houston data illustrate how a large community can effect social control through a variety of sanctioning processes. One such process, so clearly evident in the cases presented in this book, demonstrates how a community positively rewards private citizens who defend their rights, personal honor, or their property by taking the lives of those who threaten them. The data further show that homicides that result from unsatisfactory interpersonal relationships are not viewed in any way as threatening to the maintenance of social order.

For the later middle ages, Hammer, "Homicide in Fourteenth Century Oxford," p. 23, concludes:

> Although the Oxford experience seems horrendous when viewed collectively, what would have been the effect on the average, solid burgess . . . of the violent demise of some obscure and socially marginal figure every month. . . . Moreover, we know from recent experience that a high level of personal violence may be tolerated by the influential as socially innocuous if it is confined largely to people of low or marginal social status, and that societies can respond selectively to, even sanction positively, the use of physical force by individuals.

problems and grievances among the *popolo minuto* themselves. Moreover, the changes in immigration of the *popolo minuto*—the influx of
Italians from other city–states and of other foreigners, particularly
Germans—would have made it much easier for the authorities of the
Florentine Commune and the merchant class generally to perceive the
popolo minuto more consciously as "a minority group" whose rights
and needs were somehow different from those of the native Florentine
citizenry.[46] In contrast, the ecology of Trecento Florence, in which
merchants, magnates, artisans, and *sottoposti* generally resided in the
same communities and congregated in the same parish churches, and
where the immigrant supply of laborers originated from the surrounding countryside and freely intermarried with the native population,
had made less feasible the selectivity of surveillance and prosecution
indicated by the gaps in the condemnations of the mid-Quattrocento.
Unlike the late Quattrocento, the problems of the Trecento *popolo
minuto*—their altercations and violations against one another—were
problems of the urban community as a whole.

But it would be misleading to regard the geography of the city as a
pre-condition, an independent variable which operated in a different
modality of time from an event such as the Revolt of the Ciompi.[47] The
geographical fragmentation in residential patterns of the fifteenth century as well as the even sharper psychological and social fragmentation and parochialism indicated by fundamental changes in networks
of social association of the *popolo minuto* can be seen as the consequences
of the imbalance in class conflict, which the transformations in the
composition of criminality have chronicled. The ripping of community
control out of the hands of the *popolo minuto* and the consequent
class character of surveillance, prosecution and the courts that emerged
during the Quattrocento may have created more insecurity and disorder
(from the point of view of the *popolo minuto*) than we can possibly
imagine from the hundreds of fist fights and stabbings which fill the
sentences of the earlier period. Similar to the "inward turning" of
settlement patterns in Marc Bloch's first feudal age,[48] the geography and
social relations of the *popolo minuto* in fifteenth-century Florence reflected the malaise of social and psychological insecurity. But, instead

---

46. For the relationship of class geography and class segregation to racism, see Chevalier,
Laboring Classes and Dangerous Classes, pp. 433ff.

47. See Braudel's discussion of modalities of time, *The Mediterranean and the Mediterranean
World in the Age of Philip II,* 2 vols. translated by S. Reynolds (New York, 1973), pp. 1238–1244
and "Histoire et science sociale la longue durée," *Annales: E. S. C.,* 4 (1958), 725–53.

48. Marc Bloch, *Feudal Society,* 2 vols., translated by L. A. Manyon (Chicago, 1961), pp. 59–
65.

of the "insecurity of an age," it was the insecurity of a class. And its cause, instead of the disappearance of centralized authority, was its over-abundance: on the one hand, repression; on the other, the systematic neglect by the state of the community problems of artisans, laborers, and peasants.

Chapter 9

Toward an Explanation

T HE interpretation of the Revolt of the Ciompi as just another Italian *imbroglio* must be revised.[1] When the form and content of this insurrection as well as the movement of insurrections, more generally, of the mid-Trecento are compared to popular movements in France and in England from the French Revolution to the early period of industrialization, the Ciompi revolt appears remarkably modern. In the mid- and late Trecento there were strikes, secret meetings, the beginning of working men's associations. Food riots were rare and the appearance of women (concerned with the immediate well-being of the hearth), almost unknown in the crowds of insurrectionists. Instead of arising out of dire material scarcity, the riots arose against the backdrop of sharply rising wages and even, at times, falling bread prices. Most important, the Revolt of the Ciompi was not just another millennarian outburst; the designs of the Ciompi were firmly rooted in "this-worldliness." Through the formation of working-class guilds which cut across the parochialism of individual skills and trades, for a short time, they successfully integrated themselves into the citizenry and government of Florence. For the first time, workers and artisans (the *popolo minuto*) could participate in determining the economic and political policy of the state and of the largest industry in Florence, wool production.

Indeed, when placed in the framework of the models for social protest constructed for eighteenth- and nineteenth-century France and England by Charles Tilly and George Rudé, the social movements of the mid-fourteenth century in Florence appear at first sight suspiciously modern. But the forms of social protest observed during the period of

---

1. Gene A. Brucker, "The Ciompi Revolution," in *Florentine Studies,* edited by N. Rubinstein (London, 1968), p. 356.

the Ciompi cannot be understood in and of themselves, nor simply as reflections of changes in the mode of production. The historian must consider popular revolt in relation to the nature of the state, the development of its repressive apparatuses and in relation to the class formation of the ruling elites. Our study of the fourteenth and fifteenth centuries has shown, moreover, that the "modernization" of the repertoires of popular insurrection does not always follow a unilinear chronology; nor does it necessarily parallel advances in statecraft or the progression of social and economic structures. From the perspective of the laboring and artisan neighborhoods of Renaissance Florence, the fourteenth century was far more "modern" than the fifteenth. Instead of the succession of historical stages with neat correspondences among modes of production, repertoires of insurrection, and the progression of the modern state, the principle of uneven development proves to be a better key for understanding reciprocal but opposing developments: the formation of the Florentine Renaissance state and changes in the strategies of class conflict.[2]

At the time of the Revolt of the Ciompi (1378) one-third to one-half of the work force were wage laborers—a proportion that is comparable to those involved in manufactory production in Paris, 1789. These workers, brought together by new capitalist relations of production that cut across old *communal* networks of association, challenged the domination of a state which was still medieval. The courts and the organization of social control were distributed among three overlapping institutions—the Podestà, the Capitano del Popolo and the Esecutore degli Ordinamenti di Giustizia. A different foreign dignitary directed each of these judicial and executive bodies. There were no precise divisions in the functions of the three bodies, nor a clear hierarchy of control. In short, there was no sovereign body in the modern sense. The actual positions of social control, moreover, were decentralized. The most important organizations of police surveillance and law enforcement were the small parish communities—their lay chaplains and the reliance on the "hue and cry" of the inhabitants. Thus, the mid-fourteenth century presents an uneven development between the formation of the social relations of production or the mode of production and the formation of the state. Because of this uneven development, the Ciompi could assume the modern *associational* forms of protest as opposed to the *communal* ones which generally characterized insurrection in France until the late 1840s. Would the Ciompi insurrections,

---

2. See Chapter 5, note 60.

1342–1383, have been conceivable within the context of the absolutist state of the Ancien Régime?

In contrast, forms of popular protest by the middle of the fifteenth century in Florence had changed completely. The city was no longer torn periodically by civil strife taking the form of class discord, mass movements, and insurrections. Instead, the popular classes seem to have entered a period of quiescence. The expressions of class conflict that can be found in the criminal archives were mostly individual and isolated acts—arson or assaults on individual members of the merchant class. Examples of collective actions are rare; moreover, their forms—protests in the subject towns against the central authority of Florence, neighbors defending a friend accused of theft or indebtedness—reflect *communal* ties as opposed to the *associational* relations which structured the social protests of the previous century.

Concomitantly, by the middle of the fourteenth century, the polity of Renaissance Florence had been transformed. Through the successive issuing of emergency decrees called *balìa,* and through the development of its own police and court system (the Otto di Guardia), the Signoria had clearly become a sovereign power.[3] The courts and the police of the medieval courts continued to exist through the fifteenth century, but instead of exercising control over the Signoria and the Florentine patriciate, they had clearly become the instruments of the Signoria's control. The day-to-day sentences of these medieval courts during the last 12 years of Cosimo de'Medici's rule leave little doubt about the shift in the hierarchy of control. We no longer find in the sentences of the Capitano del Popolo fines levelled against members of the Signoria, individually or collectively, for certain violations in procedure explicated in the Statutes of the Capitano or of the Podestà.[4] Instead, we find the Signoria through its criminal court and law enforcing agency, the Otto di Guardia (staffed solely by members of the Florentine patriciate), intervening in and determining the outcome of all important criminal cases and especially those cases which touched on the security of the state. Second, the local *foci* of police enforcement and community re-

---

3. Cf. Anthony Molho, "The Florentine Oligarchy and the *Balìa* of the Late Trecento," *Speculum* XLIII (1968), 23–51, and Giovanni Antonelli, "La magistratura degli Otto di Guardia a Firenze," *Archivo Storico Italiano,* XCII (1954), pp. 3–40; Brucker, *The Civic World in Early Renaissance Florence* (Princeton, 1977), pp. 484 and 501; R. C. Trexler, "Florence, By Grace of the Lord Pope . . .," *Studies in Medieval and Renaissance History,* 9 (1972), 115–215; Marvin Becker, "The Florentine Territorial State and Civic Humanism in the Early Renaissance," in *Florentine Studies,* edited by N. Rubinstein (London, 1968), pp. 109–140.

4. ACP n. 19, fol. 7r–8v, 11r–12v, 19r–20v.

sponsibility, the parish and its officials, disappear from the inquisitions redacted by the courts. In the countryside, the larger secular districts of the *podesterie* and the *capitani*, staffed by Florentine patricians, absorbed the responsibilities of the parish, its rectors, and its reliance on the "hue and cry" of its inhabitants. In the city, the networks of spies and the new centralized bodies of *balestrieri* and *berrovarii* organized and controlled by the Otto abolished the old jurisdictions of mutual assistance and community responsibility.

But how do we explain these shifts from the fourteenth to the fifteenth centuries in the nature of popular protest and in the structure of the Florentine state? Can they be understood simply as political phenomena or as the consequences of changes in the mode of production?

Historians now view the Revolt of the Ciompi as the result of factionalism within the late Trecento oligarchy.[5] The political role of the *popolo minuto* has been minimized to such an extent that these historians assume that the political developments of the fourteenth and fifteenth centuries and the formation of the Renaissance state can be understood exclusively through studying the elite classes of Florence.[6] Through a statistical analysis of social networks of association among laborers and artisans we have shown that their social structure and community organization were not so static as historians have assumed. Moreover, changes in the class formation of the *popolo minuto* traced through these networks bear a direct relationship to the formation of the Florentine patriciate as a class.

Briefly, during the period of the Ciompi, 1340–1383, the social networks of association among the *popolo minuto* assumed contours across the geography of urban Florence that were very similar to those of the patriciate. But during the fifteenth century our statistics narrate a sharp bifurcation in the community structures of these classes. The patriciate emerged from the world of neighborhood enclaves and factionalism—breaking down the vestiges of old tower family formations—to create city-wide networks and to identify themselves simply as citizens of Florence; while the *popolo minuto* lost their capacity for city-wide organization and insurrection. They "turned inward" around their parish communities. The map of their fifteenth-century networks of association shows a working class fractured into many small and isolated social groups defined largely by the parochial communities of Renaissance Florence.

---

5. Brucker, *Florentine Politics and Society, 1343–1378* (Princeton, 1962), p. 388; Sergio Bertelli, "Oligarchies et gouvernment dans la Renaissance," *Social Science: Information sur les sciences sociales* XV–4/5 (1976), p. 623.

6. Cf. Brucker, *Florentine Politics and Society* and *The Civic World*.

These working-class formations of the late Quattrocento depended in part on forces (perhaps) exogenous to the political economy of urban Florence—the changes in the sources of the supply of laborers to Florentine industry. They relied on distant migrants from other Italian cities and foreign countries in lieu of the local *contadini* who so freely intermingled and intermarried with the native Florentine population during the fourteenth century. This transformation certainly contributed to the tightening of local defensiveness and parochialism. In the fifteenth century the largest single group of immigrant laborers (the Germans) lived in two distinct ghettos, isolated from the Florentine population and more narrowly enclosed within their parish communities than any other subgroup in Florentine society.

Other structural developments impinged upon the community structures of the *popolo minuto*. The growing importance of the silk industry, which relied more on the putting-out system and on quasi-independent and highly skilled laborers than did the wool industry, might have influenced the nature of social relations beyond the work place. But there was no fundamental transformation in the mode of production. According to the most recent historiography, wool production increased in the fifteenth century, and silk manufactories did not become the major employers of Florentine labor until the end of the sixteenth or even the early seventeenth century.

We have argued that the "inward turning" of the working classes of Florence during the Quattrocento—more than the automatic consequence of certain structural changes, the character of the labor supply, or a fundamental transformation in the mode of production—was the result largely of a shift in the balance of power that developed after the fall of the Ciompi and progressed through the bureaucratic developments of the oligarchy during the last decades of the fourteenth century and the early fifteenth century and finally through the statecraft of the Medici. The formation of the Renaissance state during the fifteenth century, in turn, did not occur within a social vacuum, but was itself the product of class struggle.

The crucial event for the understanding of fifteenth-century developments in class structure and state formation is in fact the Revolt of the Ciompi. Not only did it result in the exile of the Ciompi's leadership and a considerable portion of its rank and file,[7] it broke a tradition of artisan and working-class militancy and resistance.[8] Furthermore, Professor

---

7. Niccolò Rodolico, *La democrazia fiorentina nel suo tramonto (1378-1382)* (Bologna, 1905), p. 428; and Brucker, *The Civic World*, p. 71.

8. For the psychological consequences of the defeat of the Ciompi on subsequent workers' skirmishes with the state, see Brucker, *The Civic World*, p. 101: "Among the workers and artisans

Molho has shown the impact of the Ciompi on the ideology and political strategies of the oligarchy during the last decades of the Trecento and early Quattrocento. Memories of the Ciompi, kept very much alive through brilliant polemicists such as Leonardo Bruni, convinced the ruling elites of Florence to abandon ideals of neighborhood power, and ultimately certain liberties, in order to form a stronger state organization with stronger instruments for social repression.[9]

The history of class formation and the development of statecraft in Renaissance Florence, from the period of the Ciompi to the Principality, illustrates the dialectic between voluntarism (or political action) and structure, the strands which Karl Marx sensitively interwove:

> People make their own history but they do not make it just as they please, they do not make it under circumstances chosen by themselves; but under circumstances directly encountered, given and transmitted from the past.[10]

On the one hand, the fundamental changes in community and class structure described and analyzed in this book hinged on an event supposedly on the surface of history—the Revolt of the Ciompi. On the other, uneven development in economic and state structures created the possibility for the extraordinary modernity of the popular movements preceding this event, as well as the success of the event itself—a working-class regime at the end of the middle ages. In the period after the Ciompi, the instruments first developed by the government of the minor guilds— the Otto di Guardia, its summary courts, networks of spies, and centralized police—to combat the radicals among the Ciompi (the Otto di Santa Maria Novella) and to protect themselves against an aristocratic resurgence,[11] were used in the following decade to crush the government of the *Arti Minori* and to restore the oligarchic rule of the patriciate. These same instruments were then developed and turned against the patricians themselves during the years of the Medici Republic and ultimately and decisively during the absolutist regimes of the Principality to establish the hegemony of a single family.

---

who failed to respond to Bastardino's appeal (1397) were hundreds—perhaps thousands—who sympathized with the rebels, but who had seen too many comrades being escorted to the gallows by the officials of the *podestà* and *capitani*."

9. Molho, "The Florentine Oligarchy," p. 26; "Politics and the Ruling Class in Early Renaissance Florence," *Nuova Rivista Storica*, LII (1968), p. 416; and Brucker, "Some Aspects of Oligarchical, Dictatorial, and Popular *Signorie* in Florence, 1282–1382," *Comparative Studies in Society and History*, 26 (1960), 439.

10. Karl Marx, *The 18th Brumaire of Louis Bonaparte* (New York, 1963), p. 15.

11. See Rodolico, *La democrazia fiorentina*, p. 393.

Appendixes

Appendix A
Notaries Sampled for Marriage Statistics, 1340–1383

A 181 (1337–80)	B 2689 (1365–70)
A 206 (1351–53)	B 2690 (1370–81)
A 383 (1370–73)	C 4 (1340–46)
A 426 (1336–43)	C 130 (1341–60), (1360–64)
A 849 (1363)	C 335 (1378–83)
A 909 (1369–71)	C 464 (1343)
A 923 (1346)	C 452 (1373–84)
B 190 (1373–76)	C 598 (1343–44)
B 191 (1374–1417)	C 600 (1345–53)
B 192 (1376–81)	C 602 (1358–63)
B 193 (1379–81)	C 604 (1370–81)
B 194 (1381–85)	C 605 (1338–41), (1341–45)
B 381 (1345–47)	C 669 (1336–1388)
B 406 (1350–55)	F 393 (1370–1426), (1372–83)
B 708 (1348–51)	F 529 (1338–40), (1344–46)
B 1951 (1322–43)	F 535 (1355–59)
B 2567 (1343–48)	F 566 (1343–46)
B 2568 (1348–56)	G 16 (1374–77)
B 2569 (1356–63)	G 71 (1361–99)
ʙ 2570 (1361–65)	G 165 (1374–76)
B 2571 (1365–69)	

Appendix A (*Continued*)

G 167 (1326–48)	M 490 (1342)
G 384 (1355–64)	M 606 (1378–87)
G 384 (1369–75)	N 63 (1377–80)
G 394 (1365–68), (1369–72)	N 69 (1372–80)
G 395 (1377–80)	N 90 (1344–67)
G 396 (1381–84)	N 160 (1372)
G 414 (1341–47)	N 191 (1366–73)
G 438 (1379–84)	N 220 (1352–55)
G 451 (1340–42)	O 32 (1348–62)
G 583 (1316–63)	O 53 (1337–48)
I 16 (1378–84)	P 21 (1345–46)
L 75 (1375–82)	P 104 (1354–61)
L 77 (1349–62)	S 102 (1345)
L 128 (1374–85)	S 507 (1339–56)
M 272 (1375–79), (1379–93),	T 10 (1350–58)
(1384–85)	Z 58 (1369–1456)

Appendix B
Notaries Sampled for Marriage Statistics, 1450–1530

A 124 (1481–85)	G 155 (1481–87)
A 153 (1472–75)	G 158 (1484–1502)
A 374 (1447–1460)	G 192 (1446–57)
A 501 (1495–1502)	G 230 (1504–22)
A 720 (1455–58)	G 237 (1479–91), (1491–99), (1500–08)
B 775 (1449–53)	G 252 (1450–69)
B 824 (1483–1527)	G 266 (1479–85)
B 856 (1462–72)	G 271 (1461–75)
B 1304 (1489–99)	G 274 (1476–82)
B 2321 (1481–89)	G 275 (1470–81)
B 2322 (1489–91)	G 282 (1459–61)
C 150 (1486–91)	G 284 (1481–86)
C 525 (1437–55)	G 295 (1522–27)
C 676 (1472–78)	G 408 (1477–81)
D 22 (1471–82)	G 428 (1490–92)
D 87 (1458–61), (1458–67)	G 238 (1508–17), (1517–29)
D 89 (1466–69)	G 461 (1486–94)
D 91 (1474–76), (1474–76)	G 478 (1458–89)
D 92 (1481–83)	G 494 (1494)
D 93 (1488–89)	G 517 (1510–16)
D 95 (1494–1502), (1495–56),	G 518 (1460–75)
(1496–98)	G 573 (1511–24)
D 98 (1468–89)	G 579 (1514–58)
F 84 (1490–96)	G 589 (1458–67)
F 498 (1449–65), (1465–74)	G 611 (1508–11)
G 21 (1507–10)	G 616 (1458–59)
G 31 (1506–10)	G 617 (1463–65), (1466–69)
G 68 (1485–89)	G 618 (1476–78), (1482–83),
G 122 (1495–1506), (1506–15)	(1476–78)
G 152 (1524–36)	

Appendix B (*Continued*)

G 699 (1462-78)

G 738 (1513-28)

G 803 (1508-10)

G 849 (1478-81)

I 95 (1487-89)

I 119 (1494)

L 21 (1524-43)

L 33 (1508-29)

L 52 (1483-1509), (1491-1501), (1501-09)

L 60 (1488-98)

L 125 (1484-1505), (1505-26)

L 139 (1461-69), (1477-82)

L 140 (1500-17), (1463-1501)

L 141 (1488-95), (1495-99)

L 145 (1445-71)

L 149 (1486-93)

L 152 (1513-16)

L 166 (1507-14)

L 206 (1473-79)

L 284 (1465-79)

L 295 (1484-93)

L 298 (1512-23)

L 301 (1522-39)

L 341 (1466-75)

M 2 (1464-80)

M 30 (1492-97)

M 89 (1497-1506)

M 90 (1505-17)

M 103 (1453-58)

M 115 (1494-98)

M 144 (1491-97)

M 150 (1486-90)

M 196 (1442-54), (1460-67)

M 197 (1519-26)

M 203 (1454-68)

M 228 (1485)

M 233 (1459-67)

M 246 (1470-1526)

M 248 (1504-34)

M 275 (1492-97)

M 335 (1499-1504)

M 337 (1485-93)

M 339 (1509-10)

M 343 (1459-80)

M 380 (1495-1509)

M 227 (1480)

M 351 (1515-27)

M 381 (1491-98)

M 393 (1495-1512)

M 463 (1483-85)

M 530 (1468-1515)

M 531 (1512-20)

M 562 (1466-75)

M 565 (1481-84)

M 567 (1474-85) (1485-93)

M 569 (1458-60)

M 597 (1479-90)

M 604 (1453-65)

M 646 (1447-59), (1460-69)

M 647 (1484-86)

Appendix B (*Continued*)

M 666 (1481-92)	P 71 (1455-75), (1476-82),
M 669 (1488-97)	(1481-99), (1500-12)
M 701 (1513-21)	P 99 (1460-64)
M 729 (1524)	P 128 (1452-62)
M 756 (1491-1500)	P 129 (1462-65)
N 3 (1487-89), (1489-92)	P 167 (1509-13)
N 4 (1492-95)	P 204 (1525-45)
N 6 (1483-92)	P 355 (1492-94)
N 8 (1500-03)	R 30 (1518-40)
N 16 (1460-64)	R 31 (1492-1508)
N 19 (1461-69), (1470-79),	R 33 (1525-29)
(1480-89), (1490-97)	R 36 (1527-33)
N 61 (1497-1520)	R 109 (1527-29)
N 91 (1444-56)	R 167 (1520-27)
O 7 (1514-18)	R 304 (1528-30)
O 41 (1470-1500)	T 155 (1457-61)
O 83 (1523-37)	V 178 (1492-96)
P 44 (1513-23)	V 201 (1504-10)

Each set of parentheses corresponds to a separate notarial <u>filza</u>.

Appendix C.1
Marriage Endogamies for the Fourteenth Century by Period

I. BEFORE THE BLACK DEATH (1349)

PARISH	ENDOGAMIES: (a) PARISH	(b) GONFALONE	(c) QUARTER	(d) CLUSTER	(e) CROSS-QUARTER	EXOGAMIES: (f) CROSS-CLUSTER	(g) CONTADO	TOTAL
S. FREDIANO	3	–	2	2	3	3	–	8
S. MARIA IN VERZAIA	–	–	–	–	–	–	1	1
S. PIERO GATTOLINO	1	2	1	3	–	–	1	5
S. FELICITÀ	–	–	1	1	1	1	–	2
S. FELICE IN PIAZZA	11	2	1	3	5	5	–	19
S. GIORGIA	–	–	–	–	1	1	–	1
S. LUCIA OGNISSANTI	1	–	2	2	1	1	–	4
S. MARIA NOVELLA	–	–	–	–	1	1	–	1
S. PAOLO	5	2	1	2	–	1	1	9
S. PANCRAZIO	1	–	–	–	1	1	1	3
S. TRINITÀ	–	–	1	1	–	–	–	1
S. LORENZO	6	–	1	–	3	4	2	12
S. AMBROGIO	–	–	–	–	2	2	–	2
S. PIERO MAGGIORE	3	–	1	–	2	3	–	6
S. SIMONE	–	–	–	2	4	2	–	4
S. IACOPO TRA LE FOSSE	2	–	–	–	–	–	–	2
S. MARIA DEL FIORE	1	2	1	–	–	3	–	4

								Total
S. MARIA MAGGIORE	–	2	2	2	–	2	–	4
ORSANMICHELE	–	–	–	–	1	1	–	1
S. MARIA SOPRA PORTA	–	–	3	–	–	3	–	3
S. STEFANO AL PONTE	–	–	–	–	–	–	1	1
S. ROMOLO	–	–	–	1	1	–	–	1
S. FIRENZE	–	–	–	–	1	1	–	1
S. PROCOLO	–	–	–	–	–	–	1	1
S. MARIA DEGLI ALBERIGHI	1	–	1	–	–	1	–	2
S. MARIA NIPOTECOSA	–	1	–	1	–	–	–	1
S. MARIA DEGLI UGHI	–	1	–	–	–	1	–	1
S. PIERO CELORO	–	–	1	1	–	–	–	1
S. MARTINO	–	–	1	–	–	1	–	1
CONTADO	–	–	–	–	–	–	–	6
TOTAL (Women)	35	12	20	21	27	38	8	102
TOTAL (Men)	35	12	20	21	27	38	6	100
TOTAL	70	24	40	42	54	76	14	202
	.3465	.1188	.1980	.2079	.2673	.3762	.0694	
CUMULATIVE TOTAL		.4653	.6634	.5545				

217

Appendix C.2
Marriage Endogamies for the Fourteenth Century by Period

II. 1350 – 1379

| PARISH | ENDOGAMIES: | | | | EXOGAMIES: | | | TOTAL |
	(a) PARISH	(b) GONFALONE	(c) QUARTER	(d) CLUSTER	(e) CROSS-QUARTER	(f) CROSS-CLUSTER	(g) CONTADO	
S. FREDIANO	4	–	2	1	9	10	8	23
S. MARIA IN VERZAIA	–	2	1	3	1	1	–	4
S. PIERO GATTOLINI	–	–	–	–	1	1	4	5
S. IACOPO SOPR'ARNO	–	–	–	–	–	–	1	1
S. FELICITÀ	4	1	2	3	3	3	–	10
S. FELICE IN PIAZZA	8	2	2	4	8	8	8	28
S. NICCOLÒ	2	–	–	–	3	3	1	6
S. GIORGIO	–	–	–	–	2	2	1	3
S. LUCIA DEI BARDI	–	–	1	–	1	2	–	2
S. MARIA SOPR'ARNO	–	–	1	–	–	1	–	1
S. LUCIA OGNISSANTI	13	–	3	3	10	10	7	33
S. MARIA NOVELLA	–	–	6	5	4	5	–	10
S. PAOLO	7	1	6	5	6	8	4	24
S. PANCRAZIO	13	2	2	4	11	11	5	33
S. TRINITA	4	–	2	1	10	11	1	17
S. LORENZO	24	4	–	–	13	17	11	52
S. AMBROGIO	3	1	–	2	3	2	2	9
S. PIERO MAGGIORE	8	1	4	6	15	14	3	31

S. MICHELE VISDOMINI	1	–	–	2	1	3	–	4
S. SIMONE	3	–	2	2	11	11	3	19
S. REMIGIO	5	–	2	2	9	9	1	17
S. IACOPO FRA LE FOSSE	2	1	1	1	8	9	3	15
S. MARIA DEL FIORE	1	2	2	1	2	5	2	9
S. MARIA MAGGIORE	2	–	–	–	1	1	–	3
S. MICHELE BERTELDE	1	1	1	1	1	2	1	5
S. TOMMASO	–	–	–	–	2	2	–	2
S. MARIA IN CAMPIDOGLIO	–	–	–	–	1	1	–	1
ORSANMICHELE	1	–	–	–	–	–	–	1
S. MARIA SOPR'ARNO	1	–	–	–	–	–	–	1
SS. APOSTOLI	1	–	–	–	1	1	–	2
S. STEFANO AL PONTE	1	1	1	1	2	3	1	6
S. PIERO SCHERAGGIO	5	1	8	4	16	21	4	34
S. CECILIA	–	–	2	–	–	2	–	2
S. ROMOLO	–	–	–	–	1	1	–	1
S. FIRENZE	–	1	1	2	–	–	–	3
S. APOLLINARE	–	–	–	–	3	3	–	3
S. STEFANO ALLA BADIA	1	–	–	–	–	–	1	2

Appendix C.2 (*Continued*)

II. 1350 - 1379 (CONTINUED)

PARISH	ENDOGAMIES:				EXOGAMIES:			
	(a) PARISH	(b) GONFALONE	(c) QUARTER	(d) CLUSTER	(e) CROSS-QUARTER	(f) CROSS-CLUSTER	(g) CONTADO	TOTAL
S. PROCOLO	1	-	4	2	1	3	1	7
S. MARIA DEGLI ALBERIGHI	-	-	1	-	-	1	-	1
S. MARIA IN CAMPO	-	2	1	1	4	6	1	8
CANTADO								29
TOTAL (Women)	116	23	60	54	164	193	75	438
TOTAL (Men)	116	23	60	54	164	193	29	392
TOTAL	232	46	120	108	328	386	104	830
	.2795	.0554	.1446	.1301	.3952	.4651	.1253	
CUMULATIVE TOTALS		278	398	386				
		.3349	.4795	.4651				

Appendix C.3
Marriage Endogamies for the Fourteenth Century by Period

III. 1380 AND BEYOND

PARISH	ENDOGAMIES:				EXOGAMIES:			TOTAL
	(a) PARISH	(b) GONFALONE	(c) QUARTER	(d) CLUSTER	(e) CROSS-QUARTER	(f) CROSS-CLUSTER	(g) CONTADO	
S. FREDIANO	1	–	1	1	1	1	–	3
S. FELICE IN PIAZZA	2	1	1	2	–	–	–	4
S. LUCIA OGNISSANTI	7	–	1	1	5	5	1	14
S. MARIA NOVELLA	–	–	3	3	3	3	1	7
S. PAOLO	–	–	–	–	1	1	–	1
S. PANCRAZIO	1	1	–	1	1	1	–	3
S. TRINITÀ	–	–	1	1	1	1	–	2
S. LORENZO	21	–	5	–	14	19	11	53
S. MARCO	1	–	–	–	–	–	–	1
S. PIERO MAGGIORE	–	–	2	–	2	4	–	4
S. MICHELE VISDOMINI	1	–	–	–	–	–	–	1
S. SIMONE	1	–	–	–	1	1	2	4
S. REMIGIO	–	–	–	–	1	1	–	1
S. IACOPO TRA LE FOSSE	1	–	–	–	1	1	–	2
S. MARIA DEL FIORE	2	2	–	1	3	4	1	8
S. LEO	1	–	–	–	–	–	–	1
S. DONATO DEI VECCHIETTI	–	–	1	–	1	2	–	2

Appendix C.3 (*Continued*)

III. 1380 AND BEYOND (CONTINUED)

| PARISH | ENDOGAMIES: | | | | EXOGAMIES: | | | TOTAL |
	(a) PARISH	(b) GONFALONE	(c) QUARTER	(d) CLUSTER	(e) CROSS-QUARTER	(f) CROSS-CLUSTER	(g) CONTADO	
S. MARIA SOPRA PORTA	-	-	-	-	1	1	-	1
S. PIERO SCHERAGGIO	1	-	-	-	1	1	-	2
S. ROMOLO	-	-	1	-	-	1	-	1
S. MARIA IN CAMPO	1	-	4	1	1	4	1	7
CONTADO								5
TOTAL (Women)	41	4	20	11	39	52	17	121
TOTAL (Men)	41	4	20	11	39	52	5	109
TOTAL	82	8	40	22	78	104	22	230
	.3565	.0348	.1739	.0957	.3391	.4522	.0957	
CUMULATIVE TOTALS		.3913	.5652	.4522				

Appendix D.1
Marriage Endogamies for the Latter Half of the Fifteenth and the Early Sixteenth Centuries

I. 1450–1465

| PARISH | ENDOGAMIES: | | | | EXOGAMIES: | | | |
	(a) PARISH	(b) GONFALONE	(c) QUARTER	(d) CLUSTER	(e) CROSS-QUARTER	(f) CROSS-CLUSTER	(g) CONTADO	TOTAL
S. FREDIANO	66	11	6	16	30	31	11	124
S. MARIA IN VERZAIA	24	11	4	13	5	7	6	50
S. PIER GATTOLINO	10	3	2	5	1	1	2	18
S. IACOPO SOPR' ARNO	–	–	1	1	1	1	–	2
S. FELICITA	–	–	2	1	3	4	2	7
S. FELICE IN PIAZZA	6	–	10	8	5	7	7	28
S. NICCOLO	16	1	4	1	8	12	6	35
S. GIORGIO	–	–	1	–	4	5	1	6
S. LUCIA DE' BARDI	–	1	1	1	2	3	–	4
S. LUCIA OGNISSANTI	2	–	2	1	10	11	1	15
S. MARIA NOVELLA	2	1	2	3	5	5	1	11
S. PAOLO	–	–	3	3	5	5	2	10
S. PANCRAZIO	–	–	2	2	5	5	–	7
S. TRINITA	–	–	1	1	4	4	1	6

Appendix D.1 (*Continued*)

I. 1450–1465 (CONTINUED)

PARISH	ENDOGAMIES: (a) PARISH	(b) GONFALONE	(c) QUARTER	(d) CLUSTER	EXOGAMIES: (e) CROSS-QUARTER	(f) CROSS-CLUSTER	(g) CONTADO	TOTAL
S. LORENZO	32	–	11	–	19	30	10	72
S. MARCO	–	–	–	–	3	3	1	4
S. IACOPO IN CAMPO CORBOLINI	–	–	–	–	1	1	–	1
S. AMBROGIO	22	3	2	7	10	8	4	41
S. PIER MAGGIORE	2	3	9	6	11	17	5	30
S. MICHELE VISDOMINI	4	–	4	2	2	4	3	13
S. SIMONE	4	–	1	3	5	3	3	13
S. REMIGIO	4	–	–	–	5	5	3	12
S. IACOPO FRA LE FOSSI	4	–	1	–	4	5	1	10
S. MARIA DEL FIORE	–	–	1	–	7	8	4	12
S. MARIA MAGGIORE	2	–	–	–	1	1	1	4
S. LEO	–	–	–	–	2	2	–	2
S. DONATO DE' VECCHIETTI	2	–	–	–	1	1	1	4
S. TOMMASO	–	–	1	–	–	1	–	1
S. PIER BUON-CONSIGLIO	–	–	–	1	2	1	–	2

S. MARIA IN CAMPIDOGLIO	–	–	1	1	–	–	1
S. ANDREA	–	1	1	1	–	–	1
S. MARIA SOPRA PORTA	–	–	–	1	1	–	1
SS. APOSTOLI	–	2	1	–	1	–	2
S. STEFANO AL PONTE	2	1	2	5	4	–	8
S. PIERO SCHERAGGIO	4	1	–	3	4	3	11
S. ROMOLO	–	–	–	1	1	–	1
S. FIRENZE	–	–	1	2	1	1	3
S. APOLLINARE	–	2	1	1	2	–	3
S. MARIA NIPOTECOSA	–	1	–	1	2	–	2
S. MARIA DEGLI ALBERIGHI	–	1	–	–	1	–	1
S. MARIA IN CAMPO	–	1	–	1	2	–	2

225

Appendix D.I (*Continued*)

I. 1450–1465 (CONTINUED)

PARISH	ENDOGAMIES: (a) PARISH	(b) GONFALONE	(c) QUARTER	(d) CLUSTER	EXOGAMIES: (e) CROSS-QUARTER	(f) CROSS-CLUSTER	(g) CONTADO	TOTAL
TOTALS (Women)	104	17	41	41	89	106	48	299
(Men)	104	17	41	41	89	106	32	283
(Total)	208	34	82	82	178	212	80	582
	35.74%	5.84%	14.09%	14.09%	30.58%	36.43%	13.75%	
CUMULATIVE TOTALS		242	324	290				
	41.58%		55.67%	49.83%				

Appendix D.2
Marriage Endogamies for the Latter Half of the Fifteenth and the Early Sixteenth Centuries

II. 1466-1489

| PARISH | ENDOGAMIES: | | | | EXOGAMIES: | | | |
	(a) PARISH	(b) GONFALONE	(c) QUARTER	(d) CLUSTER	(e) CROSS-QUARTER	(f) CROSS-CLUSTER	(g) CONTADO	TOTAL
S. FREDIANO	8	2	2	4	8	8	6	24
S. MARIA IN VERZAIA	4	2	1	3	2	2	1	10
S. PIER GATTOLINI	4	1	2	2	5 •	6	4	16
S. IACOPO SOPR' ARNO	4	-	-	-	3	3	-	7
S. FELICITA	-	-	-	-	3	3	1	4
S. FELICE IN PIAZZA	6	1	2	3	11	11	2	22
S. NICCOLO	2	-	-	-	8	8	4	13
S. GIORGIO	2	-	-	-	1	1	1	4
S. LUCIA DE' BARDI	-	-	1	-	-	1	-	1
S. LUCIA OGNISSANTI	6	-	1	1	8	8	1	16
S. MARIA NOVELLA	2	-	1	1	1	1	3	6
S. PAOLO	2	-	-	-	5	5	-	7
S. PANCRAZIO	-	-	-	-	3	3	-	3
S. TRINITA	-	-	-	-	4	4	-	4

Appendix D.2 (*Continued*)

II. 1466–1489 (CONTINUED)

PARISH	ENDOGAMIES: (a) PARISH	(b) GONFALONE	(c) QUARTER	(d) CLUSTER	EXOGAMIES: (e) CROSS-QUARTER	(f) CROSS-CLUSTER	(g) CONTADO	TOTAL
S. LORENZO	40	1	6	1	19	25	10	76
S. MARCO	–	1	–	1	–	–	–	1
S. AMBROGIO	4	4	3	5	13	15	4	28
S. PIER MAGGIORE	8	5	5	6	8	12	7	33
S. MICHELE VISDOMINI	–	–	3	1	–	2	–	3
S. SIMONE	2	–	2	2	4	4	5	13
S. REMIGIO	–	1	–	3	2	–	–	3
S. IACOPO FRA LE FOSSE	–	1	1	3	5	4	–	7
S. CROCE	–	1	–	–	–	1	–	1
S. MARIA DEL FIORE	2	–	2	–	–	2	2	6
S. MARIA MAGGIORE	2	–	–	–	2	2	2	6

S. RUFILLO	–	–	–	–	–	3	3
S. MICHELE BERTELDE	2	–	–	1	1	–	3
S. APOLLINARE	–	1	–	–	1	–	1
S. PIERO SCHERAGGIO	–	–	–	5	5	–	5
S. PROCOLO	2	–	–	1	1	–	3
S. LEO	–	–	1	–	1	–	1
S. DONATO DE' VECCHIETTI	–	–	–	1	1	–	1
S. TOMMASO	–	–	–	–	–	1	1
S. MARIA IN CAMPIDOGLIO	–	1	–	–	1	–	1
S. MARIA SOPRA PORTA	–	–	1	1	1	–	1
S. STEFANO AL PONTE	–	–	1	5	6	1	7
S. BARTOLOMMEO AL CORSO	–	–	1	–	1	1	1
S. MARIA NIPOTECOSA	–	–	–	1	2	–	2
S. MARIA IN CAMPO	2	–	–	2	2	–	4

Appendix D.2 (Continued)

II. 1466–89 (CONTINUED)

PARISH	ENDOGAMIES: (a) PARISH	(b) GONFALONE	(c) QUARTER	(d) CLUSTER	EXOGAMIES: (e) CROSS-QUARTER	(f) CROSS-CLUSTER	(g) CONTADO	TOTAL
TOTALS (Women)	52	11	18	18	66	77	23	170
(Men)	52	11	18	18	66	77	32	179
(Total)	104	22	36	36	132	154	55	349
	29.80%	6.30%	10.32%	10.32%	37.82%	44.13%	15.76%	
CUMULATIVE TOTALS		126	162	140				
		36.10%	46.42%	40.11%				

Appendix D.3
Marriage Endogamies for the Latter Half of the Fifteenth and the Early Sixteenth Centuries

III. 1490–1530

PARISH	ENDOGAMIES: (a) PARISH	(b) GONFALONE	(c) QUARTER	(d) CLUSTER	EXOGAMIES: (e) CROSS-QUARTER	(f) CROSS-CLUSTER	(g) CONTADO	TOTAL
S. FREDIANO	14	4	6	10	17	17	17	58
S. MARIA IN VERZAIA	4	4	–	4	2	2	2	12
S. PIER GATTOLINO	4	–	3	3	5	5	5	17
S. IACOPO SOPR' ARNO	–	–	1	1	–	–	1	2
S. FELICITA	4	–	–	–	2	2	–	6
S. FELICE IN PIAZZA	4	–	2	2	9	9	4	19
S. NICCOLO	6	1	–	1	4	4	3	14
S. GIORGIO	–	1	–	1	3	3	–	4
S. LUCIA OGNISSANTI	54	–	5	5	19	19	14	92
S. MARIA NOVELLA	6	3	4	4	7	10	1	21
S. PAOLO	–	–	1	1	9	9	1	11
S. PANCRAZIO	–	–	1	1	–	–	–	1
S. TRINITA	–	–	1	1	1	1	1	3

231

Appendix D.3 (*Continued*)

III. 1490–1530 (CONTINUED)

PARISH	ENDOGAMIES: (a) PARISH	(b) GONFALONE	(c) QUARTER	(d) CLUSTER	EXOGAMIES: (e) CROSS-QUARTER	(f) CROSS-CLUSTER	(g) CONTADO	TOTAL
S. LORENZO	46	5	13	5	22	35	21	107
S. IACOPO IN CAMPO CORBOLINI	8	5	1	5	2	3	3	14
S. MARCO	2	1	1	–	–	1	–	4
S. AMBROGIO	16	3	6	5	9	13	9	43
S. PIER MAGGIORE	10	3	9	3	9	18	11	42
S. MICHELE VISDOMINI	4	–	3	–	8	11	5	20
S. SIMONE	2	–	–	1	6	5	–	8
S. REMIGIO	–	–	–	1	2	1	1	3
S. MARIA DEL FIORE	–	1	2	–	1	4	1	5
S. MARIA MAGGIORE	–	–	1	–	–	1	–	1
S. RUFILLO	–	–	–	–	1	1	–	1
S. MICHELE BERTELDE	–	1	–	–	–	1	–	1
S. LEO	–	–	1	–	–	1	–	1
S. DONATO DE' VECCHIETTI	2	2	1	1	4	6	–	9

S. TOMMASO	6	3	1	1	–	–	–	2
S. PIER BUONCONSIGLIO	3	–	1	1	–	–	–	2
S. ANDREA	2	–	1	1	1	1	–	–
S. MARIA SOPRA PORTA	1	–	–	1	1	–	–	–
SS. APOSTOLI	1	–	–	1	1	–	–	–
S. STEFANO AL PONTE	1	–	1	1	–	–	–	–
S. PIERO SCHERAGGIO	2	–	2	2	–	–	–	–
S. ROMOLO	5	1	3	4	1	–	–	–
S. FIRENZE	1	–	1	1	–	–	–	–
S. APOLLINARE	1		1	1	–	–	–	–
S. MARGHERITA DE' RICCI	1	–	1	–	–	1	–	–
S. BARTOLOMMEO AL CORSO	3	–	3	1	–	2	–	–
S. MARIA NIPOTECOSA	2	–	1	2	1	–	–	2
S. BENEDETTO	2	–	1	1	1	1	–	–

Appendix D.3 (*Continued*)

III. 1490–1530 (CONTINUED)

PARISH	ENDOGAMIES: (a) PARISH	(b) GONFALONE	(c) QUARTER	(d) CLUSTER	EXOGAMIES: (e) CROSS-QUARTER	(f) CROSS-CLUSTER	(g) CONTADO	TOTAL
S. CISTOFANO DEGLI ADIMARI	–	–	2	–	1	3	–	3
S. MARIA DEGLI UGHI	2	–	–	–	–	–	1	3
TOTALS (Women)	97	17	35	31	81	102	38	268
(Men)	97	17	35	31	81	102	67	297
(Total)	194	34	70	62	162	204	105	565
	34.34%	6.02%	12.39%	10.98%	28.67%	36.11%	18.58%	
CUMULATIVE TOTALS		228	298	256				
	40.35%	45.31%	52.74%	45.31%				

Appendix E.1

Marriage Endogamies for the Fourteenth Century According to the Size of
Dowry: Between 200 and 400 Florins

PARISH	ENDOGAMIES:				EXOGAMIES:			TOTAL
	(a) PARISH	(b) GONFALONE	(c) QUARTER	(d) CLUSTER	(e) CROSS-QUARTER	(f) CROSS-CLUSTER	(g) CONTADO	
S. FREDIANO	-	-	1	1	1	1	-	2
S. FELICITÀ	-	-	1	1	4	4	-	5
S. FELICE IN PIAZZA	2	-	1	-	-	2	2	6
S. NICCOLO	2	-	-	-	1	1	-	3
S. LUCIA DE'BARDI	-	-	1	-	-	1	-	1
S. LUCIA OGNISSANTI	2	-	1	-	1	1	-	4
S. MARIA NOVELLA	-	-	1	1	1	1	-	2
S. PAOLO	-	-	-	-	2	2	-	2
S. TRINITA	-	-	-	-	4	4	-	4
S. LORENZO	4	-	1	-	4	5	-	9
S. PIER MAGGIORE	4	-	-	1	5	4	-	9
S. MICHELE VISDOMINI	-	-	1	-	3	4	-	4
S. SIMONE	2	-	-	2	3	1	-	5
S. REMIGIO	2	-	-	-	1	1	-	3
S. IACOPO TRA LE FOSSE	4	-	-	-	1	1	-	5

Appendix E.1 (*Continued*)

PARISH	ENDOGAMIES:				EXOGAMIES:			TOTAL
	(a) PARISH	(b) GONFALONE	(c) QUARTER	(d) CLUSTER	(e) CROSS-QUARTER	(f) CROSS-CLUSTER	(g) CONTADO	
S. MARIA DEL FIORE	–	–	–	–	–	1	–	1
S. MARIA MAGGIORE	–	–	–	1	1	–	–	1
S. DONATO DE' VECCHIETTI	–	–	1	–	–	1	–	1
S. MARIA SOPR'ARNO	–	–	–	1	1	–	–	1
SS. APOSTOLI	–	–	–	–	1	1	–	1
S. PIERO SCHERAGGIO	–	–	–	1	4	3	1	5
S. ROMOLO	–	–	–	1	1	–	–	1
S. PROCOLO	–	–	–	–	1	1	–	1
S. MARIA NEPOTECOSA	–	–	–	1	1	–	–	1
S. MICHELE DELLE TROMBE	–	1	–	1	–	–	–	1
S. MARIA IN CAMPO	–	1	–	1	1	1	–	2
S. PIERO CELORO	–	–	–	1	1	–	–	1
TOTAL	22	2	10	15	44	41	3	81
	.2716	.0247	.1235	.1852	.5432	.5061	.0370	
		.2963	.4197	.4568				

Appendix E.2

Marriage Endogamies for the Fourteenth Century According to the Size of Dowry: 400 Florins or Greater

| PARISH | ENDOGAMIES: | | | | | EXOGAMIES | | TOTAL |
	(a) PARISH	(b) GONFALONE	(c) QUARTER	(d) CLUSTER	(e) CROSS-QUARTER	(f) CROSS-CLUSTER	(g) CONTADO	
S. FREDIANO	–	–	–	–	3	3	–	3
S. IACOPO SOPR'ARNO	–	1	–	1	1	1	–	2
S. FELICITÀ	4	1	2	3	2	2	–	9
S. FELICE IN PIAZZA	2	–	2	2	7	7	–	11
S. NICCOLÒ	–	–	–	–	3	3	–	3
S. GIORGIO	–	–	–	–	1	1	–	1
S. LUCIA OGNISSANTI	2	–	1	1	4	4	–	7
S. MARIA NOVELLA	–	–	2	2	6	6	–	8
S. PANCRAZIO	–	1	2	2	2	3	–	5
S. TRINITÀ	–	–	2	1	5	6	1	8
S. LORENZO	2	–	2	–	10	12	–	14
S. AMBROGIO	2	–	–	–	–	–	–	2
S. PIER MAGGIORE	–	–	1	1	4	4	–	5
S. MICHELE VISDOMINI	2	–	–	–	1	1	–	3
S. SIMONE	2	–	4	1	10	13	1	17
S. REMIGIO	–	1	–	1	5	5	–	6
S. IACOPO TRA LE FOSSE	2	1	–	1	3	3	–	6

Appendix E.2 *(Continued)*

PARISH	ENDOGAMIES:				EXOGAMIES:			TOTAL
	(a) PARISH	(b) GONFALONE	(c) QUARTER	(d) CLUSTER	(e) CROSS-QUARTER	(f) CROSS-CLUSTER	(g) CONTADO	
S. MARIA DEL FIORE	4	1	–	2	2	1	–	7
S. MARIA MAGGIORE	–	2	–	2	4	4	–	6
S. RUFILO	–	1	–	1	–	–	–	1
S. MICHELE BERTELDE	–	1	–	1	–	–	–	1
S. PIER BUONCONSIGLIO	–	–	–	1	1	–	–	1
S. MARIA SOPRA PORTA	–	–	–	–	2	2	–	2
SS. APOSTOLI	–	–	–	–	1	1	–	1
S. STEFANO	2	–	–	–	1	1	–	3
S. PIERO SCHERAGGIO	2	–	3	1	3	5	–	8
S. ROMOLO	–	–	1	–	1	2	–	2
S. APOLLINAIRE	–	–	1	1	1	1	–	2
S. PROCOLO	2	–	1	–	–	1	–	3
S. MARIA NEPOTECOSA	–	1	–	1	–	–	–	1
S. MARIA DEGLI ALBERIGHI	–	–	1	–	–	1	–	1
S. CRISTOFANO	–	1	–	1	–	–	–	1
S. MARIA DEGLI UGHI	–	1	1	–	–	2	–	2
S. PIER CELORO	–	–	–	–	2	2	2	2
TOTAL	28	13	26	28	85	96	2	154
	.1818	.0844	.1688	.1818	.5519	.6234	.0130	
		41	67					
		.2662	.4351					

238

Appendix E.3
Marriage Endogamies for the Fourteenth Century of Those Bearing Family Names

PARISH	ENDOGAMIES: (a) PARISH	(b) GONFALONE	(c) QUARTER	(d) CLUSTER	EXOGAMIES: (e) CROSS-QUARTER	(f) CROSS-CLUSTER	(g) CONTADO	TOTAL
S. FREDIANO	–	–	1	1	1	1	–	2
S. IACOPO SOPR'ARNO	–	–	–	–	1	1	–	1
S. FELICITÀ	2	–	2	2	3	3	–	7
S. FELICE IN PIAZZA	–	–	1	1	–	–	–	1
S. NICCOLÒ	–	–	–	–	4	4	–	4
S. LUCIA DE'BARDI	–	–	–	–	1	1	–	1
S. MARIA NOVELLA	–	–	–	–	2	2	–	2
S. PAOLO	–	–	–	–	1	1	–	1
S. PANCRAZIO	–	1	1	1	–	1	–	2
S. TRINITÀ	–	–	2	1	7	8	–	9
S. LORENZO	–	–	3	–	2	5	–	5
S. AMBROGIO	2	–	–	–	1	1	–	3
S. PIER MAGGIORE	4	–	3	1	5	7	–	12
S. MICHELE VISDOMINI	–	–	1	2	2	1	–	3
S. SIMONE	2	–	3	1	6	8	–	11
S. REMIGIO	–	–	–	–	5	5	–	5
S. MARIA DEL FIORE	–	1	–	1	–	–	–	1
S. MARIA MAGGIORE	2	2	–	2	2	2	–	6
S. MICHELE BERTELDE	–	1	–	1	1	1	–	2

Appendix E.3 (*Continued*)

PARISH	ENDOGAMIES:				EXOGAMIES:			
	(a) PARISH	(b) GONFALONE	(c) QUARTER	(d) CLUSTER	(e) CROSS-QUARTER	(f) CROSS-CLUSTER	(g) CONTADO	TOTAL
S. LEO	-	1	-	1	-	-	-	1
S. TOMMASO	-	-	-	-	1	1	-	1
S. MARIA SOPRA PORTA	-	-	-	-	2	2	-	2
SS. APOSTOLI	2	-	-	-	1	1	-	3
S. STEFANO	2	-	1	-	-	1	1	4
S. PIERO SCHERAGGIO	2	-	-	-	1	1	-	3
S. ROMOLO	-	-	1	-	-	1	-	1
S. FIRENZE	-	-	-	-	1	1	-	1
S. PROCOLO	2	-	1	-	1	2	-	4
S. MARIA DEGLI ALBERIGHI	-	-	1	-	-	1	-	1
S. CRISTOFANO	-	1	-	1	-	-	-	1
S. MARIA DEGLI UGHI	-	1	1	-	-	2	-	2
S. PIER CELORO	-	-	-	-	1	1	-	1
TOTAL	20	8	22	16	52	66	1	103
	.1942	.0777	.2136	.1553	.5049	.6408	.0098	
		28	50	36				
		.2718	.4854	.3495				

Appendix E.4
Marriage Endogamies for the Fourteenth Century of Those Bearing Family Names and with Dowries of 400 Florins or Greater

PARISH	ENDOGAMIES: (a) PARISH	(b) GONFALONE	(c) QUARTER	(d) CLUSTER	EXOGAMIES: (e) CROSS-QUARTER	(f) CROSS-CLUSTER	(g) CONTADO	TOTAL
S. FREDIANO	–	–	–	–	1	1	–	1
S. IACOPO SOPR'ARNO	–	–	–	–	1	1	–	1
S. FELICITÀ	2	–	–	–	1	1	–	3
S. NICCOLÒ	–	–	–	–	2	2	–	2
S. MARIA NOVELLA	–	–	–	–	1	1	–	1
S. PAOLO	–	–	–	–	1	1	–	1
S. PANCRAZIO	–	1	1	1	–	1	–	2
S. TRINITÀ	–	–	1	–	4	5	–	5
S. LORENZO	–	–	1	–	2	3	–	3
S. AMBROGIO	2	–	–	–	–	–	–	2
S. PIER MAGGIORE	–	–	–	–	2	2	–	2
S. MICHELE VISDOMINI	–	–	–	–	1	1	–	1
S. SIMONE	2	–	2	–	4	6	–	8
S. REMIGIO	–	–	–	–	2	2	–	2
S. MARIA DEL FIORE	–	1	–	1	–	–	–	1
S. MARIA MAGGIORE	–	1	–	1	1	1	–	2
S. MICHELE BERTELDE	–	1	–	1	–	–	–	1
S. LEO	–	1	–	1	–	–	–	1

Appendix E.4 (*Continued*)

PARISH	(a) PARISH	ENDOGAMIES: (b) GONFALONE	(c) QUARTER	(d) CLUSTER	EXOGAMIES: (e) CROSS-QUARTER	(f) CROSS-CLUSTER	(g) CONTADO	TOTAL
S. MARIA SOPRA PORTA	-	-	-	-	2	2	-	2
S. STEFANO	2	-	-	-	-	-	-	2
S. ROMOLO	-	1	-	-	-	1	-	1
S. PROCOLO	2	-	1	-	-	1	-	3
S. MARIA DEGLI UGHI	-	1	1	-	-	2	-	2
S. PIER CELORO	-	-	-	-	1	1	-	1
TOTAL	10	7	7	5	26	35	-	50
	.2000	.1400	.1400	.1000	.5200	.7000		
		17	24	22				
		.3400	.4800	.4400				

Appendix E.5
Marriage Endogamies of Those Bearing Family Names, 1450–1530

PARISH	ENDOGAMIES:				EXOGAMIES:			
	(a) PARISH	(b) GONFALONE	(c) QUARTER	(d) CLUSTER	(e) CROSS-QUARTER	(f) CROSS-CLUSTER	(g) CONTADO	TOTAL
S. FREDIANO	2	–	3	2	9	10	2	16
S. MARIA IN VERZAIA	–	–	1	–	–	1	–	1
S. FELICITÀ	–	–	–	–	2	2	1	3
S. FELICE IN PIAZZA	2	–	2	2	8	8	–	12
S. PIER GATTOLINO	–	–	–	–	1	1	–	1
S. NICCOLÒ	–	–	1	–	3	4	1	5
S. GIORGIO	–	–	–	–	–	–	1	1
S. LUCIA DE'BARDI	–	–	1	–	–	1	–	1
S. MARIA SOPR'ARNO	2	–	–	–	–	–	–	2
S. LUCIA OGNISSANTI	4	–	–	–	3	3	1	8
S. MARIA NOVELLA	–	2	–	–	2	4	–	4
S. PAOLO	–	–	–	–	4	4	–	4
S. PANCRAZIO	–	–	–	–	2	2	–	2
S. TRINITÀ	–	–	–	–	2	2	1	3
S. LORENZO	4	1	4	1	6	10	–	15
S. MARCO	0	1	0	1	0	0	0	1
S. AMBROGIO	4	1	1	2	4	4	–	10
S. PIER MAGGIORE	–	1	3	1	3	6	5	12
S. MICHELE VISDOMINI	2	–	1	–	3	4	–	6
S. SIMONE	2	–	–	1	2	1	2	6

Appendix E.5 (*Continued*)

PARISH	ENDOGAMIES: (a) PARISH	(b) GONFALONE	(c) QUARTER	(d) CLUSTER	EXOGAMIES: (e) CROSS-QUARTER	(f) CROSS-CLUSTER	(g) CONTADO	TOTAL
S. REMIGIO	-	-	-	-	1	1	1	2
S. IACOPO FRA LE FOSSE	-	-	-	-	1	1	-	1
S. MARIA DEL FIORE	-	-	1	-	1	2	-	2
S. MARIA MAGGIORE	-	-	1	-	1	2	-	2
S. MICHELE BERTELDE	-	1	-	-	-	1	-	1
S. DONATO DE' VECCHIETTI	-	1	1	1	2	3	-	4
S. ANDREA	-	-	1	1	-	-	-	1
S. STEFANO	-	-	-	-	1	1	-	1
S. PIERO SCHERAGGIO	-	-	-	-	2	2	-	2
S. MARIA SOPRA PORTA	-	-	-	1	1	-	-	1
SS. APOSTOLI	-	-	-	-	1	1	-	1
S. MARGHERITA DE' RICCI	-	-	1	-	-	1	-	1
S. MARIA NIPOTECOSA	-	-	-	-	3	3	-	3
S. MARIA IN CAMPO	-	-	-	-	-	-	1	1
TOTAL	22	8	22	13	68	85	16	136
	.1618	.0588	.1618	.0956	.5000	.6250	.1176	
		30	52	35				
		.2206	.3824	.2574				

244

Appendix E.6
*Marriage Endogamies of Those Identified by Professions of the Major Guilds,
1450–1530*

PARISH	ENDOGAMIES:				EXOGAMIES:			
	(a) PARISH	(b) GONFALONE	(c) QUARTER	(d) CLUSTER	(e) CROSS-QUARTER	(f) CROSS-CLUSTER	(g) CONTADO	TOTAL
S. FREDIANO	–	–	–	–	3	3	1	4
S. FELICITÀ	–	–	–	–	2	2	1	3
S. FELICE IN PIAZZA	–	–	–	–	5	5	1	6
S. NICCOLÒ	2	1	–	1	1	1	–	4
S. LUCIA DE'BARDI	–	1	–	1	–	1·	–	1
S. LUCIA OGNISSANTI	–	–	1	1	1	1	–	2
S. MARIA NOVELLA	2	1	1	1	2	3	–	6
S. PANCRAZIO	–	–	–	–	1	1	–	1
S. PAOLO	–	–	–	–	2	2	–	2
S. LORENZO	2	–	1	–	4	5	1	8
S. AMBROGIO	–	–	–	–	1	1	–	1
S. PIER MAGGIORE	–	–	–	1	2	1	2	4
S. SIMONE	–	–	–	1	1	–	2	3
S. CROCE	–	1	–	–	–	1	–	1
S. MARIA DEL FIORE	–	–	–	–	1	1	–	1
S. MARIA MAGGIORE	–	–	–	–	–	–	1	1
S. PIER BUONCONSIGLIO	–	–	–	1	1	–	1	1
S. MARIA SOPRA PORTA	–	–	–	1	1	–	–	1

Appendix E.6 (*Continued*)

PARISH	ENDOGAMIES: (a) PARISH	(b) GONFALONE	(c) QUARTER	(d) CLUSTER	EXOGAMIES: (e) CROSS-QUARTER	(f) CROSS-CLUSTER	(g) CONTADO	TOTAL
S. PIERO SCHERAGGIO	-	-	-	-	1	1	-	1
S. ROMOLO	-	-	-	1	1	-	-	1
S. FIRENZE	-	-	-	1	1	-	-	1
S. APOLLINARE	-	1	-	-	-	1	-	1
S. STEFANO ALLA BADIA	-	-	-	-	1	1	-	1
S. PROCOLO	2	-	-	-	-	-	-	2
S. DONATO VECCHIETTI	-	1	-	-	-	1	-	1
S. MARIA NEPOTECOSA	-	-	1	-	-	1	-	1
TOTAL	8	6	4	10	32	32	9	59
	.1356	.1017	.0678	.1695	.5424	.5424	.1525	
		14	18	18				
		.2373	.3051	.3051				

Appendix E.7

Patriciate Marriages from the Fifteenth Century: The Tratte *and Those Bearing Family Names with Dowries of 600 Florins or Greater*

GONFALONE	ENDOGAMIES: (b) GONFALONE	(c) QUARTER	EXOGAMIES: (e) CROSS-QUARTER	TOTAL
Q. S. SPIRITO:				
SCALA (1:1)	-	-	2	2
NICCHIO (1:2)	-	1	2	3
FERZA (1:3)	-	1	6	7
DRAGO (1:4)	-	-	2	2
Q. S. CROCE:				
CARRO (2:1)	-	1	1	2
BUE (2:2)	-	2	1	3
LEON NERO (2:3)	2	1	6	9
RUOTE (2:4)	2	2	3	7
Q. S. MARIA NOVELLA				
VIPERA (3:1)	-	-	2	2
UNICORNO (3:2)	-	-	2	2
LEON ROSSO (3:3)	-	-	2	2
LEON BIANCO (3:4)	-	-	2	2
Q. S. GIOVANNI				
LEON D'ORO (4:1)	-	2	8	10
DRAGO (4:2)	-	3	-	3
CHIAVI (4:3)	-	4	2	6
VIAO (4:4)	-	1	3	4
TOTAL	4	18	44	66
	.0606	.2727	.6667	

Appendix F.1
The Popolo Minuto, 1340–1383

PARISH		(a) PARISH	ENDOGAMIES: (b) GONFALONE	(c) QUARTER	(d) CLUSTER	EXOGAMIES: (e) CROSS-QUARTER	(f) CROSS-CLUSTER	(g) CONTADO	TOTAL
S. FREDIANO	(M)	4	–	3	3	6	6	3	16
	(W)	4	–	–	–	5	5	–	9
	(T)	8	–	3	3	11	11	3	25
S. MARIA IN VERZAIA	(M)	–	–	–	–	1	1	–	1
	(W)	–	–	1	1	1	1	1	3
	(T)	–	–	1	1	2	2	1	4
S. PIER GATTOLINI	(M)	1	2	1	3	–	–	4	8
	(W)	1	4	1	5	3	3	–	9
	(T)	2	6	2	8	3	3	4	17
S. IACOPO SOPR'ARNO	(M)	–	–	–	–	–	–	–	0
	(W)	–	–	–	–	–	–	1	1
	(T)	–	–	–	–	–	–	1	1
S. FELICITÀ	(M)	–	–	1	1	1	1	–	2
	(W)	–	–	1	1	1	1	–	2
	(T)	–	–	2	2	2	2	–	4
S. FELICE IN PIAZZA	(M)	9	4	1	5	3	3	4	21
	(W)	9	2	3	5	4	4	1	19
	(T)	18	6	4	10	7	7	5	40
S. SPIRITO	(M)	–	–	–	–	–	–	1	1
	(W)	–	–	–	–	–	–	–	0
	(T)	–	–	–	–	–	–	1	1

	Col 1	Col 2	Col 3	Col 4	Col 5	Col 6	Col 7	Col 8
S. NICCOLÒ	–	–	–	–	2	2	1	3
	–	–	–	–	1	1	–	1
	–	–	–	–	3	3	1	4
S. GIORGIO	–	–	–	–	3	3	–	3
	–	–	–	–	1	1	–	1
	–	–	–	–	4	4	–	4
S. LUCIA DE' BARDI	–	–	–	–	–	–	–	0
	–	–	–	–	1	1	–	1
	–	–	–	–	1	1	–	1
S. LUCIA OGNISSANTI	8	–	3	2	3	4	3	17
	8	–	5	5	4	4	1	18
	16	–	8	7	7	8	4	35
S. MARIA NOVELLA	–	–	2	2	1	1	–	3
	–	–	–	–	3	3	–	3
	–	–	2	2	4	4	–	6
S. PAOLO	6	3	7	7	3	6	4	23
	6	–	3	3	4	4	–	13
	12	3	10	10	7	10	4	36
S. PANCRAZIO	8	–	2	2	6	6	4	20
	8	2	2	3	6	7	–	18
	16	2	4	5	12	13	4	38
S. TRINITÀ	2	–	2	1	–	1	–	4
	2	–	5	3	3	5	–	10
	4	–	7	4	3	6	–	14

Appendix F. 1 (Continued)

PARISH	ENDOGAMIES: (a) PARISH	(b) GONFALONE	(c) QUARTER	(d) CLUSTER	EXOGAMIES: (e) CROSS-QUARTER	(f) CROSS-CLUSTER	(g) CONTADO	TOTAL
S. LORENZO	16	1	1	–	8	10	12	38
	16	–	2	–	10	12	2	30
	32	1	3	–	18	22	14	68
S. AMBROGIO	–	–	–	1	3	2	–	3
	–	–	–	–	2	2	–	2
	–	–	–	1	5	4	–	5
S. PIER MAGGIORE	2	–	–	4	6	2	2	10
	2	–	2	1	3	4	3	10
	4	–	2	5	9	6	4	20
S. MICHELE VISDOMINI	–	–	–	–	1	–	–	0
	–	–	–	–	1	1	–	1
	–	–	–	–	1	1	–	1
S. SIMONE	1	–	1	1	2	2	1	5
	1	–	1	1	3	3	–	5
	2	–	2	2	5	5	1	10
S. REMIGIO	–	–	–	1	2	1	–	2
	–	–	–	1	2	1	–	2
	–	–	–	2	4	2	–	4
S. IACOPO TRA LE FOSSE	1	–	1	–	3	4	–	5
	1	–	–	–	3	3	–	4
	2	–	1	–	6	7	–	9
S. MARIA DEL FIORE	–	–	–	–	–	–	–	0
	–	1	1	1	–	1	1	3
	–	1	1	1	–	1	1	3

S. MARIA MAGGIORE	1	–	2	–	1	–	3	–	4														
	1	–	1	–	1	1	1	1	4														
	2	–	3	–	2	1	4	1	8														
S. MICHELE BERTELDE	1	–	1	–	–	–	1	–	2														
	1	–	2	–	–	–	2	–	3														
	2	–	3	–	–	–	3	–	5														
S. LEO	1	–	–	–	–	–	1	–	1														
	1	–	–	–	1	–	1	–	2														
	2	–	–	–	1	–	1	–	3														
S. DONATO DE' VECCHIETTI	–	–	–	–	–	–	–	–	0														
	–	–	1	–	1	–	1	1	1														
	–	–	1	–	1	–	1	1	1														
S. TOMMASO	–	–	1	–	1	1	2	–	2														
	–	–	–	–	–	–	–	1	1														
	–	–	1	–	1	1	2	1	3														
S. PIER BUONCONSIGLIO	–	–	1	–	–	–	1	–	0														
	–	–	1	–	1	–	1	–	1														
	–	–	1	–	1	–	1	–	1														
S. MARIA IN CAMPIDOGLIO	–	–	–	–	–	–	1	–	0														
	–	–	1	–	1	–	1	–	1														
	–	–	1	–	1	–	1	–	1														
S. MINIATO FRA LE TORRI	–	–	–	–	–	–	1	–	0														
	–	–	1	–	1	–	1	–	1														
	–	–	1	–	1	–	1	–	1														

Appendix F.1 (*Continued*)

PARISH	ENDOGAMIES: (a) PARISH	(b) GONFALONE	(c) QUARTER	(d) CLUSTER	EXOGAMIES: (e) CROSS-QUARTER	(f) CROSS-CLUSTER	(g) CONTADO	TOTAL
ORSANMICHELE	–	–	–	–	1	1	–	1
	–	–	–	–	–	–	–	0
	–	–	–	–	1	1	–	1
S. MARIA SOPRA PORTA	1	–	2	–	–	2	–	3
	1	–	–	–	–	–	–	1
	2	–	2	–	–	2	–	4
S. STEFANO	–	1	–	1	1	1	1	3
	–	–	1	–	–	1	–	1
	–	1	1	1	1	2	1	4
S. PIERO SCHERAGGIO	1	–	3	1	4	6	2	10
	1	1	1	1	–	1	1	4
	2	1	4	2	4	7	3	14
S. CECILIA	–	–	–	–	–	–	–	0
	–	–	–	–	1	1	–	1
	–	–	–	–	1	1	–	1
S. FIRENZE	–	–	–	–	1	1	–	1
	–	–	–	–	–	–	–	0
	–	–	–	–	1	1	–	1
S. APOLLINARE	–	–	1	1	1	1	–	2
	–	–	1	1	–	–	–	1
	–	–	2	2	1	1	–	3

S. STEFANO ALLA BADIA	–	–	–	–	–	–	–	–	–	0
	–	–	1	1	1	1	–	1	1	2
	–	–	1	1	1	1	–	1	1	2
S. PROCOLO	–	–	–	–	–	1	1	1	1	1
	–	–	1	–	1	1	–	1	–	1
	–	–	1	–	1	1	–	1	–	2
S. MARIA NIPOTECOSA	–	–	–	–	1	1	1	1	–	0
	–	–	1	1	1	1	1	1	1	1
	–	–	1	1	1	1	1	1	1	1
S. MARIA DEGLI ALBERIGHI	1	–	1	–	–	–	–	–	–	1
	1	–	1	–	–	1	1	–	–	1
	2	–	1	–	–	1	1	–	–	2
S. MARIA IN CAMPO	–	–	1	1	–	–	–	–	–	1
	–	–	1	–	1	1	–	–	–	0
	–	–	1	1	1	1	–	–	–	1
S. BENEDETTO	–	–	–	–	–	–	–	1	1	1
	–	–	–	–	1	–	–	1	1	0
	–	–	–	–	1	–	–	1	1	1
S. MARIA DEGLI UGHI	–	1	–	–	–	1	–	–	–	0
	–	1	–	–	1	1	–	–	1	1
	–	1	–	–	1	1	–	–	1	1

Appendix F.1 (*Continued*)

PARISH	ENDOGAMIES: (a) PARISH	(b) GONFALONE	(c) QUARTER	(d) CLUSTER	EXOGAMIES: (e) CROSS-QUARTER	(f) CROSS-CLUSTER	(g) CONTADO	TOTAL
S. SALVADORE	–	–	–	–	–	–	–	0
	–	–	1	–	–	1	–	1
	–	–	1	–	–	1	–	1
S. PIER CELORO	–	–	2	1	–	1	–	2
	–	–	–	–	–	–	–	0
	–	–	2	1	–	1	–	2
TOTAL	64	11	38	36	65	76	44	192
	64	11	38	36	65	78	14	222
	128	22	76	72	130	156	58	414
	30.92%	5.31%	18.36%	17.39%	31.40%	37.68%	14.01%	
		150	226	200				
		36.23%	54.59%	48.31%				

Appendix F.2
The Popolo Minuto, 1450–1530: Sottoposti of the Wool and Silk Industries

PARISH		ENDOGAMIES:				EXOGAMIES:			
		(a) PARISH	(b) GONFALONE	(c) QUARTER	(d) CLUSTER	(e) CROSS–QUARTER	(f) CROSS–CLUSTER	(g) CONTADO	TOTAL
S. FREDIANO	(M)	27	9	5	14	10	10	4	55
	(W)	27	3	–	3	10	10	5	45
	(T)	54	12	5	17	20	20	9	100
S. MARIA IN VERZAIA		13	3	1	4	4	4	–	21
		13	9	–	9	3	3	4	29
		26	12	1	13	7	7	4	50
S. PIER GATTOLINI		4	3	–	3	1	1	–	8
		4	–	4	4	–	–	4	12
		8	3	4	7	1	1	4	20
S. IACOPO SOPR'ARNO		1	–	–	–	1	1	–	2
		1	–	–	–	–	–	1	2
		2	–	–	–	1	1	1	4
S. FELICITÀ		–	–	–	–	1	1	–	1
		–	–	–	–	1	1	–	1
		–	–	–	–	2	2	–	2
S. FELICE IN PIAZZA		–	–	–	–	1	1	3	4
		–	3	2	5	4	4	4	13
		–	3	2	5	5	5	7	17
S. NICCOLÒ		5	1	–	1	2	2	2	10
		5	–	–	–	1	1	–	6
		10	1	–	1	3	3	2	16

Appendix F.2 (*Continued*)

| PARISH | ENDOGAMIES: | | | | EXOGAMIES: | | | |
	(a) PARISH	(b) GONFALONE	(c) QUARTER	(d) CLUSTER	(e) CROSS-QUARTER	(f) CROSS-CLUSTER	(g) CONTADO	TOTAL
S. GIORGIO	-	-	-	-	1	1	-	1
	-	1	-	1	-	-	-	1
	-	1	-	1	1	1	-	2
S. LUCIA DE'BARDI	-	-	-	-	-	-	-	0
	-	-	-	-	1	1	-	1
	-	-	-	-	1	1	-	1
S. LUCIA OGNISSANTI	24	-	2	2	9	9	1	36
	24	-	1	1	4	4	1	30
	48	-	3	3	13	13	2	66
S. MARIA NOVELLA	1	-	-	-	1	1	-	2
	1	-	2	2	1	1	-	4
	2	-	2	2	2	2	-	6
S. PAOLO	-	-	1	1	2	2	-	3
	-	-	-	-	1	1	-	1
	-	-	1	1	3	3	-	4
S. PANCRAZIO	-	-	-	-	-	-	-	0
	-	-	1	1	-	-	-	1
	-	-	1	1	-	-	-	1
S. TRINITÀ	-	-	1	1	1	1	-	2
	-	-	-	-	-	-	-	0
	-	-	1	1	1	1	-	2
S. LORENZO	16	3	2	3	5	7	1	27
	16	1	6	1	12	18	3	38
	32	4	8	4	17	25	4	65

	Col 1	Col 2	Col 3	Col 4	Col 5	Col 6	Col 7	Total
S. MARCO	1 / 1 / 2	– / – / –	1 / – / 1	– / – / –	– / – / –	1 / – / 1	– / – / –	2 / 1 / 3
S. IACOPO IN CAMPO CORBOLINI	4 / 4 / 8	1 / 3 / 4	1 / – / 1	1 / 3 / 4	– / 2 / 2	1 / 2 / 3	1 / 1 / 1	6 / 10 / 16
S. AMBROGIO	7 / 7 / 14	– / 4 / 4	5 / – / 5	2 / 5 / 7	8 / 6 / 14	11 / 5 / 16	1 / 1 / 2	21 / 18 / 39
S. PIER MAGGIORE	3 / 3 / 6	4 / – / 4	1 / 2 / 3	4 / – / 4	4 / 1 / 5	5 / 3 / 8	2 / 2 / 4	14 / 8 / 22
S. MICHELE VISDOMINI	– / – / –	– / – / –	– / 1 / 1	– / – / –	– / – / –	– / 1 / 1	– / – / –	0 / 1 / 1
S. SIMONE	1 / 1 / 2	– / – / –	– / 1 / 1	– / 1 / 1	2 / 6 / 8	2 / 6 / 8	1 / – / 1	4 / 8 / 12
S. REMIGIO	1 / 1 / 2	– / – / –	– / – / –	1 / 1 / 2	2 / 1 / 3	1 / – / 1	– / 1 / 1	3 / 3 / 6
S. IACOPO TRA LE FOSSE	1 / 1 / 2	– / – / –	– / – / –	– / – / !	3 / – / 3	3 / – / 3	– / 1 / 1	4 / 2 / 6

Appendix F.2 (*Continued*)

PARISH	(a) PARISH	ENDOGAMIES: (b) GONFALONE	(c) QUARTER	(d) CLUSTER	(e) CROSS-QUARTER	EXOGAMIES: (f) CROSS-CLUSTER	(g) CONTADO	TOTAL
S. MARIA DEL FIORE	1	–	–	–	–	–	–	1
	1	–	3	–	–	3	–	4
	2	–	3	–	–	3	–	5
S. MARIA MAGGIORE	2	–	–	–	–	–	–	2
	2	–	–	–	–	–	–	2
	4	–	–	–	–	–	–	4
S. RUFILLO	1	–	–	–	–	–	–	1
	1	–	–	–	–	–	–	1
	2	–	–	–	–	–	–	2
S. LEO	–	–	–	1	1	–	–	1
	–	–	1	–	–	1	–	1
	–	–	1	1	1	1	–	2
S. DONATO DE' VECCHIETTI	–	–	–	–	–	–	–	0
	–	–	–	–	1	1	–	1
	–	–	–	–	1	1	–	1
S. TOMMASO	1	–	–	–	–	–	–	1
	1	–	–	–	–	–	–	1
	2	–	–	–	–	–	–	2
S. PIER BUONCONSIGLIO	1	–	–	–	–	–	–	1
	1	–	–	–	–	–	–	1
	2	–	–	–	–	–	–	2
S. MARIA IN CAMPODIGLIO	–	–	–	–	–	–	–	0
	–	–	–	–	1	1	–	1
	–	–	–	–	1	1	–	1

S. MINIATO FRA LE TORRI	– / –	– / – / –	– / – / –	– / – / –	– / 1 / 1	– / 1 / 1	– / 1 / 1	0 / 1 / 1
S. ANDREA	– / – / –	– / – / –	– / – / –	1 / – / 1	1 / – / 1	1 / – / 1	1 / – / 1	1 / 0 / 1
S. MARIA SOPRA PORTA	– / – / –	– / – / –	– / – / –	– / 2 / 2	– / 2 / 2	– / 2 / 2	– / 2 / 2	0 / 2 / 2
S. STEFANO	1 / 1 / 2	– / – / –	1 / – / 1	1 / – / 1	1 / – / 1	1 / – / 1	1 / – / 1	3 / 1 / 4
S. PIERO SCHERAGGIO	– / – / –	– / – / –	1 / 1 / 1	1 / 1 / 2	1 / 1 / 2	2 / 1 / 3	2 / 1 / 3	2 / 2 / 4
S. ROMOLO	– / – / –	– / – / –	– / – / –	– / 2 / 2	– / 2 / 2	– / 2 / 2	– / 2 / 2	0 / 2 / 2
S. APOLLINAIRE	– / – / –	– / – / –	– / – / –	– / 2 / 2	– / 2 / 2	– / 2 / 2	– / 2 / 2	0 / 2 / 2
S. PROCOLO	– / – / –	– / – / –	– / – / –	1 / – / 1	1 / – / 1	1 / – / 1	1 / – / 1	1 / 0 / 1

Appendix F.2 *(Continued)*

PARISH	ENDOGAMIES: (a) PARISH	(b) GONFALONE	(c) QUARTER	(d) CLUSTER	(e) CROSS-QUARTER	EXOGAMIES: (f) CROSS-CLUSTER	(g) CONTADO	TOTAL
S. BARTOLOMMEO AL CORSO	–	–	2	–	–	2	–	2
	–	–	–	–	–	–	–	0
	–	–	2	–	–	2	–	2
S. MARIA NIPOTECOSA	1	–	–	–	–	–	–	1
	1	–	–	–	–	–	–	1
	2	–	–	–	–	–	–	2
S. MARIA IN CAMPO	–	–	1	–	1	2	–	2
	–	–	1	–	1	1	–	1
	–	–	1	–	2	3	–	3
TOTAL (M)	117	24	23	37	65	75	16	245
(W)	117	24	23	37	65	75	28	257
(T)	234	48	46	74	130	150	44	502
	46.61%	9.56%	9.16%	14.74%	25.90%	29.88%	8.76%	
		282	328	308				
		56.18%	65.34%	61.35%				

Appendix F.3
The Popolo Minuto, 1450–1530: Non-Sottoposti with Dowries of 70 Florins or Less

PARISH		ENDOGAMIES: (a) PARISH	(b) GONFALONE	(c) QUARTER	(d) CLUSTER	EXOGAMIES: (e) CROSS-QUARTER	(f) CROSS-CLUSTER	(g) CONTADO	TOTAL
S. FREDIANO	(M)	1	–	–	–	–	–	–	1
	(W)	1	–	–	–	1	1	1	3
	(T)	2	–	–	–	1	1	1	4
S. MARIA IN VERZAIA		2	–	–	–	1	1	–	3
		2	–	–	–	–	–	1	3
		4	–	–	–	1	1	1	6
S. PIER GATTOLINI		1	–	–	–	–	–	–	1
		1	–	–	–	–	–	–	1
		2	–	–	–	–	–	–	2
S. IACOPO SOPR' ARNO		–	–	–	–	–	–	–	0
		–	–	–	–	–	–	1	1
		–	–	–	–	–	–	1	1
S. FELICITÀ		1	–	–	–	–	–	–	1
		1	–	–	–	–	–	–	1
		2	–	–	–	–	–	–	2
S. FELICE IN PIAZZA		1	–	–	–	–	–	–	1
		1	–	–	–	–	–	–	1
		2	–	–	–	–	–	–	2
S. NICCOLÒ		1	–	–	–	–	–	–	1
		1	–	–	–	1	1	1	3
		2	–	–	–	1	1	1	4

Appendix F.3 (*Continued*)

PARISH	(a) PARISH	ENDOGAMIES: (b) GONFALONE	(c) QUARTER	(d) CLUSTER	(e) CROSS-QUARTER	EXOGAMIES: (f) CROSS-CLUSTER	(g) CONTADO	TOTAL
S. GIORGIO	–	–	–	–	1	1	–	1
	–	–	–	–	–	–	–	0
	–	–	–	–	1	1	–	1
S. LUCIA	1	–	1	1	1	1	2	5
OGNISSANTI	1	–	1	–	–	–	1	2
	2	–	1	1	1	1	3	7
S. MARIA NOVELLA	–	–	–	–	–	–	–	0
	–	–	–	–	–	–	1	1
	–	–	–	–	–	–	1	1
S. PAOLO	–	–	–	–	–	1	–	0
	–	–	1	1	1	1	–	2
	–	–	1	1	1	1	–	2
S. LORENZO	8	–	1	–	–	1	1	10
	8	–	1	–	1	2	4	14
	16	–	2	–	1	3	5	24
S. AMBROGIO	1	1	–	1	2	2	1	5
	1	–	1	–	–	1	4	6
	2	1	1	1	2	3	5	11
S. PIER MAGGIORE	1	–	1	1	–	1	1	3
	1	1	–	1	–	–	1	3
	2	1	1	1	–	1	2	6
S. MICHELE	–	–	–	–	–	–	–	0
VISDOMINI	–	–	–	–	–	–	2	2
	–	–	–	–	–	–	2	2

262

	C1	C2	C3	C4	C5	C6	C7
S. SIMONE	1	–	–	–	–	–	1
	1	–	–	–	–	–	1
	2	–	–	–	–	–	2
S. REMIGIO	1	–	–	–	–	–	1
	1	–	–	–	–	–	1
	2	–	–	–	–	–	2
S. MARIA DEL FIORE	–	–	–	–	–	1	1
	–	–	–	–	–	–	0
	–	–	–	–	–	1	1
S. PIERO SCHERAGGIO	–	–	–	1	1	–	1
	–	–	–	–	–	–	0
	–	–	–	1	1	–	1
S. PROCOLO	–	–	–	–	–	–	0
	–	–	–	1	1	–	1
	–	–	–	1	1	–	1
TOTAL (M)	19	3	2	6	8	6	35
(W)	19	3	2	6	8	17	46
(T)	38	6	4	12	16	23	81
	40	46	42				
	49.38%	56.39%	51.85%				

Appendix F.4
The Popolo Minuto, 1450–1530: Sottoposti with Dowries of 70 Florins or Less

PARISH		ENDOGAMIES: (a) PARISH	(b) GONFALONE	(c) QUARTER	(d) CLUSTER	EXOGAMIES: (e) CROSS-QUARTER	(f) CROSS-CLUSTER	(g) CONTADO	TOTAL
S. FREDIANO	(M)	8	1	–	1	3	3	–	12
	(w)	8	–	–	–	7	7	4	19
	(T)	16	1	–	1	10	10	4	31
S. MARIA IN VERZAIA		5	–	–	–	–	–	–	5
		5	1	–	1	–	–	1	7
		10	1	–	1	–	–	1	12
S. PIER GATTOLINI		3	–	–	–	–	–	–	3
		3	–	–	–	–	–	3	6
		6	–	–	–	–	–	3	9
S. IACOPO SOPR' ARNO		–	–	–	–	–	–	–	0
		–	–	–	–	–	–	1	1
		–	–	–	–	–	–	1	1
S. FELICE IN PIAZZA		–	–	–	–	1	1	–	1
		–	–	–	–	1	1	1	2
		–	–	–	–	2	2	1	3
S. NICCOLÒ		1	–	–	–	1	1	–	2
		1	–	–	–	1	1	–	2
		2	–	–	–	2	2	–	4
S. LUCIA OGNISSANTI		8	–	–	–	6	6	–	14
		8	–	–	–	2	2	–	10
		16	–	–	–	8	8	–	24

	C1	C2	C3	C4	C5	C6	C7	C8
S. LORENZO	3	–	–	–	–	–	–	3
	3	–	–	–	5	5	2	10
	6	–	–	–	5	5	2	13
S. MARCO	1	–	–	–	–	–	–	1
	1	–	–	–	–	–	–	1
	2	–	–	–	–	–	–	2
S. IACOPO IN CAMPO CORBOLINI	1	–	–	–	–	–	–	1
	1	–	–	–	–	–	1	2
	2	–	–	–	–	–	1	3
S. AMBROGIO	3	–	1	–	4	5	–	8
	3	2	–	2	1	1	1	7
	6	2	1	2	5	6	1	15
S. PIER MAGGIORE	1	2	–	2	–	–	–	3
	1	–	–	–	–	–	–	1
	2	2	–	2	–	–	–	4
S. SIMONE	1	–	–	–	–	–	–	1
	1	–	–	–	–	–	–	1
	2	–	–	–	–	–	–	2
S. REMIGIO	–	–	–	–	1	1	–	1
	–	–	–	–	–	–	–	0
	–	–	–	–	1	1	–	1

Appendix F.4 (*Continued*)

PARISH	ENDOGAMIES:				EXOGAMIES:			
	(a) PARISH	(b) GONFALONE	(c) QUARTER	(d) CLUSTER	(e) CROSS-QUARTER	(f) CROSS-CLUSTER	(g) CONTADO	TOTAL
S. MARIA DEL FIORE	–	–	–	–	–	–	–	0
	–	–	1	–	–	1	–	1
	–	–	1	–	–	1	–	1
S. ANDREA	–	–	–	–	1	1	–	1
	–	–	–	–	–	–	–	0
	–	–	–	–	1	1	–	1
S. MARIA NIPOTECOSA	1	–	–	–	–	–	–	1
	1	–	–	–	–	–	–	1
	2	–	–	–	–	–	–	2
TOTAL (M)	36	3	1	3	17	18	0	57
(W)	36	3	1	3	17	18	14	71
(T)	72	6	2	6	34	36	14	128
	56.25%	4.69%	1.56%	4.69%	26.56%	28.13%	10.94%	
		78	80	78				
		60.94%	62.50%	60.94%				

Appendix G.1
Possible Units of Analysis: Estimo del Sega

QUARTER AND GONFALONE	CHURCH*	1352 NUMBER OF HOUSEHOLD HEADS		1355 NUMBER OF HOUSEHOLD HEADS	
SANTO SPIRITO					
Scala:	10	167	.0168	167	.0169
	11	127		127	
	13	78		79	
	14	62		62	
		435	.0437	435	.0439
	05	33		34	
Ferza:	03	168		170	
	(06)	578		580	
		745	.0748	750	.0757
Nicchio:	(05)	395		390	
	+05	33 428	.0430	34	
	04	254		255	
		682	.0685	679	.0686
Drago Verde:	(01)	862	.0866	860	.0868
	(02)				

Estimation by Streets

	(01)	588			
	(02)	273			

ANALYSIS:

Outer Ring: 10, 03, 06, 01, 02

		1775	.1782	1777	.1794

Inner Ring: 11, 13, 14, 05, 04

		950	.0953	947	.0956

*
Numbers correspond to parish churches listed in Table 1:3, p. 27.

Appendix G.1 (*Continued*)

QUARTER AND GONFALONE	CHURCH	1352 NUMBER OF HOUSEHOLD HEADS		1355 NUMBER OF HOUSEHOLD HEADS	
SANTA CROCE					
Carre:	65	232		237	
	64	96		101	
	66	19		20	
	67	39		40	
	61	29		29	
		415	.0417	427	.0431
Bue:	43 infra	96		85	
	(43 extra)	247		246	
		343	.0344	331	
	69	144		148	
	68	96		96	
		583	.0585	575	
Leone Nero:	45	190		190	
	44	243		244	
		433	.0435	434	
Ruota:	(71)				
	(70)	426	.0428	415	
	(83)				

ANALYSIS:

    Outer Ring:

    Inner Ring: 43, 44, 45

	776	.0780	765	.0772

    Inter City: 65, 64, 66, 67, 61, 69, 68, 71, 70, 83

1071	.1036	1086	.1097

Appendix G.1 *(Continued)*

QUARTER AND GONFALONE	CHURCH	1352 NUMBER OF HOUSEHOLD HEADS		1355 NUMBER OF HOUSEHOLD HEADS	
SANTA MARIA NOVELLA					
Vipera:	(63)				
	(62)	252	.0253	239	
Unicorno:	(24)	228		254	
	20	447		396	
		675	.0678	650	
Leon Rosso:	(22) (59)				
	(23)	604	.0600	603	
	(80)				
Leon Bianco:	(21)				
	(53)				
	(55)	538	.0540	536	
	(57)				
ANALYSIS:					
Outer Ring: 20					
		447	.0449	396	.0400
Inner Ring: 24, 22, 23, (21, 53, 55, 57)					
		1370	.1376	1393	.1410
Inter City: 63, 62					
		252	.0254	239	.0241

QUARTER AND GONFALONE	CHURCH	1352 NUMBER OF HOUSEHOLD HEADS		1355 NUMBER OF HOUSEHOLD HEADS	
SAN GIOVANNI					
Leon d'Oro	(30 infra)	815		801	
	(30 extra)				
	(32)	401		400	
		1216	.1221	1201	.1213
Drago:	50	240		243	
	52	11		11	
	58	19		19	
	54	33		33	
	82	57		56	
	79	34		34	
	53	47		47	
	51	242		241	
	56	28		28	
		711	.0714	712	.0719
Chiave:	(40)				
	(41)				
	(71)	870	.0839	869	.0877
	(73)				
Vaio:	74	47		47	
	75	18		18	
	81	37		38	
	78	28		28	
	77	92		93	
	72	19		19	
	71*	6		6	
	73	16		16	
	76	48		48	
		311	.0312	313	.0316
	42	206		206	
		517	.0519	519	

ANALYSIS:

       Outer Ring: 30, 32, (40, 41, 71, 73)

2086	.2095	2070	.2090

       Inner Ring: 42

206	.0207	206	.0208

       Inter City: 50, 52, 58, 54, 82, 79, 53, 51, 56, 74, 75, 81, 78, 77, 72, 71, 73, 76

1022	.1027	1025	.1035

Appendix G.2
Possible Units of Analysis: The Marriage Sample, 1343–1383

QUARTER AND GONFALONE	CHURCH	NUMBER	
SANTO SPIRITO			
Scala:	10	16	.0119
	11	6	
	13	5	
	14	1	
		28	.2078
Ferza:	03	26	
	06	110	
		136	.1009
Nicchio:	05	30	
	04	6	
	07	1	
		37	.0274
Drago Verde:	01	68	
	02	9	
		77	.0571

ANALYSIS:

Outer Ring: 10, 03, 06, 01, 02

	229	.1699

Inner Ring: 11, 13, 14, 05, 04, 07

	49	.0364

Appendix G.2 (*Continued*)

QUARTER AND GONFALONE	CHURCH	NUMBER	
SANTA CROCE			
Carro:	65	48	
	64	18	
	66	3	
	67	6	
	61	5	
		80	.0593
Bue:	43	49	.0364
	69	10	
	68	8	
		67	.0497
Leon Nero:	45	33	
	44	33	
		66	.0490
Ruota:	71	12	
	70	4	
	83	3	
		19	.0141

ANALYSIS:

Outer Ring:

Inner Ring: 43, 44, 45

115   .0853

Inter City: 65, 64, 66, 67, 61, 69, 68, 71, 70, 83

117   .0868

Appendix G.2 (*Continued*)

QUARTER AND GONFALONE	CHURCH	NUMBER	
SANTA MARIA NOVELLA			
Vipera:	63	4	
	62	8	
		12	.0089
Unicorno:	24	44	
	20	110	.0816
		154	.1142
Leon Rosso:	22	68	
	23	80	
		148	.1098
	80	3	
	89	1	
		152	.1128
Leon Bianco:	21	29	
	55	5	
	57	3	
		37	.0274

ANALYSIS:

Outer Ring:	20			
		110	.0816	
Inner Ring:	24, 22, 23, 21, 55, 57, 80, 59			
		233	.1728	
Inter City:	63, 63			
		12	.0089	

Appendix G.2 (*Continued*)

QUARTER AND GONFALONE	CHURCH	NUMBER	
SAN GIOVANNI			
Leon d'Oro:	30	224	
	31	3	
	32	4	
		231	.1714
Drago:	50	41	
	52	–	
	58	2	
	54	5	
	82	1	
	79	1	
	53	14	
	51	20	
	56	4	
		88	.0653
Chiavi:	40	24	
	41	87	
		111	.0830
Vaio:	74	4	
	75	2	
	81	3	
	78	1	
	77	17	
	72	–	
	73	1	
	76	6	
		34	.0252
	42	19	
		53	.0482

ANALYSIS:

        Outer Ring: 30, 31, 32, (40, 41,)

                              342   .2545

        Inner Ring: 42

                              19   .0141

        Inter City: 50, 52, 58, 54, 82, 79, 53, 51, 56, 74, 75, 81, 78, 77, 72, 73, 76

                             122   .0305

Appendix H.1
The Composition of Criminality—1344–1345

TYPE OF CRIME	PODESTÀ	CAPITANO	ESECUTORE	TOTAL
I. Assault				
1. fist	108	4	12	124
2. stones	42			42
3. weapon	135	2		137
Collective:				
4. fists	18	2		20
5. stones	1	4		5
6. weapons	42	4		46
7. slander	8			8
8. slander and assault	6			6
9. kidnapping	12			12
II. Murder				
10. singular	19		2	21
11. collective	2			2
III. Theft				
12. normal	27		2	29
13. famosum*	11			11
IV. Rural crimes				
Poaching:				
14. pigeons	6			6
15. farm animals			2	2
16. wood	5			5
17. grain	4			4
18. arson	5		2	7
Trespass:				
19. with animals	2	2		4
20. occupation	58	6	6	70
21. neglecting work	3			3

*
The courts invariably sentenced the criminal convicted of <u>furta famosa</u>
to death. Usually the criminal thus convicted had committed a long series
of robberies over a period extending often a decade or more.

Appendix H.1 (*Continued*)

TYPE OF CRIME	PODESTÀ	CAPITANO	ESECUTORE	TOTAL
V. Urban Trespass				
22. occupation	17	2		17
23. breaking and entering	41	2		43
VI. Fraud and Swindle				
24. counterfeit	1			1
25. swindle	3			3
VII. Morality				
26. sodomy/pederasty				
27. sodomy				
28. heterosexual rape	7			7
29. adultery	7		4	11
30. prostitution	7			7
31. blasphemy	10			10
32. games			2	2
VIII. Indebtedness				
33. personal	137		8	145
34. guild consules	1			1
35. Mercanzia				
36. arrears in rent				
IX. Contempt of Court				
37. contumacy	11		2	13
38. false testimony	40		2	42
X. Miscellaneous				
39. miscellaneous	5		2	7
40. political crimes	34	20	4	58
41. uncertain	27		10	37
42. false arrest or police violation	12	12	22	46
43. violation of street ordinances	5			5
TOTAL CITY	886	58	82	1026
CONTADO	614	32	10	656
TOTAL	1500	90	92	1628

Appendix H.2
The Composition of Criminality—1374–1375

TYPE OF CRIME	PODESTÀ	CAPITANO	ESECUTORE	TOTAL
I. Assault				
1. fist	14	6		20
2. stones	13	6		19
3. weapon	17	18		35
Collective:				
4. fists	1	2		3
5. stones		2		2
6. weapons	1			1
7. slander	5			5
8. slander and assault	4	2		6
9. kidnapping				
II. Murder				
10. singular	6			6
11. collective	3			3
III. Theft				
12. normal	2	2		4
13. famosum	2	2		4
IV. Rural crimes				
Poaching:				
14. pigeons	1			1
15. farm animals	3			3
16. wood				
17. grain	3			3
18. arson				
Trespass:				
19. with animals				
20. occupation	2	2		4
21. neglecting work	7			7

Appendix H.2 (*Continued*)

TYPE OF CRIME	PODESTA	CAPITANO	ESECUTORE	TOTAL
V. Urban Trespass				
22. occupation	1	2		3
23. breaking and entering	7	10		17
VI. Fraud and Swindle				
24. counterfeit	1			1
25. swindle	1			1
VII. Morality				
26. sodomy/pederasty				
27. sodomy				
28. heterosexual rape		4		4
29. adultery	2			2
30. prostitution	1			1
31. blasphemy	2			2
32. games				
VIII. Indebtedness				
33. personal	18	10		28
34. guild consules	2			2
35. Mercanzia	4			4
36. arrears in rent	4			4
IX. Contempt of Court				
37. contumacy	3			3
38. false testimony	1			1
X. Miscellaneous				
39. miscellaneous	6			6
40. political crimes	5			5
41. uncertain				
42. false arrest or police violation	12	12		24
43. violation of street ordinances				
TOTAL CITY	154	80		234
CONTADO	134	72		206
TOTAL	288	152		440

Appendix H.3
The Composition of Criminality—1455–1466

TYPE OF CRIME	PODESTÀ	CAPITANO	TOTAL
I. Assault			
1. fist	5	4	9
2. stones	2	4	6
3. weapon	19	20	39
Collective:			
4. fists	3	-	3
5. stones	-	-	-
6. weapons	2	11	13
7. slander	2	1	3
8. slander and assault	2	4	6
9. kidnapping	-	-	-
II. Murder			
10. singular	10	14	24
11. collective	1	2	3
III. Theft			
12. normal	5	2	7
13. famosum	7	22	29
IV. Rural crimes			
Poaching:			
14. pigeons	1	-	1
15. farm animals	2	2	4
16. wood	10	5	15
17. grain	-	2	2
18. arson	3	-	3
Trespass:			
19. with animal	-	-	-
20. occupation	23	5	28
21. neglecting work	6	5	11

Appendix H.3 (*Continued*)

TYPE OF CRIME	PODESTÀ	CAPITANO	TOTAL
V. Urban Trespass			
22. occupation	4	1	5
23. breaking and entering	9	5	14
VI. Fraud and Swindle			
24. counterfeit	5	-	5
25. swindle	1	5	6
VII. Morality			
26. sodomy/pederasty	-	5	5
27. sodomy	4	-	4
28. heterosexual rape	-	3	3
29. adultery	-	2	2
30. prostitution	-	-	-
31. blasphemy	2	1	3
32. games	1	6	7
VIII. Indebtedness			
33. personal	15	4	19
34. guild consules	14	5	19
35. Mercanzia	30	9	39
36. arrears in rent	7	8	15
IX. Contempt of Court			
37. contumacy	2	4	6
38. false testimony	5	4	9
X. Miscellaneous			
39. miscellaneous	4	6	10
40. political crimes	3	42	45
41. uncertain	2	-	2
42. false arrest or police violation	-	-	-
43. violation of street ordinances	-	-	-
TOTAL CITY	230	217	447
CONTADO	32	52	84
TOTAL	262	269	531

Sources

Manuscript Sources

Archivio di Stato, Firenze
Arte della Lana
Atti del Capitano del Popolo (ACP)
Atti del Esecutore di Ordinamenti di Guistizia (AEOG)
Atti del Podestà (AP)
Carte Strozziane
Catasti
Estimi
Notarile Antecosimo (NAC)
Otto di Guardia della Repubblica
Statuti della Repubblica di Firenze
Tratte
Ufficiali di Notte
Archivio dell'Opera del Duomo di Firenze
Registro delle fedi di battesimo

Published Sources

Alberti, Leon Battista. *The Family in Renaissance Florence* (*I Libri della famiglia*). Translated by Renée Neu Watkins. Columbia: University of South Carolina Press, 1969.
Bruni, Leonardo. *Laudatio Florentinae Urbis*. In *From Petrarch to Leonardo Bruni. Studies in Humanistic and Political Literature*. Edited by Hans Baron. Chicago: University of Chicago Press, 1968.
Compagni, Dino. *La cronica*. In *Rerum Italicarum Scriptores*, new ed., Vol. 9, Pt. 2. Edited by I. Del Lungo. Città di Castello: S. Lapi, 1913.
Cronache e memorie sul tumulto dei Ciompi. In *Rerum Italicarum Scriptores*, new ed., Vol. 18, Pt. 3. Edited by G. Scaramella. Bologna: N. Zanichelli, 1917–1934.
Da Certaldo, Paolo. *Libro di buoni costumi*. Edited by Alfredo Schiaffini. Florence: F. Le Monnier, 1945.
Dati, Gregorio. *Il Libro segreto*. Edited by Carlo Gargiollo. Bologna: G. Romagnoli, 1869.

della Casa, Giovanni. *Il Galateo*. Edited by Ruggiero Romano. Turin: G. Einaudi, 1975.

Diario d'anonimo fiorentino dall'anno 1358 al 1389. In *Cronache dei secoli XIII e XIV*. Documenti di Storia Italiana, 6. Edited by A. Gherardi. Florence: 1876.

Documenti. In *Il Tumulto dei Ciompi*. Edited by Carlo Falletti-Fossati. Florence: R. Istituto di Studi Superiori, 1873.

Documenti. In *Storia della Repubblica di Firenze*, 2nd. ed., 1. Edited by Gino Capponi. Florence: G. Barbèra, 1876.

Documenti. In *La democrazia fiorentina del suo tramonto, 1378–1382*. Edited by Niccolò Rodolico. Bologna: N. Zanichelli, 1905.

Documenti. In *Il Popolo Minuto. Note di storia fiorentina, 1343–1378*, 2nd. ed. Edited by Rodolico. Florence: Olschki, 1968.

Landucci, Luca. *Diario fiorentino dal 1450 al 1516*. Edited by Iodaco del Badia. Florence: G. C. Sansoni, 1883.

Machiavelli, Niccolò. *Istorie fiorentine*. Edited by Franco Gaeta. Milan: Feltrinelli, 1962.

Morelli, Giovanni di Pagolo. *Ricordi*. Edited by Vittore Branca. Florence: F. Le Monnier, 1956.

Statuta Populi et Communis Florentiae (1415), 3 vols. Freiburg: M. Kluch, 1778–83.

Statuto dell'Arte della Lana di Firenze, 1317–1319. Edited by Anna Maria Agnoletti. Florence: F. Le Monnier, 1940.

Statuti dell'Arte di Por Santa Maria del tempo della Repubblica. Edited by Umberto Dorini. Florence: Olschki, 1934.

Statuti della Repubblica Fiorentina. Edited by Romolo Caggese, I: *Statuto del Capitano del Popolo, 1322–1325*. Florence: Galileiana, 1910. 2: *Statuto del Podestà, 1325*. Florence: E. Ariani, 1921.

Stefani, Marchionne di Coppo. *Cronaca fiorentina*. In *Rerum Italicarum Scriptores*, new ed., Vol. 30, Pt. 1. Edited by N. Rodolico. Città di Castello: S. Lapi, 1903–55.

La Tavola antica di tutti popoli. In *Delizie degli eruditi Toscani*, Vol. 13. Edited by Fr. Idelfonso di San Luigi. Florence: Gaetano Cambiagi, 1780.

Villani, Giovanni. *Cronica*, 4 vols. Edited by F. G. Dragomanni. Florence: S. Coen, 1844–1845.

Secondary Sources

Abbiateci, A., Billacois, F., Castan, Y., Petrovich, P., Bongert, Y., and Castan, N. *Crimes et Criminalité en France suos l'Ancien Régime, 17e–18e siècles*. Cahiers des Annales, n. 33. Paris: A. Colin, 1971.

Abel, W. *Agrarkrisen und Agrarkonjunktur in Mitteleuropa Vom. 13 bis 19. Jahrhundert*. Berlin: Paul Parey, 1935.

Annales de démographie historique, Vol. 7, 1970.

Antonelli, Giovanni. "La magistratura degli Otto di Guardia a Firenze," *Archivio Storico Italiano*, 92 (1954):3–40.

Barbadoro, Bernardino. "Finanza e demografia nei ruoli fiorentini d'imposta del 1352–55," in *Atti del congresso internazionale per gli studi sulla popolazione*, Vol. 11, pp. 615–45. Rome, 1933.

Baron, Hans. *The Crisis of the Early Italian Renaissance: Civic Humanism and Republican Liberty in an Age of Classicism and Tyranny*, 2 vols. Princeton: Princeton University Press, 1955.

Battara, Pietro. *La popolazione di Firenze alla metà del 1500*. Florence: Scuola di Statistica della R. Università di Firenze, 1935.

Becker, Marvin B. "Changing Patterns of Violence and Justice in Fourteenth and Fifteenth Century Florence," *Comparative Studies in Society and History,* 18 (1976):281–296.

Becker, Marvin B. "An Essay on the 'Novi Cives' and Florentine Politics, 1343–82," *Mediaeval Studies,* 24 (1962):35–82.

Becker, Marvin B. *Florence in Transition,* 2 vols. Baltimore: Johns Hopkins Press, 1967–1969.

Becker, Marvin B. "Florentine Politics and the Diffusion of Heresy in the Trecento: A Socioeconomic Inquiry," *Speculum,* 34 (1959):60–75.

Becker, Marvin B. "The Florentine Territorial State and Civic Humanism in the Early Renaissance." In *Florentine Studies,* pp. 109–139. Edited by N. Rubinstein. London: Faber, 1968.

Becker, Marvin B., and Brucker, G. "The *Arti Minori* in Florentine Politics, 1342–1378," *Mediaeval Studies,* 18 (1956):93–104.

Bernocchi, M., and Fantappie, R. *Le Monete della Repubblica di Firenze,* Vol. 1, *Il Libro di Zecca.* Florence: Olschki, 1974.

Bertelli, Sergio. "Oligarchies et gouvernment dans la Renaissance," *Social Science: Information sur les sciences sociales,* 15-4/5 (1976):601–623.

Bettleheim, Charles. *Class Struggles in the U.S.S.R.: First Period, 1917–23.* Translated by Brian Pearce. New York: Monthly Review Press, 1977.

Blanshei, Sarah R. *Perugia, 1260–1340. Conflict and Change in a Medieval Italian Urban Society.* Transaction of the American Philosophical Society, new ser., Vol. 66, Pt. 2. Philadelphia: American Philosophical Society, 1976.

Bloch, Marc. *Feudal Society.* 2 vols. Translated by L. A. Manyon. Chicago: University of Chicago Press, 1961.

Bonolis, Guido. *La Giurisdizione della Mercanzia in Firenze nel secolo XIV saggio storico-giuridico.* Florence: B. Seeber, 1901.

Braudel, Fernand. "Histoire et science sociale: la longue durée," Annales, E.S.C., 4 (1958): 725–753.

Braudel, Fernand. *The Mediterranean and the Mediterranean World in the Age of Philip II.* 2 vols. Translated by S. Reynolds. New York: Harper & Son, 1972.

Brucker, Gene A. "The Ciompi Revolution." In *Florentine Studies: Politics and Society in Renaissance Florence,* pp. 314–356. Edited by Nicolai Rubinstein. London: Faber, 1968.

Brucker, Gene A. *The Civic World of Early Renaissance Florence.* Princeton: Princeton University Press, 1977.

Brucker, Gene A. "The Florentine *Popolo Minuto* and Its Political Role, 1340–1450." In *Violence and Disorder in Italian Cities,* pp. 155–83. Edited by Lauro Martines. Berkeley: University of California Press, 1972.

Brucker, Gene A. *Florentine Politics and Society, 1343–1378.* Princeton: Princeton University Press, 1962.

Brucker, Gene A. *Renaissance Florence.* New York: Wiley, 1969.

Brucker, Gene A., ed. *The Society of Renaissance Florence. A Documentary Study.* New York: Harper & Row, 1971.

Cantini, Lorenzo. "Dell'Ufizio del Podestà di Firenze." In *Saggi istorici d'antichità toscane.* Edited by Cantini. Florence: S. Maria in Campo, 1796.

Carr, E. H. *A History of Soviet Russia,* Vol. 1: *The Bolshevik Revolution, 1917–1923.* London: Macmillan, 1950.

Carus-Wilson, E. "The Woolen Industry." In *The Cambridge Economic History,* pp. 355–428. Edited by M. M. Postan and E. E. Rich. Cambridge: Cambridge University Press, 1952.

Catoni, G., and Fineschi, S., eds. *L'Archivio arcivescovile di Siena. Inventario.* Rome: Pubblicazioni degli archivi di Stato, 1970.

Chevalier, Louis. *Laboring Classes and Dangerous Classes in Paris During the First Half of the Nineteenth Century.* Translated by F. Jellinek. New York: H. Fertig, 1973.

La chiesa fiorentina. Florence: Curia Arcivescovile, 1970.

Cipolla, Carlo. *Before the Industrial Revolution*. New York: Norton, 1976.

Cocchi, Arnaldo. *Le chiese di Firenze del secolo IV al secolo XX*. Vol. 1. Florence: Pellas, Cocchi & Chiti successori, 1903.

Cockburn, J.S. "The Nature and Incidence of Crime on England 1559–1625: A Preliminary Survey." In *Crime in England, 1550–1800*. Edited by Cockburn. Princeton: Princeton University Press, 1977.

Cohn, Jr., Samuel. Review of Dale Kent, *The Rise of the Medici* in *Renaissance Quarterly*, 33 (1980):74–76.

Cohn, Jr., Samuel. "Rivolte popolari e classi sociali nella Toscana del Rinascimento," *Studi Storici*, 20 (1979):747–758.

Constant, A. "The Geographical Background of Inter-Village Population Movements in Northamptonshire and Huntingdonshire, 1754–1943," *Geography*, 33, pt. 2 (1948):78–88.

Corazzini, G.O. "Cenni Sulla procedura penale in nel secolo XIV," *Miscellanea Fiorentina*, 2:17–23.

De Meo, Giuseppe. *Saggi di statistica, economica e demografica sull'Italia meriodionale nei Secoli XVII e XVIII*. Rome: Istituto di Statistica Economica dell'Università di Roma, 1962.

de Roover, Raymond. "Labour Conditions in Florence Around 1400: Theory, Policy and Reality." In *Florentine Studies*, pp. 277–313. Edited by Nicolai Rubinstein. London: Faber, 1968.

de Tocqueville, Alexis. *The Old Régime and the French Revolution*. Translated by Stuart Gilbert. Garden City, N.Y.: Doubleday, 1955.

Doren, Alfred. *Deutsche Handwerker und Handwerkerbruderschaften im mittelalterlichen Italien*. Berlin: R. L. Prager, 1903.

Doren, Alfred. *Studien in der Florentiner Wirtschaftgeschicte: I. Die Florentiner Wollentuchindustrie vom 14. bis zum 16. Jahrhundert*. Stuttgart: Cotta, 1901; *II. Das Florentiner Zunftwesen vom 14. bis zum 16. Jahrhundert*. Stuttgart: Cotta, 1908. (*Le arti fiorentine*, 2 vols. Translated by G. B. Klein. Florence: F. Le Monnier, 1940).

Dorini, Umberto. *Il diritto penale e la delinquenza in Firenze nel secolo XIV*. Lucca: D. Corsi, 1923.

Engels, Friedrich. *The Condition of the Working Class in England*. Translated by W. O. Henderson and W. H. Chaloner. Oxford: Basil Blackwell, 1958.

Falletti-Fossati, Carlo. *Il Tumulto dei Ciompi*. Florence: Istituto di Studi Superiori, 1873.

Fei, Silvano. *Nascità e Sviluppo di Firenze. Città Borghese*. Florence: Sansoni, 1971.

Fonti archivistiche per lo studio della popolazione fino al 1848. Comitato Italiano per lo studio dei problemi della popolazione. Rome: Istituto poligrafico dello stato, 1933–1941.

Fossier, Robert. *La terre et les homes en Picardie*. 2 vols. Paris and Louvain: B. Nauwelaerts, 1968.

Foster, John. *Class Struggle and the Industrial Revolution. Early Industrial Capitalism in Three English Towns*. New York: St. Martin's Press, 1974.

Foster, John. "Nineteenth-Century Towns—A Class Dimension." In *The Study of Urban History*, pp. 281–99. Edited by H. J. Dyos. London: Edward Arnold, Ltd., 1968.

Garden, Maurice. *Lyon et les Lyonnais au XVIIIe siécle*. Paris: les Belles lettres, 1970.

Garin, Eugenio. *L'Umanesimo italiano: filosofia e vita civile nel Rinascimento*. Bari: Laterza, 1952.

Genovese, Eugene D. *Roll, Jordan Roll: The World the Slaves Made*. New York: Pantheon Books, 1974.

Gherardi, A. "Il Podestà e il Capitano del Popolo," *Miscellanea fiorentina di erudizione e storia*, Vol. 3 (1902):43–45.

Giddens, Anthony. *Capitalism and Modern Social Theory. An Analysis of the Writings of Marx, Durkheim and Max Weber*. Cambridge: Cambridge University Press, 1971.

Gilmore, Myron P., ed. Introduction to *Machiavelli. The History of Florence and Other Selections.* New York: Washington Square Press, 1970.

Goldthwaite, Richard A. "I prezzi del grano a Firenze dal XIV al XVI secolo," *Quaderni Storici,* 28 (1975):5–36.

⚹ Goldthwaite, Richard A. *Private Wealth in Renaissance Florence.* Princeton: Princeton University Press, 1968.

Goldthwaite, Richard A. and Rearick, W. R. *Michelozzo and the Ospedale di San Paolo in Florence.* Mitteilungen des Kunsthistorichen Institutes in Florenz. Vol. 21, pt. 3 (1971): 221–306.

Goodman, Jordan. "The Florentine Silk Industry in the 17th Century." Ph. D. dissertation, University of London, 1977.

Graesse, Benedict, and Plechl. *Orbis Latinus. Lexikon lateinischer geographischer Namen des Mittelalters und der Neuzeit.* 3 vols. Braunschweig: Klinkhardt & Biermann, 1972.

Green, James. "The Brotherhood of Timber Workers, 1910–1913," *Past and Present,* no. 60 (1973):161–200.

Guida d'Italia del Touring Club Italiano. Firenze e dintorni. Milan: Garzanti, 1974.

Guida d'Italia del Touring Club Italiano. Toscana. Milan: Garzanti, 1974.

Gutkind, Curt. *Cosimo de'Medici, Pater Patriae.* Oxford: The Clarendon Press, 1938.

Gutman, Herbert. *World, Culture, and Society in Industrializing America.* New York: Knopf, 1976.

Hale, J. R. "The End of Florentine Liberty: The Fortezza da Basso." In *Florentine Studies,* pp. 501–32. Edited by Rubinstein. London: Faber, 1968.

Hammer, Jr., Carl I. "Patterns of Homicide in a Medieval University Town, Fourteenth Century Oxford," *Past and Present,* no. 78 (1978):3–23.

Hanawalt, Barbara (Westman). "The Peasant Family and Crime in Fourteenth Century England," *Comparative Studies in Society and History,* 18 (1976):297–320.

Herlihy, David. "Deaths, Marriages, Births, and the Tuscan Economy (ca. 1300–1550)." In *Population Patterns in the Past,* pp. 135–64. Edited by R. D. Lee. New York: Academic Press, 1977.

⚹ Herlihy, David. "The Distribution of Wealth in a Renaissance Community: Florence 1427." In *Towns in Societies: Essays in Economic History and Historical Sociology,* pp. 131–157. Edited by Abrams and Wrigley. Cambridge: Cambridge University Press, 1978.

Herlihy, David. *Medieval and Renaissance Pistoia. The Social History of an Italian Town, 1200–1430.* New Haven and London: Yale University Press, 1967.

Herlihy, David, and Klapisch, Christiane. *Les Toscans et leurs familles. Une étude du castato florentin de 1427.* Paris: Editions de l'école des hautes études en sciences sociales, 1978.

Hobsbawm, Eric J. *Bandits.* New York: Delacorte Press, 1969.

Hobsbawm, Eric J. "Labor History and Ideology," *Journal of Social History* (1974):371–381.

Hobsbawm, Eric J. *Primitive Rebels. Studies in Archaic Forms of Social Movement in the 19th and 20th Centuries.* Manchester: Manchester University Press, 1959.

Hoshino, Hidetoshi. "Per la Storia dell'Arte della Lana in Firenze nel Quattrocento: Un riesame," *Istituto Giopponese di Cultura,* 10 (1972–1973):33–80.

Hours, Henri. "Émeutes et émotions populaires dans les campagnes du Lyonnaise au XVIIIᵉ siécle," *Cahiers d'histoire,* 9 (1964):137–153.

Hughes, Diane O. "Urban Growth and Family Structure in Medieval Genoa," *Past and Present,* no. 66 (1975):3–28.

Hunnisett, R. F. *The Medieval Coroner.* Cambridge: Cambridge University Press, 1961.

Hyman, Isabella. *Fifteenth Century Florentine Studies. The Palazzo Medici and a Ledger from the Church of San Lorenzo.* New York: Garland Publications, Inc., 1977.

Jones, Gareth Stedman. "Working-Class Culture and Working-Class Politics in London, 1870–

1900: Notes on the Remaking of a Working Class," *Journal of Social History*, 7 (1974): 460–508.

Judt, Tony. "A Clown in Regal Purple: Social History and the Historians," *History Workshop*, no. 7 (1979):66–94.

Kent, Dale. "The Florentine *Reggimento* in the Fifteenth Century." *Renaissance Quarterly*, 28 (1975):575–638.

Kent, Dale. *The Rise of the Medici. Faction in Florence, 1426–1434.* Oxford: Oxford University Press, 1978.

Kent, F. W. *Household and Lineage in Renaissance Florence. The Family Life of the Capponi, Ginori and Rucellai.* Princeton: Princeton University Press, 1977.

Kohler, J., and degli-Azzi, G. *Das Florentiner Strafrecht des XIV. Jahrhunderts.* Mannheim-Leipzig: 1909.

Klapisch, Christiane. " 'Parenti, amici e vicini': il territorio urbano d'una famiglia mercantile nel XV secolo," *Quaderni Storici*, 33 (1976):953–982.

✕ Kirshner, Julius. "Paolo di Castro on *Cives Ex Privilegio*: A Controversy over the Legal Qualification for Public Office." In *Renaissance Studies in Honor of Hans Baron.* Edited by A. Molho and J. Tedeschi. Dekalb, Ill: Northern Illinois University Press, 1971.

Kirshner, Julius. "Pursuing Honor While Avoiding Sin. The Monte delle doti." In *Quaderni di "Studi Senesi,"* n. 41. Edited by Domenico Maffei. Milan, 1978.

Landini, da Placido. *Istoria dell'oratorio di S. Maria del Bigallo e della venerabile compagnia della misericordia della città di Firenze.* Florence: P. Allegrini, 1779.

La Roncière, Charles-M. de. *Florence. Centre économique régional au XIVe siècle: Le Marche des denrées de premiere necessité à Florence et dans sa campagna et les conditions de vie des salaries, 1320–1380.* 5 vols. Aix-en-Provence, 1977.

La Roncière, Charles–M. de. "Pauvres et Pauvreté à Florence au XIVe siècle." In *Études sur l'histoire de la Pauvreté* (Moyen Age–XIVe siècle). 2 vols., pp. 661–745. Edited by M. Mollat. Paris: Publications de la Sorbonne, 1974.

Lastri, Marco. *Recerche sull'antica e moderna popolazione della città di Firenze.* Florence: G. Cambiagi, 1775.

Lefebvre, Georges. *The Coming of the French Revolution.* Translated by R. R. Palmer. Princeton: Princeton University Press, 1947.

Limburger, Walther. *Die Gebäude von Florenz. Architekten, Strassen und Plätze in alphabetischen Verzeichissen.* Leipzig: F. A. Brockhaus, 1910.

Lopes-Pegna, Mario. *Le più antiche chiese fiorentine.* Florence: Del Re, 1972.

Lundsgaarde, Henry P. *Murder in Space City. A Cultural Analysis of Houston Homicide Patterns.* New York: Oxford University Press, 1977.

Manacorda, Gustone. "Introduction to Jean Jaurès." In *Storia Socialista della Rivoluzione Francese*, xiii–liii. Milan: Libro Popolare, 1953.

Mao Tse-Tung. "The Role of the Merchants in the National Revolution" and "Analysis of All Classes in Chinese Society." In *The Political Thought of Mao Tse-Tung.* Edited by Stuart R. Schram. New York: Praeger, 1963.

Martines, Lauro. *Lawyers and Statecraft in Renaissance Florence.* Princeton: Princeton University Press, 1968.

Martines, Lauro, ed. *Violence and Disorder in Italian Cities, 1200–1500.* Berkeley: University of California Press, 1972.

Marx, Karl. *The 18th Brumaire of Louis Bonaparte.* New York: International Publishers, 1963.

Marx, Karl. *Grundrisse. Foundations of the Critique of Political Economy.* Translated by Martin Nicolaus. New York: Random House, 1973.

Mason, Timothy W. *Sozial politik im Dritten Reich. Arbeiterklasse und Volksgemeinschaft.* Opladen: Westdeutscher Verlag, 1977.

Mathiez, Albert. *La Révolution Française.* Paris: A. Colin, 1922–1927.

Molho, Anthony. "Cosimo de'Medici: Pater Patriae or Padrino?" *Stanford Italian Review* (Spring 1979):5–33.

Molho, Anthony. "The Florentine Oligarchy and the Balìa of the Late Trecento," *Speculum,* 43 (1968):23–51.

Molho, Anthony. *Florentine Public Finances in the Early Renaissance, 1400–1433.* Cambridge, Mass.: Harvard University Press, 1971.

✗Molho, Anthony. "Politics and the Ruling Class in Early Renaissance Florence," *Nuova Rivista Storica,* 52 (1968):401–420.

Molho, Anthony, and Kirshner, Julius. "The Dowry Fund and the Marriage Market in Early Quattrocento Florence," *Journal of Modern History,* 50 (1978):403–438.

Mollat, M., and Wolff, P. *Ongles Bleus, Jacques et Ciompi. Les révolutions populaires en Europe aux XIVe et XVe siècles.* Paris: Calmann-Lévy, 1970.

Mols, Roger. *Introduction à la démographie historique des villes d'Europe du XIVe au XVIIIe siècle.* 3 vols. Gembloux-Louvain: J Duculot, 1954–1956.

L'oreficeria nella Firenze del Quattrocento. Florence: S.P.E.S., 1977.

Najemy, John. "Guild Republicanism in Trecento Florence: The Successes and Ultimate Failure of Corporate Politics," *American Historical Review,* 84 (1979):53–71.

Nolan, Molly. "Social Policy, Economic Mobilization and the Working Class in the Third Reich: A Review of the Literature," *Radical History Review,* 4 (1977):

Ottokar, Nicola. *Il Comune di Firenze al fine del Dugento.* Florence: Vallecchi, 1926.

Paatz, Walter and Elisabeth. *Die Kirchen von Florenz. Ein kunstgeschichtliches Handbuch.* 6 vols. Frankfurt am Main: V. Klostermann, 1952–1955.

Pagnini dell Ventura, Giovanni F. *Della decima e di varie altre gravezze imposte dal Commune di Firenze della moneta e della mercantura de'Fiorentini fino al Secolo XVI.* Lisbon and Lucca: 1765–66.

Pampaloni, Guido. "Fermenti di rifiorme democratiche nella Firenze medicea del Quattrocento," *Archivio Storico Italiano,* 119 (1961):11–62.

Pampaloni, Guido. *Firenze al tempo di Dante. Documenti sull'urbanistica fiorentina.* Rome: Publicazioni degli archivi di Stato, 1973.

Paoli, Cesare. *Mercato, scritta e denaro di Dio.* Florence: T. Galileiana, 1895.

Papi, Massimo. "Per un censimento delle fonti relative alle confraternite laiche fiorentine: Primi resultati." In *Da Dante a Cosimo I. Richerche di storia religiosa e culturale toscana nei secoli XIV–XVI,* pp. 92–121. Edited by Domenico Maselli. Pistoia: Tellini, 1976.

Peel, R. F. "Local Intermarriage and the Stability of Rural Population in the English Midlands," *Geography,* 27 (1942):22–30.

Pöhlmann, Robert. *Die Wirtschaftspolitik der Florentiner Renaissance und das Prinzip der Verkehrsfreiheit.* Leipzig: Jablonowski'schen Gesellschaft, 1878.

Prunai, Giulio. *Gli archivi storici dei comuni della Toscana.* In Quaderni della "Rassegna degli archivi di Stato." Vol. 22. Rome: Pubblicazioni degli archivi di Stato, 1963.

Reddy, William M. "The Textile Trade and the Language of the Crowd at Rouen, 1752–1871," *Past and Present,* no. 74 (1977):62–89.

Repetti, E. *Dizionario geografico fisico storico della Toscana,* 8 vols. Florence: Presso l'autore e editore, 1833–43.

Richa, G. *Notizie istoriche della chiese fiorentine divise ne'suoi quartieri,* 10 vols. Florence: P. G. Viviani, 1754–1762.

Rodolico, Niccolò. *Il Popolo Minuto. Note di Storia fiorentina, 1343–1378,* 2nd ed. Florence: Olschki, 1968.

Rodolico, Niccolò. *La democrazia fiorentina nel suo tramonto 1378–1382.* Bologna: N. Zanichelli, 1905.

Romby, Giuseppina C. *Descrizioni e rappresentazioni della città di Firenze nel XV secolo.* Florence: Libreria editrice fiorentina, 1976.

Rubinstein, Nicolai. "The Beginning of Political Thought in Florence: A Study in Medieval Historiography," *Journal of the Warburg and Courtauld Institutes* 5 (1952):198–227.

Rubinstein, Nicolai. *The Government of Florence Under Medici, 1434–1494.* Oxford: Clarendon Press, 1965.

Rubenstein, Nicolai, ed. *Florentine Studies. Politics and Society in Renaissance Florence.* London: Faber, 1968.

Rudé, George. *The Crowd in the French Revolution.* London: Oxford University Press, 1959.

Rudé, George. *Paris and London in the Eighteenth Century. Studies in Popular Protest.* London: Collins, 1974.

Rutenburg, Victor. *Popolo e movimenti popolari nell'Italia del '300 e '400.* Translated by G. Borghini. Bologna: Il mulino, 1971; Moscow, 1958.

Salvemini, Gaetano. *Magnati e popolani in Firenze dal 1280 al 1295.* Florence: Tip. G. Carnesecchi e figli, 1899.

Santoni, Luigi. *Raccolta di notizie storiche riguardanti le chiese dell'arcidiogesi di Firenze.* Florence: G. Mazzoni, 1847.

Scaramella, Gino. *Firenze allo scoppio del Tumulto dei Ciompi.* Pisa: F. Mariotti, 1914.

Sewell, Jr., William H. "Social Change and the Rise of Working Class Politics in Nineteenth Century Marseille," *Past and Present,* no. 65 (1974):75–109.

Sjoberg, Gideon. *The Preindustrial City. Past and Present.* New York: The Free Press, 1960.

Soboul, Albert. *The French Revolution, 1787–1799. From the Storming of the Bastille to Napoleon.* Translated by A. Forrest and C. Jones. New York: Random House, 1974.

Stradario storico e amministrativo della città e del commune di Firenze. Florence: Comune di Firenze, 1913.

Taine, Hippolyte A. *The Ancien Régime.* Translated by John Durand. New York: H. Holt, 1876.

Thompson, Edward P. "Crimes of Anonymity." In *Albion's Fatal Tree.* Edited by D. Hay, P. Linbaugh, J. Rule, Thompson and C. Winslow. New York: Pantheon Books, 1975.

Thompson, Edward P. *The Making of the English Working Class.* London: Penguin Books, 1963.

Thompson, Edward P. "The Moral Economy of the English Crowd in the Eighteenth Century," *Past and Present,* no. 50 (1971):76–136.

Thompson, Edward P. "Patrician Society, Plebeian Culture," *Journal of Social History,* 7 (1974): 382–405.

Thompson, Edward P. *Whigs and Hunters. The Origins of the Black Act.* New York: Pantheon Books, 1975.

Tilly, Charles. "Collective Violence in European Perspective." In *Violence in America. History and Comparative Perspectives.* Edited by H. Graham and T. Gurr. Beverly Hills: Sage Publications, Inc., 1979.

Tilly, Charles, ed. *The Formation of the National States in Western Europe.* Princeton: Princeton University Press, 1975.

Tilly, Charles. "Getting It Together in Burgundy, 1675–1975," *Theory and Society,* 4 (1977): 478–504.

Tilly, Charles. "Hauptformen kollektiver Aktion in Westeuropa, 1500–1975." In *Geschichte und Gesellschaft,* pt. 2, *Sozialer Protest,* pp. 154–163. Edited by Richard Tilly. Göttingen, 1977.

Tilly, Charles. "How Protest Modernized France, 1845–55." In *The Dimensions of Quantitative Research,* pp. 192–256. Edited by Aydelotte, Boque, and Fogel. Princeton: Princeton University Press, 1972.

Tilly, Charles. "The Routinization of Protest in Nineteenth Century France." Center for Research on Social Organization, University of Michigan. Working Paper No. 181 (1978).

Tilly, Charles. "Social Movements and National Politics," CRSO, no. 197 (1979).

Tilly, Charles. *The Vendée*. Cambridge: Harvard University Press, 1964.

Tilly, Charles. "The Web of Collective Action in Eighteenth Century Cities," CRSO, no. 174 (1978).

Todd, Emmanuel. "Mobilité, géographique et cycle de vie en Artois et en Toscane au XVIIIᵉ siècle," *Annales, E.S.C.*, 30 (1974):726–744.

Tönnies, Ferdinand. *Community and Society*. Translated by C. Loomis. East Lansing: Michigan State University Press, 1957.

Trexler, Richard C. "Le célibat à la fin du moyen âge: Les religieuses de Florence," *Annales, E.S.C.*, 27 (1972):1329–1350.

Trexler, Richard C. "Charity and the Defense of Urban Elites in the Italian Communes." In *The Rich, the Well-Born, and the Powerful*, pp. 64–109. Edited by F. C. Jaher. Urbana: University of Illinois Press, 1973.

Trexler, Richard C. *Economic, Political and Religious Effects of the Papal Interdict on Florence, 1376–1378*. Frankfurt-am-Main, 1964.

Trexler, Richard C. "Florence By Grace of the Lord Pope. . .," *Studies in Medieval and Renaissance History*, 9 (1972):115–215.

Trexler, Richard C. *Public Life in Renaissance Florence*. New York: Academic Press, 1980.

Trotsky, Leon. *The Russian Revolution. The Overthrow of Tzarism and the Triumph of the Soviets*. Edited by. F. W. Dupree. New York: Simon and Schuster, 1932.

Weber, Max. *The Theory of Social and Economic Organization*. Translated by A. M. Henderson and T. Parsons. New York: Oxford University Press, 1947.

van Onselen, Charles. *Chibaro. African Mine Labor in Southern Rhodesia, 1900–1933*. London: Pluto Press, 1976.

van Onselen, Charles. "Worker Consciousness in Black Miners in Southern Rhodesia, 1900–1920," *Journal of African History*, 14 (1973):237–255.

Warner, Jr., Sam Bass. *The Private City. Philadelphia in Three Periods of Its Growth*. Philadelphia. University of Pennsylvania Press, 1968.

Weinstein, Donald. *Savonarola and Florence. Prophecy and Patriotism in the Renaissance*. Princeton: Princeton University Press, 1970.

Weissman, Ronald. *Florentine Confraternities, 1200–1600*. New York: Academic Press, 1981.

Zanelli, A. *Le shiave orientali a Firenze nei secoli XIV e XV*. Contributo alla storia della vita privata di Firenze. Florence: Loescher, 1885.

Index

STUDIES IN SOCIAL DISCONTINUITY

Under the Consulting Editorship of:

CHARLES TILLY
University of Michigan

EDWARD SHORTER
University of Toronto

PIANTA DEL di LA CITTÀ
FIRENZE
nelle sue vere misure colla descrizione
dei luoghi più notabili di ciascun
Quartiere.

IN QUESTO QUARTIERE SONO
Chiese curate numero 13
Chiese senza cura num.o 7
Monasteri di Regolari n.o 7
Monasteri di Monache n 2
Oratorij e Compagnie num.o . . . 16
Conservatorij di Monache n . . . 2
Conservatorij di Femmine n . . . 1
Spedali per gl'Infermi n 2
Spedali per i Pellegrini n 2
Accademie numero 2
Teatro numero 1

IN QUESTO QUARTIERE
SONO
Chiese curate numero 10
Chiese senza cura n . . . .
Monasteri di Regol.i n.o . . . . .
Monasteri di Monache 21
Oratorij e Compagnie 20
Conservatorij di Ma . . . . . .
Conservatorij di Femmine . . .
Spedali per gl'Infer . . . . . .
Spedali per i Pellegrini . . . . .
Accademie numero . . . .
Teatro numero 2